NEW THEORETIC
ON DYLAN

WRITING WALES IN ENGLISH

CREW series of Critical and Scholarly Studies
General Editors: Kirsti Bohata and Daniel G. Williams (*CREW*, Swansea University)

This *CREW* series is dedicated to Emyr Humphreys, a major figure in the literary culture of modern Wales, a founding patron of the *Centre for Research into the English Literature and Language of Wales*. Grateful thanks are due to the late Richard Dynevor for making this series possible.

Other titles in the series

Stephen Knight, *A Hundred Years of Fiction* (978-0-7083-1846-1)
Barbara Prys-Williams, *Twentieth-Century Autobiography* (978-0-7083-1891-1)
Kirsti Bohata, *Postcolonialism Revisited* (978-0-7083-1892-8)
Chris Wigginton, *Modernism from the Margins* (978-0-7083-1927-7)
Linden Peach, *Contemporary Irish and Welsh Women's Fiction* (978-0-7083-1998-7)
Sarah Prescott, *Eighteenth-Century Writing from Wales: Bards and Britons* (978-0-7083-2053-2)
Hywel Dix, *After Raymond Williams: Cultural Materialism and the Break-Up of Britain* (978-0-7083-2153-9)
Matthew Jarvis, *Welsh Environments in Contemporary Welsh Poetry* (978-0-7083-2152-2)
Harri Garrod Roberts, *Embodying Identity: Representations of the Body in Welsh Literature* (978-0-7083-2169-0)
Diane Green, *Emyr Humphreys: A Postcolonial Novelist* (978-0-7083-2217-8)
M. Wynn Thomas, *In the Shadow of the Pulpit: Literature and Nonconformist Wales* (978-0-7083-2225-3)
Linden Peach, *The Fiction of Emyr Humphreys: Contemporary Critical Perspectives* (978-0-7083-2216-1)
Daniel Westover, *R. S. Thomas: A Stylistic Biography* (978-0-7083-2413-4)
Jasmine Donahaye, *Whose People? Wales, Israel, Palestine* (978-0-7083-2483-7)
Judy Kendall, *Edward Thomas: The Origins of His Poetry* (978-0-7083-2403-5)
Damian Walford Davies, *Cartographies of Culture: New Geographies of Welsh Writing in English* (978-0-7083-2476-9)
Daniel G. Williams, *Black Skin, Blue Books: African Americans and Wales 1845–1945* (978-0-7083-1987-1)
Andrew Webb, *Edward Thomas and World Literary Studies: Wales, Anglocentrism and English Literature* (978-0-7083-2622-0)
Alyce von Rothkirch, *J. O. Francis, realist drama and ethics: Culture, place and nation* (978-1-7831-6070-9)
Rhian Barfoot, *Liberating Dylan Thomas: Rescuing a Poet from Psycho-Sexual Servitude* (978-1-7831-6184-3)
Daniel G. Williams, *Wales Unchained: Literature, Politics and Identity in the American Century* (978-1-7831-6212-3)
M. Wynn Thomas, *The Nations of Wales 1890–1914* (978-1-78316-837-8)
Richard McLauchlan, *Saturday's Silence: R. S. Thomas and Paschal Reading* (978-1-7831-6920-7)
Bethan M. Jenkins, *Between Wales and England: Anglophone Welsh Writing of the Eighteenth Century* (978-1-7868-3029-6)
M. Wynn Thomas, *All that is Wales: The Collected Essays of M. Wynn Thomas* (978-1-7868-3088-3)
Laura Wainwright, *New Territories in Modernism: Anglophone Welsh Writing, 1930–1949* (978-1-7868-3217-7)
Siriol McAvoy (ed.), *Locating Lynette Roberts* (978-1-78683-382-2)

New Theoretical Perspectives on Dylan Thomas

'A Writer of Words and Nothing Else'?

WRITING WALES IN ENGLISH

Edited by Kieron Smith
and Rhian Barfoot

UNIVERSITY OF WALES PRESS
2020

www.uwp.co.uk

British Library CIP Data
A catalogue record for this book is available from the British Library.

ISBN: 978-1-78683-520-8
e-ISBN: 978-1-78683-521-5

THE *ASSOCIATION FOR*
WELSH WRITING IN ENGLISH
CYMDEITHAS LLÊN SAESNEG CYMRU

Typeset by Marie Doherty
Printed by CPI Antony Rowe, Melksham

CONTENTS

Series Editors' Preface

The aim of this series, since its founding in 2004 by Professor M. Wynn Thomas, is to publish scholarly and critical work by established specialists and younger scholars that reflects the richness and variety of the English-language literature of modern Wales. The studies published so far have amply demonstrated that concepts, models and discourses current in the best contemporary studies can illuminate aspects of Welsh culture, and have also foregrounded the potential of the Welsh example to draw attention to themes that are often neglected or marginalised in anglophone cultural studies. The series defines and explores that which distinguishes Wales's anglophone literature, challenges critics to develop methods and approaches adequate to the task of interpreting Welsh culture, and invites its readers to locate the process of writing Wales in English within comparative and transnational contexts.

Professor Kirsti Bohata and Professor Daniel G. Williams

Founding Editor: Professor M. Wynn Thomas (2004–15)

CREW (*Centre for Research into the English Literature and Language of Wales*)
Swansea University

Acknowledgements

This book resulted from the many stimulating papers, panels, conversations and ideas shared during 'Dylan Unchained: the Dylan Thomas Centenary Conference' at Swansea University, September 2014. The editors wish to acknowledge all delegates who contributed to that important event. We especially wish to thank the conference organiser, Professor Kirsti Bohata.

Warm thanks also to all of the contributors to this collection for their excellent work and, indeed, tremendous patience, while the manuscript was being prepared.

In addition, our gratitude to Sarah Lewis of the University of Wales Press, for her help and support at every stage of the project.

The editors and the publisher wish to thank the following for the permission to use the copyright material: 'A Dream of Winter', 'Altarwise by owl-light', 'A Refusal to Mourn the Death, by Fire, of a Child in London', 'Among Those Killed in the Dawn Raid was a Man Aged a Hundred', 'And Death shall have no Dominion', 'Ceremony After a Fire Raid', 'Especially when the October Wind', 'Fern Hill', 'I, in my intricate image', 'I see the boys of summer', 'In the White Giant's Thigh', 'Our eunuch dreams', 'Over St John's Hill', 'Poem in October', 'Poem on his birthday', 'The force that through the green fuse', 'The hunchback in the park', 'Then was my neophyte', 'Twenty-four years', 'When, like a running grave' by Dylan Thomas, from *The Poems of Dylan Thomas* copyright © 1952, 1953 by Dylan Thomas, copyright © 1937, 1945, 1955, 1956, 1957, 1962, 1966, 1967, 1971, 1977 by the Trustees for the Copyrights of Dylan Thomas, copyright © 1938, 1939, 1943, 1946, 1971, 2003 by

ABBREVIATIONS

Quotations from the poetry of Dylan Thomas are taken from *Collected Poems*, edited by John Goodby (London: Weidenfeld & Nicolson, 2014); references to this will be made using the abbreviation *CP*, followed by the page number. Quotations from the stories of Dylan Thomas are taken from *Collected Stories*, edited by Walford Davies (London: Weidenfeld & Nicolson, 2014); references to these will be made using the abbreviation *CS*, followed by the page number. Quotations from the letters of Dylan Thomas are taken from *The Collected Letters*, edited by Paul Ferris (London: Dent, 1985); references to these will be made using the abbreviation *CL* followed by the page number. References to *Under Milk Wood* are taken from the Walford Davies edition (London: Penguin, 2000); references to this will be made using the abbreviation *UMW*, followed by the page number. References to *Quite Early One Morning: Poems and Stories*, ed. Aneirin Talfan Davies (London: Dent, Aldine Paperbacks, 1974) will be made using the abbreviation *QEOM*, followed by the page number.

Notes on Contributors

Rhian Barfoot is an honorary research associate of CREW (The Centre for Research into the English Literature and Language of Wales) at Swansea University. She is the author of *Liberating Dylan Thomas: Rescuing a Poet from Psycho-sexual Servitude* (University of Wales Press, 2015). Her research interests include Modernist and Postmodern poetry and poetics and post-Freudian literary theory.

Tony Brown is Emeritus Professor of English at Bangor University and co-director of the R. S. Thomas Research Centre, and a Fellow of the Learned Society of Wales. The founding editor of *Welsh Writing in English: A Yearbook of Critical Essays* (1995–2007), he has lectured and published widely on Welsh writing in English, especially on the work of R. S. Thomas and Glyn Jones. He has a particular interest in the anglophone short story in Wales.

John Goodby is a Professor at Swansea University, where he is director of CREW's Dylan Thomas Research Project. He has published widely on Thomas and is author of *The Poetry of Dylan Thomas: Under the Spelling Wall* (Liverpool University Press, 2013), *Discovering Dylan Thomas: A Companion to the* Collected Poems *and Notebook Poems* (University of Wales Press, 2017), and the co-editor of the New Casebook title on Dylan Thomas (Palgrave, 2001). In 2014, he published the annotated centenary edition of Dylan Thomas's *Collected Poems* (Weidenfeld & Nicolson/New Directions). With Ade Osbourne, he is currently editing the recently-discovered fifth notebook of Dylan

Thomas for publication in Bloomsbury's Modernist Archives series in 2020.

James Keery teaches English in Wigan. He is currently editing an anthology of mid-century modernist poetry, entitled *Apocalypse*, to be published by Carcanet in 2019. He has published a collection of poems, *That Stranger, The Blues*, and has contributed to a number of magazines and books including *PN Review*, *Angel Exhaust* and *Resounding Dylan Thomas*.

Tomos Owen is Lecturer in English Literature at the School of English, Communication and Philosophy, Cardiff University. His research focuses principally on the literatures of Wales and on modern and contemporary writing. He has published on topics including London-Welsh literary culture and industrial fiction, and on authors including Amy Dillwyn, Caradoc Evans, Arthur Machen and Rhys Davies.

Kieron Smith is a researcher working in the field of Welsh writing in English. He is the author of *John Ormond's Organic Mosaic: Poetry, Documentary, Nation* (Cardiff: University of Wales Press, 2019). He completed a PhD at CREW (Centre for Research into the English Literature and Language of Wales), Swansea University, in 2014, where he is currently Honorary Research Fellow.

M. Wynn Thomas is Professor of English and Emyr Humphreys Professor of Welsh Writing in English, Swansea University, and a Fellow of the British Academy and a Fellow of the Learned Society of Wales. *All That is Wales*, the latest of his two dozen volumes on American poetry and on the two literatures of Wales, was shortlisted for the Welsh Book of the Year award in 2018.

Andrew Webb is Senior Lecturer and Head of the Department of English Literature and Creative Writing, at Bangor University, where he specialises in Welsh writing in English.

Introduction: '[A] Writer of Words, and Nothing Else'

Kieron Smith and Rhian Barfoot

Dylan Thomas once claimed that he was 'a writer of words, and nothing else'.[1] The statement is eminently quotable. It contains everything the popular literary quotation should: arch wittiness, ludic self-referentiality, as well as an underlying seriousness about the vocation of writing. Now a well-worn favourite among Thomas aficionados the world over, it was originally spoken in conversation with a student on one of the poet's American tours, the transcript of which was later published in a 1961 issue of *Texas Quarterly* as 'Poetic Manifesto'. This text is a veritable repository of quotables: 'Eggs laid by tigers'; 'I read . . . with my eyes hanging out'; 'I could never have dreamt that there were such goings-on in the world between the covers of books'; all these stock Thomasisms and more can be found here. Perhaps an important part of the appeal of 'Poetic Manifesto' is that, read in a certain light, it bespeaks a disarmingly disarmed Thomas: unintentional, confessional, exposed.

> I wanted to write poetry in the beginning because I had fallen in love with words. The first poems I knew were nursery rhymes, and before I could read them for myself I had come to love just the words of them, the words alone. What words stood for, symbolised, or meant, was of very secondary importance; what mattered was the *sound* of them as I heard them for the first time on the lips of those remote and incomprehensible grown-ups who seemed, for some reason, to be living in my world. And these words were, to me, as the notes of bells, the sounds

of musical instruments, the noises of wind, and sea, and rain, the rat-
tle of milk carts, the clopping of hooves on cobbles, the fingering of
branches on a window pane, might be to someone, deaf from birth,
who has miraculously found his hearing. I did not care what the words
said, overmuch, nor what happened to Jack & Jill & the Mother Goose
rest of them. I cared for the shape of sound that their names and the
words describing their actions, made in my ears; I cared for the colours
the words cast on my eyes. I realise that I may be, as I think back all
that way, romanticizing my reactions to the simple and beautiful words
of those pure poems; but that is all I can honestly remember, however
much time might have falsified my memory. I fell in love with – that is
the only expression I can think of – . . . words.[2]

In one sense, this is the voice of a born poet carried away on a drift of
nostalgic reverie. The passage feigns innocence; it conjures an infant,
a prelapsarian Thomas, a young boy enamoured with words and the
world, gleefully unsullied by the grubby realities of adulthood. Words
are this child's playthings, and reading a joyous, wholesome activity.
Part of the power of the passage lies in its evocation of the language
of unmediated honesty. Here and elsewhere in 'Poetic Manifesto',
Thomas employs phrases that declare a sincere effort to be plain,
open, truthful: 'that is all I can honestly remember'; 'time might have
falsified my memory'; 'that is the only expression I can think of'; elsewhere: 'quite simply and truthfully'.[3] The language evokes a speaker
striving to recall a past without artifice or equivocation.

This potent strain of apparently pure, unpolluted idealism is a
key feature of Thomas's writing, and is an important aspect of his
appeal as one of the best known and most popular English-language
poets of the twentieth century. This is the Thomas of 'Fern Hill',
with its seemingly idyllic youthful easiness. It is the Thomas of *Under
Milk Wood*, lulled and dumbfounded. It is the Thomas of *A Child's
Christmas in Wales*, swaddled in a dreamy, never-ending childhood,
forgetting 'whether it snowed for six days and six nights when [he] was
twelve, or whether it snowed for twelve days and twelve nights when
[he] was six'.[4] Indeed, often, this is the picture of Thomas that prevails
in the popular imagination. State-approved imagery during the 2014
centenary celebrations presented a virtuous, visionary Thomas, the
wide-eyed figurehead of approved creative activity. *Love the Words*
was the title given to the major new permanent exhibition housed at
Swansea's Dylan Thomas Centre in that year. This is, moreover, a
version of Thomas that has the power to induce a particular brand of

sentimentalism from his admirers. One anthology published in 2014 contained testimonials from a range of big-name dignitaries, and the result is a peculiarly excessive outpouring of sentimentality. Rarely in *Dylan Thomas: A Centenary Celebration* is Thomas referred to by his full name; rather, the cloyingly familiar 'Dylan' is preferred. The book brims with gratuitous intimacies: Thomas 'brings tears to my eyes';[5] 'make[s] my head swim and my skin prickle and my heart pound'.[6] 'My English teacher introduced me to Dylan Thomas';[7] I got to know Dylan Thomas about ten years ago'[8]. Where in all this is the drink-addled, bombastic, showboating, modernist Thomas – writer of sophisticated, charged, infuriatingly complex verse? Where is the laggard of Laugharne and London, the Rimbaud of Cwmdonkin Drive?

It is now commonly accepted that Dylan Thomas divides opinion. While some indulge in mawkish nostalgia for a genius with a warm, lyrical heart, others scathe a scabrous, sinning malingerer. This mixed reputation can arguably be traced to the complex relationship Thomas possessed with language itself. A purveyor of linguistic and stylistic excess, Thomas's use of the English language is everywhere playful and elusive, resistant to straightforward precis and paraphrase. This can be seen upon further examination of 'Poetic Manifesto'. Phrases that appear to speak of an innocent, artless 'love' of language are, at the same time, deviously charged with ambiguity:

> I fell in love with – that is the only expression I can think of – at once, and am still at the mercy of words, though sometimes now, knowing a little of their behavior very well, I can influence slightly and have even learnt to beat them now and again, which they appear to enjoy . . . [As] I read more and more, and it was not all verse, by any means, my love for the real life of words increased until I knew that I must live *with* them and *in* them always. I knew, in fact, that I must be a writer of words, and nothing else.[9]

The child with an unconditional love of language has evidently matured. Here the register of 'Poetic Manifesto' shifts towards the postlapsarian; this is not the language of loving affection, but of adult awareness and power, of 'mercy' and 'behavior'. The voice veers towards the obsessive, beating into submission that which he loves. Thomas elsewhere describes himself as a 'devious craftsman in words' who uses 'everything and anything to make my poems work and move them in the directions I want them to'.[10] Is he, then, a writer, and nothing else, or a writer of *words*, and nothing else? Parting with 'Poetic

Manifesto', we are left with a sense of a dastardly poet, the 'brassy orator . . . strid[ing] on two levels' (*CP*, 71): child and man, lover and sadist, a poet professing 'honestly' to recall an unsullied past through deviously deliberate language.

One of the broader consequences of Thomas's complex, obsessive-compulsive, perhaps sado-masochistic relationship with language is that while he is probably best known as a poet, his art was in no way confined to verse alone. Thomas was a polyamorous writer who delighted in challenging and exceeding formal and generic boundaries. Arguably, it was precisely this obsession with the excessive qualities of language that enabled his work to take shape within and across multiple forms, genres and media. Beyond his intricate, form-testing poetry, he was a writer of black-comic surrealist fiction, experimental propaganda film scripts, rambunctious correspondence, and path-breaking popular radio. The inherently heteroglossic nature of his work makes it difficult – perhaps futile – to categorise. If he possessed a 'genius', this was surely for flaunting and destabilising formal and generic containers, and as such, his work is alchemically available to interpretation and transmogrification. This aspect of Thomas's work was in superabundance during the centenary festivities of 2014. Countless activities engaged with and celebrated his work during this year, and the full catalogue of festivities is indeed too excessive to enumerate. Some notable experiments included *Wordy Shapes of Women*, a show in which 'the work of one of Wales's greatest wordsmiths collide[d] with burlesque';[11] *Dylathon* – the self-proclaimed 'thrilling live climax of the Dylan Thomas 100 Festival'[12] – a thirty-six hour marathon reading of Thomas's work at Swansea's Grand Theatre; *Dylan Live*, a collaborative spoken-word and jazz-infused performance exploring Thomas's transatlantic legacy; and *Under Milk Wood: An Opera*, which needs no explanation. There were numerous new filmic treatments of Thomas's life and work, as well as innumerable radio and television adaptations and expositions, coffee-table books, and tourist-attracting extravaganzas.

While it is indeed tempting to revel in the Bacchanalia of Thomas worship, it is also necessary to step back to engage in a more level-headed scholarly engagement with what Thomas did with words. Yet, even from the sober detachment of the critic's desk, Thomas is a notoriously difficult writer to pin down. Since the first publication of *18 Poems* in 1934, he has consistently divided critical opinion, and in ways that run deeper than those who consider him lovable and those who consider him unlovely. The overdetermined, form-testing, boundary-straddling energy of Thomas's work meant that, as John Goodby notes, he was not only troublesomely 'non-recruitable',[13] but often wilfully shunned by critics, viewed as 'too avant-garde by the mainstream, too mainstream by the avant-garde, too Welsh by the English, too English by the Welsh, too popular by a cultural elite'.[14] Indeed, the history of Thomas criticism by now has its own historiography, and while this is not the place to rehearse all these arguments in their entirety,[15] it is worth sketching a brief outline.

Thomas's intrinsic refusal to accommodate fixed meaning posed a serious challenge to early critical efforts to 'make sense' of his work. As E. B. Cox noted in an early collection of critical essays, 'for twenty years he proved incomprehensible to some of the most perceptive critics and poets of his time'.[16] Yet at the same time as critics complained of his inscrutability, Thomas enjoyed an almost unprecedented popularity as a public poet. This, combined with the bohemian bombast of his reputation, confounded critics, and in an era before theoretical developments in literary criticism were informed by, for one, Roland Barthes's 'The Death of the Author',[17] Thomas was fair game for scholars professionally concerned with the 'life' of the poet: that is, his alleged personality, biography and psychology. For a poet who wrote of being 'shut in a tower of words' (*CP*, 67), Thomas can at this time be understood as having been shut in a tower of his own reputation. The result was the persistence of a style of literary criticism that spent as much energy evaluating the man as the work. Often the two endeavours were conflated: for decades, it was, as Goodby and Wigginton note, 'all too easy, for detractors and champions alike, to read the writing in terms of the life, and vice versa.'[18]

However, even after the advent of theoretical approaches to literary criticism provided critics with new lenses through which to refocus their attention on the textual features of Thomas's output as a writer (rather than, for example, his alleged taste for whisky), it would appear that the sheer scale of the mythology of the 'Dylan Legend', as R. B. Kerschner has it,[19] continued to obscure interpretation. As Barfoot notes, the bibliography in Walford Davies's important *Dylan Thomas* (1986) lists no criticism written after the mid-1970s, and nothing influenced by any of the developments that took place in literary theory in those years.[20] Efforts to apply theoretical approaches to Thomas's work did not happen in earnest until *Under the Spelling Wall*, an academic conference held at Swansea University in 1998. Bringing together critics working with a range of new theoretical tools – feminism, new historicism, Marxism, postcolonialism – this conference resulted in *Dylan Thomas: New Casebook* (2001), a collection of essays which contained pathbreaking entries into new, previously uncharted areas of Thomas's work. This important book enabled new ways of conceptualising the hybrid, liminal, intertextual dimensions of Thomas's writing as earlier, crudely psycho-biographical readings could not.

Nevertheless, after 2001, while the drip-feed of reissues, popular commentary and new biographies continued, serious critical examination of Thomas's work dried up for some years. It was not until the run-up to the 2014 centenary that scholarly interest was reignited in earnest. John Goodby's comprehensive *The Poetry of Dylan Thomas: Under the Spelling Wall* was published in 2013, and in the same year the Research Institute for Arts and Humanities at Swansea University published a call for papers that invited a new scholarly reassessment of Thomas's life and legacy. Importantly, where the majority of earlier criticism of Thomas's work had justifiably focused on the poetry, *Dylan Unchained: the Dylan Thomas Centenary Conference* was to break free of earlier assessments and re-evaluate the enormous scope of Thomas's work and its legacy. It is worth quoting the call for papers at length:

'Unchaining' Dylan might involve looking at his work from psychoanalytic, postcolonial, feminist and deconstructionist perspectives; it might involve reclaiming the regional specificity of his work from those who locate him as an international modernist; it could, alternatively, involve seeking to tear him away from nationalist attempts at Welsh or British canon formation in order to underline the transnational and hybrid character of his work; it might seek to place him amongst his contemporaries, or his literal or metaphorical ancestors; it might look at his influences across literary traditions and languages; it might involve seeing his review of Djuna Barnes's *Nightwood* as key moment in the re-gendering of modernism, or his review of Amos Tutuola's *Palm-Wine Drinkard* as a key moment in the global impact of anglophone African literatures; it might involve close and detailed readings of his work and analyses of his poetic practice; or it might draw on more distanced forms of reading which address locations of publication, sales, readership and dissemination; it might think of Thomas as late Romantic, or as early Beat; it might consider Thomas's voice in the age of mechanical reproduction, or his texts in the age of digital humanities. Thomas is a figure who transcends the 'now' to which he incessantly returned in his work.[21]

This book is the product of the new scholarly engagements enabled by that 2014 conference. Like *Dylan Unchained*, it is not designed to offer 'coverage' of a particular area or moment in Thomas's life or reception, nor does it seek a particular grand theory or narrative on the development of the poet. Rather, we invited contributors to consider themselves 'unchained' and free to address what seemed to them the most interesting and pertinent themes, debates and modes of expression in Thomas's works and in Thomas criticism. Our only stipulation as editors was that this book should cover the broad range of forms and genres that Thomas's work embodied. And while we are disappointed not to be able to include all of the excellent contributions made to the centenary conference in this book, we are delighted to showcase these eight exciting new perspectives on his work. What follows are some established voices, some new; some close and some distant readings; some highly theoretical, some more historically-focused chapters; overviews of his work as it exists across range of forms and contexts; as well as analyses of Thomas's wider reputation and legacy in letters and in wider society.

Given that this book was inspired by the resurgence of interest in Thomas at the time of the centenary of his birth, we feel the appropriate place to begin is with Tomos Owen's analysis of Thomas's 'anniversary poetics'. Thomas famously wrote four birthday poems: 'Especially when the October wind', 'Twenty-four years', 'Poem in October', and 'Poem on his Birthday', and, as Owen suggests, 'Thomas's poetry is already and has always been involved in its own commemoration'. Taking his cue from Derrida's work on Paul Celan, this nuanced chapter demonstrates the ways in which poststructuralist literary theory can illuminate new and fascinating aspects of Thomas's work. Owen argues that Thomas's sensitivity to the significance of the birthday reveals key features of his wider poetics. In particular, Thomas's conception of the birth day, and his repeated return to the act of commemorating the date of his own birth through poetry, was in a sense a feature of his fundamental conception of language. Just as birth dates are both utterly arbitrary, yet forever loaded with meaning – both transient and forever fixed – language for Thomas, too, has a peculiarly recurring, unfinished infinitude. Poems are always destined to spill over and outside themselves, as utterances that are both singular and endlessly dependent on those around them. Thomas's birthday poems therefore have a particular significance within his oeuvre. As Owen suggests, 'they each carry the uncanny, enigmatic, ghostly traces of past commemorations and those still to come,' commemorating and celebrating the recurrence of an arbitrarily important date, as well as reminding us of the two immutably fixed dates that bookend our lives.

However, while Owen emphasises the sense in which, in 'Poem on his Birthday', the 'tolling' of the birthday bell 'summons a connection with the grave-bound toil which is our life on earth', we choose in this instance to hear only its celebratory resonances and take this to signal the start of the collection. Next, Tony Brown's chapter examines the 'remarkably neglected' prose fiction, with an emphasis on the early 'Jarvis Hills' short stories, but also *Portrait of the Artist as a Young Dog*, as well as a look at the tantalising early sections of Thomas's unfinished novel, *Adventures in the Skin Trade*. Brown draws from psychoanalytic literary theory to uncover the unconscious drives behind certain features of Thomas's prose fiction. In doing so, he reveals that the short stories share with the poetry not only space in the pages of Thomas's early notebooks but also their 'anxieties about sexuality, about the processes of the body and, frequently . . . a sense of isolation and alienation'. Brown's particular focus is on the ways in which Thomas's sense of what Freud famously termed 'das unheimlich' – the 'unhomely' – can be read in part as a psychic manifestation of his situation as a young man brought up in a profoundly alienating, liminal, frontier Swansea: a town riven by class, linguistic and cultural difference, at once urban and anglophone, whilst simultaneously on the edge of another, rural, cymrophone Wales. This sense of estrangement was compounded by Thomas's journeys out of his home town – firstly to rural Carmarthenshire, but later to London – and found expression in his creation of grotesque, disorientatingly irrational 'dream worlds', both narrated and populated by characters agonisingly estranged from the landscapes they inhabit.

Brown is keen to stress that while these stories are not strictly autobiographical, their intensely stylised visions are nevertheless expressions of the experience of a particular social and historical positionality. His chapter is therefore an important contribution to recent developments in work on the sociocultural specificity of Thomas's writing, in particular the argument that Thomas was not simply a 'modernist' writer responding to new 'metropolitan' modes and forms of expression established elsewhere, but a modern subject who found ways to express the psychological fractures that were key features of his sociocultural experience. Indeed, literary and cultural critics now increasingly view 'modernism' not in the singular, as an inventory of certain forms and modes of creative expression established in major European and north American cities, but in the plural, as a nexus of creative responses to complex historical forces that played out in different ways in different locations.[22] In this sense, Thomas's writing can be viewed as a key example of what critics now increasingly refer to as 'Welsh modernism',[23] a set of creative responses to sweeping changes in a Welsh society transitioning rapidly from, as Daniel Williams writes, 'country to city; from Liberal to Labour; from Nonconformity to secularism'.[24] From this perspective, Thomas's Swansea was not simply a passive, parochial recipient of new ideas fermenting within metropolitan London, but the site and centre of its own state of transition, experiencing its own manifestations of the contradictions of modernity.

Andrew Webb's chapter pursues this view by reading Thomas's short stories specifically against the backdrop of a Swansea in the throes of these profound socio-spatial and cultural changes. Thomas was of course well aware of his own liminal 'inbetweenness' – he spoke of himself as a 'border case'[25] – and Webb demonstrates the extent to which this figured in his work through attentive readings of Thomas's semi-fictional construction of a complex, shifting urban geography. In *Portrait of the Artist as a Young Dog*, Thomas's self-described 'provincial autobiography' (*CL*, 426), this is partly registered through the figure of a child narrator straddling the socio-cultural border between urban Swansea and a rural west Wales hinterland. Webb demonstrates the extent to which Thomas's excessive, overdetermined linguistic mode constituted a powerful means of registering the sense in which such borders are not only permeable but permanently unfixed and in flux. For Webb, Thomas's use of a language that is resistant to literal interpretation enabled him to 'solve the problem' of how to represent a Swansea that was undergoing rapid changes in its social and physical geography. Thomas's construction of the semi-fictional 'Tawe' brilliantly registers Swansea's complex identity, which is, like all identities, always unfinished, overdetermined and contested, as evidenced in the young journalist's inscription of his address in 'One Warm Saturday': '*Tawe News*, Tawe, South Wales, England, Europe, The Earth' (*CS*, 215). Indeed, Swansea/Tawe was perhaps an appropriate home for a writer obsessed with excess; as Webb notes, Tawe is presented as a 'carnival town, impossible to contain'. Webb's chapter constitutes an important contribution to our understanding of Welsh modernism as a creative response to a rapidly changing social and physical environment. At the same time, in showing that Thomas's writing inhabited not only the complex temporal and spatial border between two different societies, but also the membrane between literary textuality and physical space – that which geographer Edward Soja called the 'real-and-imagined'[26] – it is a welcome new example of the applications of literary geography in a Welsh context.

Although Thomas can certainly be understood a 'border case' in the sense that his writing both depicted and embodied discursive boundaries, it is worth remembering that his writing also crossed borders in a rather more literal sense. Dylan Thomas was, of course, a prolific poster of letters, and M. Wynn Thomas's chapter reads this extensive correspondence as the site of some of Thomas's best comic writing. This chapter contends that the 'superadundance' of reverent praise and analysis of the poet's sullen art misses the fact that Thomas was also a dazzlingly irreverent comic writer, and makes the provocative claim that the poet 'may have been naturally gifted with a greater talent for comedy than for poetry'. Whether or not you agree with this assessment, it is certainly true that critics who laud Thomas's dexterity across a range of poetic devices – as the 'Poetic Manifesto' enumerates, 'puns, portmanteau-words, paradox, allusion, paranomasia, paragram, catachresis',[27] and so on – they often overlook the fact that he was also a virtuosic purveyor of comic techniques, having at his fingertips 'manic verbal pyrotechnics, through fantastic characterisations and mockingly astute depictions of social mores and human relations to satiric sketches'. M. Wynn Thomas himself dexterously connects these to other important features of Thomas's work, notably the early strain of gothic surrealism identified by others in this collection, suggesting that Thomas's comedy was most frequently an instinctive, nervous response to those 'terrors . . . by which he was chronically haunted.' The chapter therefore provides further evidence to support the view that Dylan Thomas can fruitfully be understood as a Welsh modernist whose work stemmed from the anxieties generated by a radically unstable, fissuring modern Wales. It is also a long-overdue reminder not to take such matters too seriously.

While M. Wynn Thomas suggests that the 'exhilarating edge' of the humour of Thomas's letter-writing rewards further reading, he argues that, contrary to popular opinion, delving into the 'extravagantly light souffle' of *Under Milk Wood* provides less sustenance. Rhian Barfoot, on the other hand, insists that there is in fact a psycho-social depth to this comic mid-century modern pastoral that has, hitherto, been overlooked, and her chapter attempts to close this gap by placing Thomas in dialogue with Freudian and post-Freudian psychoanalysis. In an important letter to the editor of the Rome-based magazine *Botteghe Oscure*, Thomas described his 'entertainment' as developing directly from the 'darkness of the town'. Reading this statement in the light of his old adage that 'whatever is hidden should be made naked', Barfoot suggests that the radio play involves a dynamic confrontation with the unconscious and, like the 'Circe' episode in Joyce's *Ulysses*, might be understood as a 'comedy of the unconscious'. Evidencing her argument with close textual analysis, she insists that the unconscious has both a thematic and a structural significance in *Under Milk Wood*. The wider view of Thomas that underpins this approach is that of a belated but positive and critically engaged modernist, who, like his precursors, recognised the enhanced aesthetic and artistic opportunities made available by the new paradigm of psychoanalysis. Thomas is known to have been an assiduous reader of the surrealist journal *transition*, a publication whose output was richly informed by contemporary developments of Freud, in particular the work of Jung and Lacan. Given their shared emphasis on the role of the unconscious, she suggests that there are a number of urgent and illuminating parallels to be drawn between Thomas's work and, in particular, that of Lacan, which bear interestingly upon our understanding of Thomas's 'Play for Voices'.

Following Barfoot's uncovering of the unconscious drives powering Thomas's foray into the popular medium of radio, John Goodby pursues this collection's effort to make whatever is hidden naked by revealing the intimate ways in which another popular medium made itself felt in Thomas's poetic imagination. This chapter argues that film was a constant, vital presence in Thomas's creative life and, in doing so, Goodby further complicates our understanding of Thomas's relationship with modernism. He develops recent interpretations of Thomas's modernism as one that blurred distinctions of 'high' and 'low' by arguing that, while it has long been understood that Thomas's poetry harnessed and tested the boundaries of complex *poetic* modes, it simultaneously engaged with and absorbed the features of the *filmic*. Goodby's chapter begins with a pioneering analysis of Thomas's engagement not only with the surface imagery of the burgeoning American, European and Russian cinema of the 1920s and 1930s, but further with its narrative and structural techniques, so much so that it could be said that Thomas's process poetic can be understood also as a process filmic. From here, Goodby goes on to examine Dylan Thomas's tantalising filmscripts for both the documentary and feature film industries. The chapter convincingly argues that there was a 'dialectical interaction in Thomas's work between "reel" and "real"'.

The final two chapters in this collection depart from critical analysis of Thomas's oeuvre. Pursuing the overdetermined, uncontainable nature of Thomas's writerly mode, they instead widen the frame to other areas into which Thomas's complex legacy has spilled over. Indeed, in a post-centenary era, when Thomas has been read and reified, cited and situated across so many domains, it seems remiss to overlook the various ways in which Thomas exists not only in the pages of his own works but further, elsewhere in culture and society. Firstly, James Keery examines what might be understood as the origin of the widespread antipathy towards Thomas from certain areas of English letters. His keenly observed chapter traces this to Kingsley Amis's sneering yet influential contempt for Thomas in the early days of The Movement, a perception that Keery suggests went 'viral, to be endlessly repeated for sixty years'. Yet as this chapter notes, a closer look at Amis's first collection of poetry, *Bright November* (1947), a volume consistently overlooked, perhaps suppressed (even repressed) by Amis's critics and celebrants, reveals a strong sub-Thomasian pungency that appears to have haunted Amis throughout his career. Keery's careful reading of this early work, alongside Amis's numerous later jibes, reveals an anxiety of influence that provides further evidence that Thomas can be read as the Oedipal father of The Movement, the irrepressible progenitor of its plain-talking, anti-excess poetics. Keery's chapter ends with an intriguing reading of Amis's late work *The Old Devils* (1986) as suggestive of a kind of atonement for past wrongs.

Finally, Kieron Smith's chapter looks beyond the page to take us on a tour of the innumerable 'extra-textual' traces of Dylan Thomas that are both visible and invisible within the cultural and public spheres, particularly so during the 2014 centenary celebrations. Starting with a walk around Swansea, a city whose urban architecture is plastered with images and references to its most famous son, Smith uses a critical cultural policy studies approach to examine the extent to which the image and idea of Dylan Thomas were employed at various levels of state administration in the months leading up to 2014. He homes in on local (City and County of Swansea) and national (Welsh Government) policy documents released through Freedom of Information requests, and argues that the reifications of Thomas endorsed and funded at the level of the state were too often shaped around bluntly neoliberal economic priorities. While Thomas, as Goodby notes, may have once been 'non-recruitable' by literary scholars, the centenary celebrations proved he was easy to enlist by state administrators. Smith suggests that an approach to cultural policy that starts instead from the very culture the state purports to 'administrate' might lead the way to more progressive forms of cultural policymaking.

We hope that this diverse collection of perspectives captures something of the spirit of Thomas's mode – which, as we have seen, famously contained 'a beast, an angel, and a madman' within it. We stress that this book is in no way an effort to fix or pin down a definitive, singular Dylan Thomas. Any attempt to do so would involve an act of occlusion or omission, be this an aspect of his often-contradictory life, his complex literary modality, or part of his oeuvre. Indeed, readers will note significant omissions in this book. For one, there is little discussion of Thomas's place within the contemporary poetic imagination. This is certainly not due to any lack of material; Wales in particular has, since the vote in favour of devolution in 1997, been the locus of an enormous amount of literary activity. Indeed, there is exciting work being done, particularly in avant-garde poetry; see, for example, the work of Nia Davies, Steven Hitchens, Zoë Skoulding, Rhys Trimble, and Nerys Williams. Yet, while such writers may seem the obvious inheritors of a Welsh modernist tradition set in motion by Thomas and his contemporaries – Lynette Roberts and David Jones in particular – much of this new writing draws upon the disjunctive experience of twenty-first-century life, and the energies generated by the interaction within and between languages and cultures, rather than any overt connection to writers of the 1930s and 1940s.[28] These poets certainly aren't the first generation to sidestep Thomas; as John Goodby and Lyndon Davies have noted, poets in Wales have a long history of detaching themselves from the 'distorting gravitational field of Thomas's style and reputation'.[29] As Matthew Jarvis concludes in his recent assessment of post-devolution writing in Wales, the latest generation of poets appear to be steering clear of Thomas's umbra: 'the complexities of writing in Wales . . . are as much to do with working away from or in the absence of distinctively Welsh models [such as Dylan Thomas] as they are of writing under their influence'.[30] There is evidently much further work to be done in tracing this absence.

There is, moreover, a serious lack of female voices in this collection. Indeed this appears to be a serious and significant 'lack' in Thomas criticism more generally, and we hope this collection is a provocation for further discussion, and in particular for long-needed applications of feminist and queer readings to Thomas's life and work. Furthermore, while we currently live in an age in which it is no longer radical to talk of hybridity, liminality or intersectionality, yet simultaneously an age in which walls and borders are being rebuilt, it is surely a timely opportunity to re-read a writer who speaks from and to the ambivalences, contradictions and complexities of social and personal experience. Thomas's work, in its very 'essence', so to speak, is always excessive, processual, and always eludes final interpretation; indeed, it is a testament to the scope of Thomas's work that it demands a never-complete diversity of critical approaches. And while Thomas's oeuvre rewards a multiplicity of readings from a range of different and, sometimes, differing perspectives, its power perhaps resides in the fact that it never closes down further readings. Thus, where *Under Milk Wood* was playfully subtitled a 'play for voices', we view this collection as a play *of* voices, some harmonious, some dissonant, but hopefully, as a collection, resonant. If the power of Thomas's mode as a 'writer of words, and nothing else' was radically to destabilise what that phrase meant and could mean, it is hoped that this diverse range of critical perspectives responds to the rich potentialities of this.

Notes

1 Dylan Thomas, 'Poetic Manifesto', in *Early Prose Writings*, ed. Walford Davies (London: Dent, 1971), p. 155.
2 Thomas, 'Poetic Manifesto', in *Early Prose Writings*, p. 154.
3 Thomas, 'Poetic Manifesto', in *Early Prose Writings*, p. 156.
4 Dylan Thomas, *A Child's Christmas in Wales* (London: Orion, 2014), p. 7.
5 Terry Jones, 'Foreword', in Hannah Ellis (ed.), *Dylan Thomas: A Centenary Celebration* (London: Bloomsbury, 2014), p. vii.
6 Philip Pullman, 'Dylan Thomas', in Ellis (ed.), *Dylan Thomas: A Centenary Celebration*, p. 222.
7 George Tremlett, 'The Kind of Man He Was', in Ellis (ed.), *Dylan Thomas: A Centenary Celebration*, p. 188.

8 Griff Rhys Jones, 'Reading Dylan Thomas', in Ellis (ed.), *Dylan Thomas: A Centenary Celebration*, p. 248.

9 Thomas, 'Poetic Manifesto', in *Early Prose Writings*, p. 155.

10 Thomas, 'Poetic Manifesto', in *Early Prose Writings*, p. 156.

11 See *http://www.dylanthomas.com/events/wordy-shapes-women/* (accessed 23 February 2018).

12 See *http://www.visitwales.com/prize-draws/dylathon* (accessed 23 February 2018).

13 John Goodby, *The Poetry of Dylan Thomas: Under the Spelling Wall* (Liverpool: Liverpool University Press, 2013), p. xv.

14 Goodby, *The Poetry of Dylan Thomas*, p. 452.

15 This has been done recently in John Goodby's *The Poetry of Dylan Thomas* (2013) and Rhian Barfoot's *Liberating Dylan Thomas: Rescuing a Poet from Psycho-sexual Servitude* (Cardiff: University of Wales Press, 2014).

16 E. B. Cox (ed.), *Dylan Thomas: A Collection of Critical Essays* (London: Prentice-Hall, 1966), p. 3.

17 Roland Barthes, 'The Death of the Author', in *Image Music Text*, trans. Stephen Heath (London: Fontana, 1977 [1967]).

18 John Goodby and Chris Wigginton, 'Introduction', in John Goodby and Chris Wigginton (eds), *Dylan Thomas: New Casebook* (Basingstoke: Palgrave, 2001), p. 2.

19 R. B. Kerschner, *Dylan Thomas: The Poet and His Critics* (Chicago: American Library Association, 1976), p. 24.

20 For a fuller discussion of this, see Goodby and Wigginton, 'Introduction', in Goodby and Wigginton (eds), *Dylan Thomas: New Casebook*.

21 See *http://www.swansea.ac.uk/riah/news/archive/2013-2014/dylanunchainedcall-forpapers.php* (accessed 23 February 2018).

22 See Daniel G. Williams, 'Welsh Modernism', in Brooker et al., *The Oxford Handbook of Modernisms* (Oxford: Oxford University Press, 2010).

23 See Laura Wainwright, *New Territories in Modernism: Anglophone Welsh Writing, 1930–1949* (Cardiff: University of Wales Press, 2018).

24 Williams, 'Welsh Modernism', in Brooker et al., *The Oxford Handbook of Modernisms*, p. 799.

25 Dylan Thomas, quoted in E. W. Tedlock (ed.), *Dylan Thomas: The Legend and the Poet*, (London: William Heinemann, 1960), p. 8.

26 Edward Soja, *Thirdspace: Journeys to Los Angeles and Other Real-and-Imagined Places* (Oxford: Blackwell, 1996).

27 Dylan Thomas, 'Poetic Manifesto', in *Early Prose Writings*, p. 157.

28 See Daniel G. Williams, 'In Paris or Sofia? Avant-Garde Poetry and Cultural Nationalism after Devolution', in Matthew Jarvis (ed.), *Devolutionary Readings*, pp. 115–56.

29 John Goodby and Lyndon Davies, 'Introduction', in *The Edge of Necessary: An Anthology of Welsh Innovative Poetry 1966–2018* (Llangattock: Aquifer, 2018), p. 17.

30 Matthew Jarvis, 'Devolutionary Complexities: Reading Three New Poets', in Matthew Jarvis (ed.), *Devolutionary Readings: English-Language Poetry and Contemporary Wales* (Oxford: Peter Lang, 2017), p. 113.

2

SHIBBOLETH: FOR DYLAN THOMAS

Tomos Owen

INTRODUCTION: BIRTH/DAY

The 27th of October is Dylan Thomas's birthday. He was born on this date in 1914, at 5 Cwmdonkin Drive, Swansea. A hundred years later, that same address played host to a series of events to commemorate that same date, with 'all eyes' trained on the front bedroom.[1] 'Dylan Thomas 100' was the name given to a high-profile year-long commemoration of the poet's centenary, backed by the Welsh Government, the Arts Council of Wales, and Literature Wales. The birthday itself saw the culmination of these activities, in Wales and beyond; indeed, the birthday could scarcely have evaded us: books were published, column inches filled, documentaries produced, adaptations performed, programmes broadcast, conferences organised, lectures delivered. In many important ways, however, Thomas's poetry is already and has always been involved in its own commemoration. As Walford Davies has written,

> No wonder Thomas is everywhere memorably found remembering. At the centenary of his birth, it is worth also *our* remembering that he wrote some of the best birthday poems in the English language . . .[2]

And, while birthday poems are quite capable of marking an anniversary, Davies continues by noting importantly Thomas's significance 'not just on birthdays, but on days of birth': for Thomas, 'each diurnal round had always a somewhat "creationist" resonance' extending beyond the merely calendrical.[3]

This chapter accepts Walford Davies's invitation to remember by considering these birthday poems and their own commemorative qualities in relation to what it terms Thomas's 'anniversary poetics'. It argues that the birthday poems bring into view a crucial element of Thomas's process poetic: while the birthday may commemorate origins in time and place, the birthday poem inevitably reaches out beyond its spatial and temporal boundedness. Moreover, in staging the experience of the birthday, the poems discussed in this chapter reveal the radical uncertainty of the date, and its ghostly non-contemporaneity with itself. The broader scope of this chapter, then, is to contribute to new ways of thinking about modernist literature and the everyday, and, most crucially, to further our understanding of Thomas's distinctively Welsh modernism. Spanning across his publishing career, Thomas's birthday poems are dated – not in the sense of their being out of fashion, but rather in the sense that they are marked by the date. They reflect on the specific singularity of the birthday, on what 'Poem in October' specifies as 'that second' (*CP*, 160). But they are never about 'that second' alone; by inevitably extending beyond the immediacy of the birthday, these poems are marked by what Jacques Derrida describes as 'the enigma of the date'.[4] The birthday poem is after all a poem occasioned by the birthday, which is called into being by it; but it is also a poem *about* the birthday, reflecting or constructing the experience of that anniversary occasion. Taken together, each of the birthday poems speak to each other; indeed, they speak because of each other, each unique yet also echoing and returning in different ways. Both cause and effect, they each carry the uncanny, enigmatic, ghostly traces of past commemorations and those still to come.

In 'Shibboleth: For Paul Celan', Derrida outlines the 'enigma of the date' by considering the enigmatic function of the motifs of passwords, ash, circumcision and (importantly for this present chapter) the date. The enigma resides in the tension between the singularity of the date (the way that, through dating, we fix a moment in time and place) and the inevitable necessity that the date must repeat. The poem, argues Derrida, 'is *due* its date, *due to* its date, owes itself to its date as its own inmost concern': immutable and indelible, the poem is dated to a singular occasion and abides by it.[5] But the poem must also efface the date, or acquit itself of it, so that it may be properly addressed beyond the date:

the date, by its mere occurrence, by the inscription of a sign as memorandum, will have broken the silence of pure singularity. But to speak of it, one must also efface it, make it readable, audible, intelligible *beyond the pure singularity* of which it speaks.[6]

A consideration of Dylan Thomas's birthday poems must be attentive to this tension, that they mark the birthday but are also marked by it, and emerge from its specific singularity. Yet no sooner are the poems given utterance than that singularity is effaced and erased. This must be the case if we are to be able to read and to address the specificity – what Derrida describes as the 'impossible repetition' – of the birthday.[7] How, asks Derrida,

can one date what does not repeat if dating also calls for some form of recurrence, if it recalls in the readability of a repetition? But how date anything else than that which does not repeat?[8]

Derrida illustrates how the enigmatic quality of the date is inscribed in what he terms the 'semantics of the everyday'.[9] He does this by unpicking the distinctions in what is meant by the word '*time*' in the phrase 'one time', and by the word 'once'. 'One speaks of "time" in the English "one time", but not in "once"', Derrida suggests.[10] When we say 'once' in English, or *einmal* in German, or any of the French, Italian or Spanish forms (*une fois, una volta, una vez* respectively) – or, as the poet's own parents might have said in Welsh, *un tro* – we resort, notes Derrida, 'to the figure of the turn or the volte, the turnabout'.[11] In speaking of what once happened, we inevitably conjure the sense of the turnaround, the circling back, the commemoration or anniversary. Thomas's birthday poems enact precisely this commemoration of the singularity of the date, but also (or while also, or and inevitably also) reaching beyond that singularity. The date for Derrida, and the birthday for Thomas, is thus '[a] thing from our past that comes back in memory, but also a problem for the future, an eternal problem, and above all a way toward poetry'.[12]

Birthdays, of course, do not happen every day, though we should keep in mind Davies's claim that for Dylan Thomas every day may still be a day of birth. The present chapter limits its focus to the birthday poems: 'Especially when the October wind', from *18 Poems* (1934); 'Twenty-four years', from *The Map of Love* (1939); 'Poem in October', from *Deaths and Entrances* (1946); and 'Poem on his Birthday', from

In Country Sleep (1952). There are, of course, other works by Thomas in which an 'anniversary poetics' is at play: *Under Milk Wood* is structured by the day yet also extends beyond it; likewise, the 1943 US-published version of 'On a Wedding Anniversary' negotiates the tension between the 'original voices of the air' and the 'torn' sky across the 'ragged anniversary'.[13] In each of these examples, poems open out onto a world of textuality – what John Goodby has described as their 'word-world' – in radically open and decentred ways.[14] Every day is remarkable in Thomas's poems, birthdays especially.

ESPECIALLY

'Especially when the October wind' was included in Thomas's first collection, *18 Poems*, published in 1934. Ralph Maud dates the poem to 1932 from an early typescript version, in which it is the November wind that blows through its lines.[15] Maud and Davies note that 'If it is one of Thomas's birthday poems, it became so when revised for publication in *The Listener*, 24 October 1934, with the title "Poem in October"'.[16] This is to say that the poem was first published a few days short of Thomas's twentieth birthday and with an initial title which, like a birthday bell, would ring down the years to become the title of the 1946 poem published in *Deaths and Entrances*. Maud does more than state the obvious when he asserts 'without fear of contradiction that it was written by a born poet'.[17] The earliest of the four, 'Especially when the October wind' is a poem about the birth of a born poet, the coming-into-being of what he always-already was, the inauguration of what had ever been the case. Such are the temporal gymnastics required of a birthday celebration.

Across the four stanzas, the poet-speaker moves from the shore in stanza one, to the 'tower of words' overlooking the 'star-gestured children in the park' in stanza two, to the suburban interior with its pot of ferns and grandfather clock in stanza three, to a wider Welsh landscape in stanza four (*CP*, 67–8). From the shore, where the October wind roughs and ruffles the speaker's hair, there is an outward movement which correlates with how the speaker's 'busy heart . . . / Sheds syllabic blood' (*CP*, 67) in exuberantly meeting the world but also, crucially, constructing and defining that world through language – through poetry, perhaps. Davies's earlier-quoted suggestion that Thomas's poems have a 'creationist' impulse is seen here in the poem's refrain: 'some let me make you' (lines 13, 16, 21, 24, 26,

29). The making in the poem is the making of the poem, the interface between words and wider worlds. Simultaneously, however, the energy of that 'busy heart' is immediately and already, inevitably, being spent, spilled and drained. The speaker is given access and permission to greet the environs which are simultaneously constructed through language. But this permission, being let or let out to this word-world, also suggests a connection to the *letting* of that same vital life blood. We might read the line, then, as 'Some [poems] let me make [for] you'. 'Especially when the October wind' thus connects the birthday with poetic identity: the speaker may be a poet all year round, but he is especially so when the October wind blows through his hair in his birthday month. As Maud brilliantly puts it, this is an example that 'shows the young poet going all out: and that is the poem's subject as well. A poem about writing your heart out.'[18] Going out and going all out are connected activities for the born poet; at a stroke, writing the wider world into existence also lets the syllabic blood. Here, the speaker of 'Especially when the October wind' might himself be referring to the way that the *poems* are what allow or what let him make the world. In a kind of self-address in the second person, the speaker also states simultaneously how he is granted license by poetry to make himself ('you'). As will become evident later in this chapter, asking permission, seeking access, is an important thread of continuity across several of the birthday poems. If they let you do anything on your birthday, the world outside is let out to the poet-tenant for a short term only. Marking the birthday is both a confirmation of one's own life and a portent of one's own demise.

Welsh modernism can be thought of as a product of the enabling yet difficult tension between Welsh and English; thus, in Thomas's poem, the 'spider-tongued' poet operates between the two languages of the 'loud hill of Wales' (*CP*, 68). This gives an abundance of linguistic raw material, yet also means that he is never fully at home in it either. It is in this sense that Daniel Williams writes of how Thomas, 'the non-Welsh speaking son of Welsh-speaking parents deployed English with such an original virtuosity that it seemed to be tearing the language apart.'[19] And in this poem, the poet is a temporary resident, a tenant in a linguistic universe which has been 'let' out to him and for which his verse constitutes rent. (That Thomas himself was famously impecunious, always late with the rent, is not the main concern of this chapter; however, Thomas's next birthday poem, 'Twenty-four years', would exhibit a concern with the question

of payment and spending.) Set against the poem's creative impulse is
another meaning of the word 'let', namely that of shedding or spilling.
That the phrase 'let me make you' should juxtapose the making and
letting of this creative force is an indicator of the poem's oscillation
between creation and destruction, composition and decomposition.
The wagging clock in the second stanza enacts this oscillation, so
appropriate on a birthday when the commemoration of one's making
is always accompanied by the ghostly reminder of one's own mortality. 'Wagging' may be a chastising or warning gesture to the young
poet who is himself something of a wag here ('a mischievous boy',
OED, n.2.1). Moreover, the *OED* reminds us that wagging is also a
form of speech, meaning to 'move [tongue or lips] briskly in animated
talk' (*OED*, v.4b). Yet however loquacious the birthday boy may be,
wagging can also mean to 'dangle from the gallows' (*OED*, v.3d).[20]
The wagging clock, like the date, links the loquacious lad with the
dead silence that is inescapably to come. The permissive nature of that
word 'let' was commented upon by no less a figure than Thomas himself. 'I make one image,' he said, in a letter to Henry Treece in 1938,

> though 'make' is not the word, I let, perhaps, an image be 'made' emotion-
> ally in me and then apply to it what intellectual & critical forces I possess
> – let it breed another, let that image contradict the first, make, of the third
> image bred out of the other two together, a fourth contradictory image,
> and let them all, within my imposed formal limits, conflict. (*CL*, 281)

By this account Thomas makes poetry and is made by it, much as
the speaker of 'Especially when the October wind' is let (in the sense
of being permitted) to make poems from the 'wordy shapes' of the
world he encounters. A dynamic tension between 'make' and 'let', the
active and the passive, underlies many of Thomas's poems. Can he
make them? Will language let him?

STRUT

'Twenty-four years' sets out, sets off, again: it is a poem which
advances, but also retreats; it struts, but also frets. It was included
in Thomas's 1939 collection *The Map of Love*, but had also been
published under the title 'Birthday Poem' in *Life and Letters Today* in
December 1938, and Thomas had initially sent it to Vernon Watkins
in October. John Milton's sonnet 'On Being Arrived at Twenty-Three

Years of Age' – with its exclamation of 'How soon hath Time, the subtle thief of youth, / Stolen on his wing my three-and-twentieth year!' – stands as a poetic template for Thomas's poem.[21] Both poems tell the time, and both speakers are told, by the time, how fleeting is their earthly existence. Critics have identified in Milton's sonnet an ambiguity – a contestation or conflation – of meanings which, though seemingly incompatible, are sustained by the poem.[22] In its ability to sustain two seemingly incompatible readings, Milton's sonnet would appear to have plenty in common with Thomas's process poetic.

The speaker, on his birthday, sets out – of the womb, of the house – in the heat and light of the 'meat-eating sun' (*CP*, 107), which both gives life and takes it away, to encounter the 'death-oriented life-to-come' (*CP*, 346, note by Goodby). Rachel Bowlby has identified the uncanny echoes, reverberations and correspondences bound up in the way we measure time: short times can mirror or echo long times, and vice versa; epochal and fleeting time may be condensed or expanded to correlate with each other.[23] The twenty-four years of age that this second birthday poem commemorate also invoke the length, in hours, of a single day – a silent, impossible repetition in chronological time which may nonetheless be sustained by the poem. Sharply dressed, and with the swagger of the 'sensual strut', the speaker sets out. Red veins 'full of money' combines the sense of having pockets full of money and veins coursing with the vitality of life blood. In its first line this poem marks the birthday as an occasion which is also a reminder; the image of the veins serves perhaps as a reminder of the image of the 'syllabic blood' of 'Especially when the October wind'. If this is a poem about a 24-year-old embarking on a night on the town, it is also a poem which commemorates the very first birthday, the very first moment of embarking on a journey: birth itself. Crouched in the space of the 'natural doorway' of the womb, the pre-natal tailor figure (Goodby describes him as the 'tailor embryo' of the poem) sews his own shroud (*CP*, 346). Echoes of the tailor's sartorial talents are heard in the sixth line, which has the speaker 'Dressed to die', punning on the notion of being dressed to kill: the dapper young man sets out, dressed to die, for the night of his life. In this way, the poem links the setting out (from the mother's womb, towards the town) by moving the speaker '[i]n the final direction of the elementary town': in his element, in the elements, the speaker's going out on the town combines with the going out of the light most memorably described in 'Do not go gentle into that good night'. The birthday in its singularity

– even the singularity of the very first birthday – is never 'pure' or totally consistent with itself. A repetition always occurs, is always occurring, is always set to occur again.

The provenance of the poem's final line seems also to enact its temporal circuitry at a meta-textual level. Maud and Davies point to a manuscript for an unpublished poem that begins with the line, 'For as long as forever is'.[24] Thomas himself mentions the line in a letter to Vernon Watkins, dated 24 October 1938, three days shy of his twenty-fourth birthday:

> I know you'll hate the use of the 'Forever' line, but there it is. I scrapped the poem beginning with that line long ago, and at last – I think – I've found the inevitable place for it: it was a time finding that place . . . Try to read the end of the poem as though you didn't know the lines. I do feel they're right. (*CL*, 334)

While this letter tells us something about Thomas's writing practice, what has the greatest bearing for this chapter is the curious status of that final inevitable line: in order to arrive at its final, inevitable place, the line needed first to appear in the wrong place, at the start of the jettisoned manuscript poem buried in the archive. Thomas's request for Watkins to read the poem as though he did not know the lines – coupled with the striking phrase that 'it was a time finding that place' – enacts the curious and ghostly troubling of origins, death and commemoration symptomatic of the birthday. Dating a letter and a poem assigns it a time and a place. For Thomas and this poem it was a time to find that right and inevitable place where the line should always have been. For all its inevitability, the line's provenance hovers around the poem; Watkins must try to read the end of the poem as though he does not know the lines, yet he – and we – must at the same time be aware that the line is a kind of ghost. Watkins must know and not know, must begin while remembering, must commence the poem while repeating. The line's inevitability and rightness in its final advance is a feature of its repeatability, its potential for reinscription to and from other contexts.

That other phrase – the end of the poem – is itself echoed in the title of a book by Paul Muldoon. Muldoon's lectures, delivered during his tenure as the Professor of Poetry at the University of Oxford, address a range of different interpretations of the 'end', and argue that in several important regards poetry and individual poems are endless, without end. Pausing to think about the ways poems end, Muldoon claims that the end of the poem 'has to do with the influence of one poem on another within the body of work of a single poet, whereby "gaps" or "blanks" in one poem are completed or perfected by another'.[25] One feature of Thomas's anniversary poetics is that his birthday poems do speak to each other across his body of work; contra Muldoon, however, they never fully complete each other, and gaps remain. Thus each birthday poem of Thomas's is ghosted and echoed by the others in a bringing-together that is a function of the enigma of the date. But a line like the 'inevitable' conclusion to 'Twenty-four Years' troubles rather than confirms the finality of its ending.

SHIBBOLETH

It would seem, then, that if a birthday is a cause for celebration, it is also a kind of mourning. Appearing in both Derrida's title and my own is 'shibboleth'. Derrida's text puts a great deal of effort into exploring the functions and valences of the word as it appears in the poetry of Paul Celan. A shibboleth is a kind of belief or code of behaviour that distinguishes one group of people from another. As the *OED* notes, it may denote '[a] custom, habit, mode of dress, or the like, which distinguishes a particular class or set of persons' (n.2c); but it may also mean figuratively a form of speech, '[a] catchword or formula adopted by a party or sect, by which their adherents or followers may be discerned, or those not their followers excluded' (n.3a). A shibboleth is, therefore, also a password. While nowadays a whole range of words, habits or customs may serve the purpose, the word shibboleth itself comes from the Hebrew, literally meaning 'an ear of corn'. Its use as a password, something uttered at a border crossing, comes from the Book of Judges, where the surviving Ephraimites, returning home from their defeat in battle at the hands of the Gileadites, were required to prove their identity at the crossing of the river Jordan:

> [5] And the Gileadites took the passages of Jordan before the Ephraimites: and it was so, that when those Ephraimites which were escaped said, Let me go over; that the men of Gilead said unto him, Art thou an Ephramite? If he said, Nay; [6] Then said they unto him, say now Shibboleth: and he said Sibboleth: for he could not frame to pronounce it right. Then they took him, and slew him at the passages of Jordan: and there fell at that time of the Ephraimites forty and two thousand.[26]

The shibboleth, the ear of corn, is used at the border to distinguish the Ephraimites, whose speech lacked the *sh* phoneme and so pronounced it *sibboleth*, from the Gileadites, who could pronounce it correctly. Correctly giving the password is a matter of vouchsafing one's identity, of confirming one's origins, of being granted access at the frontier. (We may betray our own origins in the way we say the poet's name: Thomas once wrote to a fan that his name rhymes with 'villain'.)[27]

Thomas himself gives the password in the one example of the shibboleth found in his work. This comes in 'A Refusal to Mourn the Death, by Fire, of a Child in London', from *Deaths and Entrances*, when the speaker mentions entering again

> . . . the round
> Zion of the water bead
> And the synagogue of the ear of corn . . . (*CP*, 172)

Goodby has noted how the insertion of this cluster of images into the poem's published form constitutes a 'glancing' but significant response to the Holocaust, news of which was emerging when Thomas was completing the poem.[28] Comparing the published poem with the early unpublished draft entitled 'A Refusal for an Elegy', Goodby argues that 'the addition of "Zion" and "synagogue" reflected news of the Nazi death camps, not liberated by the Allies until 1945, when Thomas completed the poem'.[29] We can add to this list the ear of corn.

In a notably bad-tempered reading, Terry Eagleton accuses this poem of 'an elaborateness of form' concealing 'a paucity of content'.[30] The bone of Eagleton's contention is the 'imbalance of form and content' that governs the poem: 'The reader has to wait ten lines, until the arrival of the main verb "Shall I let pray", to see that this "Never" clause [which opens the poem] is modifying, as though the poet is so absorbed in his own metaphorical pyrotechnics that he comes near to losing track of what he was about to say.'[31] By this account, too much effort is wasted on the modifying clause, and not enough dedicated to the work of mourning; too much verbose positioning, and not enough meaning; too much form, not enough content. Countering Eagleton's reading, Goodby emphasises how 'A Refusal to Mourn', typically for Thomas, is a literary object which produces rather than carries meaning: reading a Thomas poem is an event, unique in its every repetition. 'A Refusal to Mourn' is in many ways more than a simple rejection of meaning, a callous spurning or indifference to the reality of the dead child. As Goodby points out, the 'minimally punctuated clauses and unhyphenated compounds of the early lines of the poem', rather than being self-indulgent posturing, constitute a struggle 'to define the conditions under which mourning may take place'.[32] While Eagleton's claim is that Thomas does not get on with the job of mourning, the poem suggests instead that mourning is no simple job, not merely a prosaic sentiment to be communicated. Crucially, in this poem, the phrase which transitions from subordinate clause – from the 'Never until' to the 'Shall I let pray' – is the shibboleth. The 'ear of corn' is the password uttered at the frontier of the line break at the end of line nine. It is this which enables the transition from the painful explorations on the possibility or impossibility of adequately memorialising the dead child to the prayer uttered on her behalf. If, for Derrida, the date is a 'way towards poetry', then the shibboleth in Thomas's refusal might be thought of as a way towards mourning.

Nicholas Royle's words on Derrida's attitude towards mourning hold equally true for Dylan Thomas: 'there is no such thing as normal mourning, unless we grant that the normal is impossible . . . The concept of mourning entails the logic of the double-bind, an aporia whereby "success fails" and "failure succeeds". A refusal to mourn . . . is thus for Derrida an inseparable part of mourning. Mourning is necessarily divided, semi, demi, double mourning.'[33] The poem's apparent contradictoriness, its grappling with the conditions of mourning, its simultaneous refusal of and participation in the act of lament and commemoration, all betoken the peculiar and normal-impossible experience. The memory of the loved one is faithfully preserved and memorialised while simultaneously, as Royle argues, 'one has to let the other remain other, in other words to ensure that the other is not assimilated or effectively wiped out as other'.[34] Thomas's poem, in its very refusal, enacts this obligation towards the dead.

'A Refusal to Mourn' may be a notable poem for the presence of a dead child and an actual instance of the shibboleth in Thomas's work. 'London's daughter', however, is not the only image of a dead child, nor is the 'ear of corn' the only instance of the function of the shibboleth. The dead child, or the lost childhood, reappear as frequent images in other poems, too; perhaps unsurprisingly, the birthday poems contain other memorable, memorialised examples. Derrida, too, links the shibboleth with the function of the date and, adapting this line of thinking, we might suggest that the birthday, like the shibboleth, can give confirmation of one's origins and identity. Thomas's birthday and his birthday poems serve as a kind of shibboleth, grant-ing access to the particular qualities of his modernism – even his Welsh modernism. Yet, as we have seen already, the repetition of the birthday and the shibboleth – or the birthday-as-shibboleth – obeys a deconstructive double logic. As Derrida describes: 'There is no one meaning, from the moment that there is date and *shibboleth*, no longer a sole originary meaning.'[35] Like the date, the shibboleth performs its 'impossible repetition': in their uniqueness, both date and password can – and indeed must – be repeated, must come around again, must be renewed by repetition. In their repetition, birthday and password trouble our sense of origins and of originality, of beginnings and endings, of first and final things.

THAT SECOND

That shibboleth should include among its meanings a kind of pass-word given at a border crossing seems especially appropriate for a consideration of Thomas's anniversary poetics. In 'Poem in October', it is the poet's thirtieth birthday itself that functions as a kind of shib-boleth, as he describes how

> . . . I took the road
> Over the border
> And the gates
> Of the town closed as the town awoke. (*CP*, 160)

Setting off by once again setting out, 'Poem in October' continues the advance of the previous birthday poems, but also echoes and chimes with them. The 'October blood' of line 67 flows directly from the 'syllabic blood' of 'Especially when the October wind'; that same 'October wind' blows through as the 'rain wringing / Wind' of 'Poem in October' (*CP*, 160). These are two shoreline poems. 'Poem in October' is structured by a walk around the seaside town on the birthday morning: it is the speaker's 'thirtieth year to heaven' which 'Woke' 'the morning beckon', and which drives the poem and the speaker out of doors (*CP*, 160). While this outward motion drives the poem on, other elements turn it around, and pull it back: the uniqueness of the birthday conjures the remembrance of lost times. Rather than dampening the experience, the birthday rain brings down on the speaker 'a shower of all my days' (*CP*, 160). The poem details the birthday, and the speaker's stroll, in careful and evocative detail so that the singularity of the day – its condition of experience in the here and now – is directly emphasised:

> Myself to set foot
> That second
> In the still sleeping town and set forth. (*CP*, 160)

That second, and no other: the uniqueness of the moment is marked out, set down on a line of its own. Yet even 'that second' of time is a second time, a turnabout or repetition, twice told. If the rain is falling here, now, at 'that second', then it is also a shower of memories. The tension identified by Derrida – that when we say 'once' in English 'we resort to the figure of the turn' – is the governing force structuring the poem whose speaker, on his birthday, has gone out for a spin.[36] Indeed, this revolutionary poem continues its spin by enumerating images of return and repetition; as the speaker would marvel his birthday away at the end of the fourth stanza, 'the weather turned around' (*CP*, 161). Goodby identifies the importance of the turn and its variants as they appear in lines 40, 41, 46, 62, and 70, noting that '[t]here are two "turns" and three states, or landscapes in the poem: the present on the hill, a "blithe country" of lost faith or utopian belief, and a childhood vision'.[37] This turning is crucially linked to Thomas's exploration of the function of memory in this and other poems (the recollection of childhood in 'Fern Hill' is another notable instance figured by time, 'In all his tuneful turning' (*CP*, 178).)

Childhood, therefore, is always 'twice told', always entailing some sort of return, and never experienced during childhood *as* childhood: it is always and inevitably an adult construction. A birthday by this reckoning becomes an uncanny event, ghosted in the present by both past and future. A celebration of origins, the birthday confirms one's identity – like a password. But this returning day also troubles those same origins in a process that has implications for the poet's conception of place as well as time. 'Poem in October' defamiliarises Laugharne, the home patch, the square mile. Walking 'abroad', the speaker is both outdoors, out of his house or abode (*OED*, *adv*. 3.a) and out of his own country, 'in or into foreign lands' (*OED*, *adv*. 4.a); he is both at home and estranged from it. On his birthday, he is simultaneously himself and someone else. *Pace* Derrida, the date comes to us in the present from the past, and is a problem for our future.

Here, the encounter of the birthday is an encounter with the poet's younger self: the turn of the weather turns back the clock to 'a child's / Forgotten mornings' alongside his mother (*CP*, 161). The date thereby summons the 'fields of infancy', which are always and already 'twice told' (*CP*, 161), repeated in their uniqueness.

Identifying the similarity between birthdays and passwords, Bowlby notes that the date of birth is the only detail on a birth certificate that remains immutable. Parents, name, sex – all these may be changed, but the date of birth remains. However, as Bowlby remarks, 'one day, unknown to us now, the DOB will be matched by a second, echoing set of numbers. It is like the most private of passwords administered by the most security-conscious of companies, and we will never be asked for it, not till the day we die.'[38] The quality of the shibboleth and the anniversary lies in their ability to gather together a discontinuous array of events at the same instant. But for an anniversary poetics to function, a poem must also surrender its claims to authenticity or finality: it may be summoned by the date, and owe its existence to it, but it cannot be bound by it. Derrida exclaims that 'The date provokes the poem, but the latter speaks!'[39] The enigma of the date, and the birthday in particular, therefore, is that it is positioned at the crossroads between linguistic and cultural contexts which give it meaning, but that also and at the same time represents a singular encounter in the here and now. 'The date provokes the poem, but the latter speaks!': this declaration places its emphasis on the text as the speaking agent carrying the work of signification. While the poem is *due* its date, and *due to* its date, it is only the poem which can speak. Paradoxically, however, the condition for doing so is that the poem open itself up and free itself of the very particularities which give birth to it.

MIDLIFE

'Poem on his Birthday' is the poem of midlife crisis. Thomas's final birthday poem is, of the four he produced, the one that reflects most seriously and gravely on the mortality that is also secretly commemorated on the day. 'Poem on his Birthday' confronts the end unsmilingly, and with more solemnity: this is a poem of mourning as much as it is a poem of celebration. The thirty-fifth birthday that it commemorates is the tipping point, the halfway stage through god's allotted three-score years and ten, when suddenly comes the realisation that there is more behind than there is yet to come. 'Oh, let me midlife mourn . . .

/ The voyage to ruin I must run' (*CP*, 200), exclaims the poet (the crucial word 'let' appearing here again). Thomas himself, though he did not know it, of course, was much nearer his own end than the poem presents, and would be dead before reaching forty years of age. But if this poem is the 'mourning' of midlife, it is also an articulation of much broader troubling and wide-reaching concerns. James A. Davies has identified how anxieties about nuclear war inflected Thomas's poems of childhood in *Deaths and Entrances*, including the 'apparently idyllic' 'Fern Hill', while Goodby contends that in 'Poem on His Birthday', alongside 'Over St John's Hill', 'the threat of atomic weapons to humanity and nature produced an ecological perspective, in what might be called . . . "Cold War pastoral".'[40] The ending of this last poem delivers a reminder of the ending that awaits us all (like Bowlby's encrypted password); the final word of its final line – die – is what awaits us upon reaching the end of our reading and the end of our lives. And in its apocalyptic tone the poem's ending transforms it into a poem of the end, a poem about the end of all poems.

The philosopher Giorgio Agamben has discussed the problems and anxieties surrounding poetic endings. Like Paul Muldoon's study mentioned earlier in this chapter, Agamben's book – also entitled *The End of the Poem* – develops a consideration of what happens at the end of poems into an unfolding concern with what are the ends of poetry. For Agamben in particular, the end of the poem is a pressure point: 'if poetry is defined precisely by the possibility of enjambment', then the last line of a poem cannot meet this criterion.[41] As Michael Wood puts it, '[e]njambment occurs when a poetic line stops, but the sentence or clause doesn't'.[42] Thus if poems are energised by the tension between metrical and syntactical limits – between how and what a poem signifies – then the last line of a poem signals for Agamben a 'state of poetic emergency' in resolving this tension into 'an exact coincidence of sound and sense'.[43] Poems are by this reading forever attempting to stave off their endings lest sound 'be ruined in the abyss of sense'.[44] Intrigued by Agamben's counter-intuitive claims, Wood nonetheless sounds a note of scepticism and caution at his 'high stakes, all-or-nothing' style of argument, and posits another 'more familiar criterion for distinguishing poetry from prose: rhyme'.[45] As we shall see, both of these elements – rhyme and the end of the poem – are key features of Thomas's birthday poems, which, fearful of the end, might prefer to keep going, 'for as long as forever is' (*CP*, 107). The theme of setting out and setting down which is common to each is simultaneously an advance towards the grave and a putting off of that final destination.

'Poem on his Birthday', at 108 lines, is the longest of Thomas's birthday poems; it keeps going longer than the others. Active in this poem, and in keeping with the process poetic, is the tension between creation and destruction; and on this midlife birthday, this tension is especially powerful. Rhyme and the end of the poem become curiously commingled, triangulating a relationship between the birth(day), death and the act of writing itself. Scattered across the poem are several images and words that call back to mind the returning quality of the date.[46] The poet 'tolls his birthday bell', 'celebrates and spurns / His driftwood thirty-fifth wind turned age' (*CP*, 197). From the 'slant, racking house' the poet looks out over the Laugharne estuary and observes the herons, wildfowl and other fauna of the scene through the 'hewn coils' of his trade (*CP*, 198). That the poet's age be 'turned' shows that repetition is present as soon as there is a date. In conjunction with those hewn coils, it also suggests a sense in which the poet and his work are turned like an object, in the craftsman's sense. Having described himself as 'the rhymer in the long tongued room', those hewn coils of the poet's trade summon to mind Wood's 'more familiar' criterion for poetry, namely rhyme itself. For what is a rhyme if not a unit of sound that coils around and upon itself? Hewn coils, rhyming, recall themselves. But to hew also means to cut, and the circularity of the coil, in its turning, is interrupted by the incision. (Derrida identifies a tension with a similar structure in 'Shibboleth', where it is the motif of circumcision that provides the 'cut' in the poetry of Celan.) Thomas's 'Poem on his Birthday' contains both full and assonantal rhyme at line endings, as well as a host of internal rhymes within lines, or ghost rhymes and echoes across the poem as a whole. Thus the lines describing how

> the rhymer in the long tongued room,
>   Who tolls his birthday bell,
> Toils towards the ambush of his wounds

link the 'tolls' of the birthday bell with the toil leading towards death (*CP*, 198). The long tongued room where writing takes place might also recall the arachnid spider-tongued imagery of 'Especially when the October wind'. Here, the tolling of the celebratory birthday bell summons a connection with the grave-bound toil that is our life on earth. The 'slant racking house' is, as Goodby notes, a place where the poet racks his brains.[47] It is also a place of half rhymes, or *slant*ing rhymes, where the toil takes its toll on the poet, on the rack.

The fifth stanza of the poem again indicates the troubling of identity that a birthday brings about, at the level of form as well as content. The internal rhyme of the 'white angelus knells' in line 38, with the 'Thirty-five bells' of the next line, summon up a ghostly co-existence of birth and death. Angelus knells are bells commemorative of the Annunciation and Incarnation – they are very much linked, therefore, to birth, to taking flesh. Yet Thomas's choice, 'knells', is that of a solemn slow ringing, often 'immediately after death or at a funeral' (*OED*, n. a; see also definition b.: 'A sound announcing the death of a person or the passing away of something; an omen of death or extinction'). Following shortly afterwards, in line 41, comes the apocalyptic image of falling stars. In the rhyming of 'knells' and 'bells' across the line comes the combination of birth and demise. Yet the function of rhyme itself is, like the birthday, similarly deconstructive: the first word 'knells' must wait until the arrival of the second word 'bells' in order for the rhyme to sound. Likewise, for the second word to rhyme requires the earlier appearance of its counterpart. Rhymes, therefore, summon an interdependent relationship where the origin disappears as soon as we hear it: it makes little sense to say that the rhyme 'originates' with one sound or the other. Repetition of sound is already inscribed within language, just as the date, in spite of its uniqueness, always comes around again.

CONCLUSION: HAPPY RETURNS

With a radical impetus, Thomas's birthday poems launch themselves out beyond their origin, their dates, times and places. Recent work by scholars of literary modernism has foregrounded the connections between modernist writing and the everyday, including what Bryony Randall has termed the 'dailiness' of modernism.[48] Randall has pointed out how 'much modernist literature is, precisely, engaged in the questioning or defamiliarisation of practices, objects and environments assumed to be "everyday"',[49] and while a birthday comes but once a year (not every day), for Thomas it never comes alone. The birthday is a day that searchingly interrogates and defamiliarises environments from which it emerges – cultural, linguistic, national. Following Derrida's 'Shibboleth: for Paul Celan', the poetry speaks because, and in spite of, that which provokes it. It is in this vein – of absent presences, of unfamiliar familiarity, of an alienation of the self through the commemoration of its origins – that we might think of the uncanniness or ghostliness of the birthday and of the birthday poems.

Thomas is a vivid example among writers of his generation for whom that uncanniness stems from Welsh origins. As Daniel Williams has argued, anglophone Welsh modernism 'emerges from an uneasy relationship between two languages; it is a literature in translation'.[50] Tony Brown, meanwhile, maintains that this uneasiness gives rise to a particular structure of feeling for writers of Thomas's generation in particular. In developing a definition of the 'Welsh Uncanny', he notes how Thomas and his Welsh contemporaries – including Gwyn Thomas and Glyn Jones – were the first for whom Welsh was their parents' language, but not their own, and that this 'psycho-cultural situation' gave rise to 'a sense of the world as an insecure, uncanny place'.[51] If the 'loud hill of Wales' from 'Especially when the October wind', or the Laugharne of 'Poem in October' and 'Poem on his Birthday' are, like the birthday, among the elements that provoke these poems and bring them about, then they are never so completely. Rather, Thomas's Welsh modernism emerges from dateable and locatable times and places, but it is never reducible to them and always exceeds them. Indeed, the anniversary qualities of Thomas's birthday poems – their impossible repetitions – both efface and commemorate that which gives them life. A necessary condition inherent in the work, and this is the nature of the shibboleth, is that it remain both secret and open, commemorating what is destined to be forgotten. The turning and returning of time at the end of 'Poem in October' leads the speaker to wish

> O may my heart's truth
>   Still be sung
> On this high hill in a year's turning. (*CP*, 162)

Sailing out to die, advancing as long as forever is, we are thus greeted by Thomas's birthday poems and invited by their own anniversary poetics to wish many happy returns.

Notes

[1] *http://www.5cwmdonkindrive.com/events.php* (accessed May 2017). The house is now a museum, and between 17–28 October 2014 hosted 'The Beginning', a series of events that included the performance of a specially commissioned play.

2 Walford Davies, *Dylan Thomas* (Cardiff: University of Wales Press, 2014), p. xii.

3 Davies, *Dylan Thomas*, p. xii.

4 Jacques Derrida, 'Shibboleth: for Paul Celan', in *Acts of Literature*, ed. Derek Attridge (New York and London: Routledge, 1992), pp. 370–413 (378).

5 Derrida, 'Shibboleth', p. 382. Original italics retained in this and each subsequent citation from the text.

6 Derrida, 'Shibboleth', p. 382.

7 Derrida, 'Shibboleth', p. 376.

8 Derrida, 'Shibboleth', p. 374.

9 Derrida, 'Shibboleth', p. 373.

10 Derrida, 'Shibboleth', p. 373.

11 Derrida, 'Shibboleth', p. 373.

12 Derrida, 'Shibboleth', p. 377.

13 Thomas, 'On a Wedding Anniversary', earlier version reproduced in John Goodby, *Discovering Dylan Thomas: A Companion to the 'Collected Poems' and Notebook Poems* (Cardiff: University of Wales Press, 2017), pp. 174–5 (174).

14 John Goodby, *The Poetry of Dylan Thomas: Under the Spelling Wall* (Liverpool: Liverpool University Press, 2014), p. 154.

15 Dylan Thomas, *The Notebook Poems 1930–1934*, ed. Ralph Maud (London: Dent, 1990). Maud speculates that the poem derives from the missing notebook of 1932. The poem in its typescript form appears on pp. 121–2.

16 Walford Davies and Ralph Maud (eds), Dylan Thomas, *Collected Poems 1934–1953* (London: Phoenix, 2000), note p. 187.

17 Ralph Maud, *Where Have the Old Words Got Me? Explications of Dylan Thomas's Collected Poems* (Cardiff: University of Wales Press, 2003), p. 87.

18 Maud, *Where Have the Old Words Got Me?*, p. 87.

19 Daniel G. Williams, 'Welsh Modernism', in Peter Brooker, Andrzej Gąsiorek, Deborah Longworth and Andrew Thacker (eds), *The Oxford Handbook of Modernisms* (Oxford: Oxford University Press, 2010), pp. 797–816 (815).

20 Hangmen, hanged men and images of hanging recur throughout Thomas's poetry. We encounter the 'hangman's lime' in 'The force that through the green fuse' (*CP*, 43), the 'hangman's silks' in 'See, says the lime' (*CP*, 47), the 'hangman's raft' in 'I, in my intricate image' (*CP*, 73) and the hawk that 'hangs still' and 'hangs looped with flames' in 'Over St John's Hill' (*CP*, 184, 185). Of the latter poem, Walford Davies notes that Thomas's idiom is '*to hang fire* – death itself holding back but with that menacing delay that only makes death seem more cruel'. See Davies, *Dylan Thomas*, p. 154.

21 See note by Goodby in *CP*, 346. John Milton, 'On Being Arrived at Twenty-Three Years of Age', in *The Works of John Milton* (Hertfordshire: Wordsworth, 1994), p. 29.

22 Ryan Netzley, for instance, identifies both 'Time' and 'the will of Heav'n' as the two agents that 'appear to be in control' of the speaker's developmental process – 'and they are not compatible directors'. See Ryan Netzley, 'Milton's Sonnets', in Thomas N. Corns (ed.), *A New Companion to Milton* (Oxford and Malden, MA: Wiley Blackwell, 2016), pp. 270–81 (279).

23 Rachel Bowlby, *Everyday Stories* (Oxford: Oxford University Press, 2016), p. 44.

24 Davies and Maud, *Collected Poems 1934–1953*, n. p. 232.
25 Paul Muldoon, *The End of the Poem: Oxford Lectures in Poetry* (London: Faber and Faber, 2006), p. 58.
26 Judges 12: 5–6 (King James Version).
27 You say ˈdɪlən, I say ˈdəlan, let's call the whole thing off.
28 Goodby, *Under the Spelling Wall*, p. 32.
29 Goodby, *Discovering Dylan Thomas*, p. 206.
30 Terry Eagleton, *How to Read a Poem* (Oxford and Malden, MA: Blackwell, 2007), p. 74.
31 Eagleton, *How to Read a Poem*, p. 75.
32 Goodby, *Under the Spelling Wall*, p. 352.
33 Nicholas Royle, *Jacques Derrida* (London and New York: Routledge, 2003), p. 152. 'Success fails' and 'failure succeeds' are quoted by Royle from Derrida's *Mémoires: for Paul de Man*.
34 Royle, *Jacques Derrida*, p. 152.
35 Derrida, 'Shibboleth', p. 404.
36 Derrida, 'Shibboleth', p. 373.
37 Goodby, *Under the Spelling Wall*, p. 357.
38 Bowlby, *Everyday Stories*, p. 43.
39 Derrida, 'Shibboleth', p. 382.
40 James A. Davies, 'Dylan Thomas and his Welsh Contemporaries', in M. Wynn Thomas (ed.), *Welsh Writing in English* (Cardiff: University of Wales Press, 2003), pp. 120–64 (128); Goodby, *Under the Spelling Wall*, p. 378.
41 Giorgio Agamben, *The End of the Poem: Studies in Poetics*, trans. Daniel Heller-Roazen (Stanford, CA: Stanford University Press, 1999), p. 112.
42 Michael Wood, *Yeats and Violence* (Oxford: Oxford University Press, 2010), p. 117.
43 Agamben, *The End of the Poem*, p. 113.
44 Agamben, *The End of the Poem*, p. 113.
45 Wood, *Yeats and Violence*, p. 118.
46 The 'turnturtle dust', the 'horseshoe bay', the 'spun slime', the image of the sphere and the world that 'spins its morning of praise' all mark this out as another revolutionary work (*CP*, 197–200).
47 Goodby, in *CP*, p. 421.
48 Bryony Randall, *Modernism, Daily Time and Everyday Life* (Cambridge: Cambridge University Press, 2007). See her introduction, entitled 'Dailiness', pp. 1–28. See also Bowlby's *Everyday Stories*.
49 Randall, 'Modernist Literature and the Everyday', *Literature Compass*, 7/8 (2010), 824–35 (p. 826).
50 Daniel G. Williams, '"Speaking with the Elgin Marbles in his Mouth?": Modernism and Translation in Welsh Writing in English', *Translation Studies*, 9.2 (2016), 183–97 (p. 184).
51 Tony Brown, 'Glyn Jones and the Uncanny', *Almanac: Yearbook of Welsh Writing in English*, 12 (2007–8), 89–114 (pp. 90–1).

3

THE 'STRANGE' WALES OF
DYLAN THOMAS'S SHORT STORIES

Tony Brown

I

In 1935, Dylan Thomas, then twenty-two, wrote a letter home from
where he was staying on holiday in rural Ireland to his friend, Bert
Trick. Dylan writes about his 'homesicknesses' for the familiar routines of Swansea:

> I think of me writing by my gas-fire . . . of walking to your house in
> the Sunday rain and sitting by the fire until we've set the whole world
> straight . . . But I wouldn't be at home if I were at home. Everywhere I
> find myself seems to be nothing but a resting place between places that
> become resting places themselves . . . It may be a primary loneliness that
> makes me out-of-home. It may be this or that, & this and that is enough
> for to-day. Poor Dylan, poor him, poor me.[1] (*CL*, 191)

While evidently missing Swansea and his friendships, Thomas is
clearly aware of some more profound lack of security. He moves
from a sense of homesickness to a deep sense of insecure and divided
identity: 'Poor Dylan, poor him, poor me'. While it is an insecurity thrown into relief by his stay in remote rural Ireland – 'a wild,
unlettered and unfrenchlettered country' (*CL*, 190) – the insecurity
is something, Thomas realises, which is also present wherever he is,
even when he is in his home town.

'Home', or where we feel at home, is, of course, crucial to our sense of knowing who we are, to our sense of secure identity. This is an idea that is fundamental to Freud's notion of the uncanny in his essay of that title, published in 1919; the title of Freud's essay in the original German was '*Das Unheimlich*', 'the unhomely'.[2] In his 2003 study of the uncanny, Nicholas Royle summarises Freud's concept thus:

> The uncanny involves feelings of uncertainty, in particular regarding the reality of who one is and what is being experienced. Suddenly one's sense of oneself [. . .] seems strangely questionable.[3]

Thus, the uncanny is a sense of not feeling entirely at home with one's self. Sometimes, as Freud points out, this can be associated with a sense of 'doubleness', a kind of doppelgänger effect: 'Poor Dylan, poor him, poor me'. Relatedly, one can feel disorientated from one's immediate, ordinary surroundings. One suddenly experiences one's surroundings as unfamiliar, even if one knows where one is, the place usually familiar. Indeed, in many ways the essence of Freud's 'uncanny', the unhomely, what makes it disturbing is, for Royle,

> a peculiar commingling of the familiar and unfamiliar. It can take the form of something . . . strange and unfamiliar unexpectedly arising in a familiar context.[4]

I want to suggest that this insecurity of identity, about exactly who he is, a sense of being 'unhomed', is something that recurs in Dylan Thomas's writing. It is an insecurity which is reflected in the way in which the world in Thomas's writing can seem 'strange', alien, even hostile. It repeatedly manifests itself in sensations of the uncanny, of loneliness and disorientation, and occasionally in manifestations of the kind of doubleness we see in the letter to Bert Trick. The present discussion concentrates on Thomas's short stories, which have been remarkably neglected when compared to the volume of critical work that has been devoted to Thomas's poetry, though I would want to argue that the same sense of estrangement and alienation features there too, and is especially visible in *18 Poems* and *25 Poems*.

One might of course argue that the Swansea in which Thomas grew up was itself less than conducive to a secure sense of personal and cultural identity. As Chris Wigginton has pointed out, it occupied very much 'a frontier, liminal situation', at the western edge of English-speaking south Wales, a position that marked not only a boundary between urban and rural, English-speaking and Welsh-speaking cultures, but also the class division between the culture of rural labour and the culture of middle-class respectability to which the upwardly mobile families of Swansea's growing suburbs aspired.[5] These were differences of which Thomas was, of course, especially aware, given that his parents had crossed that cultural frontier to achieve a life of respectability at 5 Cwmdonkin Drive, the house in which he was brought up. But his parents' reaching of the semi-detached suburbia of the Uplands was not a once-and-for-all crossing of cultural borders in the family's past. As Thomas grew up, his continued crossing and re-crossing of the cultural frontier between anglicised, bourgeois Cwmdonkin Drive and rural, Welsh-speaking Carmarthenshire, during repeated visits, as a boy and a young man, to aunts, uncles and cousins at Fernhill and at Blaen Cwm, clearly kept him aware of the family shift that had taken place and of that other way of life in which he was inescapably implicated. In other words, rural, Welsh-speaking Wales was not safely in the past, but was unavoidably a part of the cultural processes that had made Thomas who he was. With other areas of Wales, of course, he was even less at home. Looking back in the 1940s on his childhood in Swansea, Thomas wrote that outside Swansea 'a *strange* Wales, coal-pitted, mountained, river-run, full, so far as I knew, of choirs and sheep and story-book tall hats, moved about its business which was none of mine'.[6]

The social aspiration of Welsh-speaking families like the Thomases as they migrated to suburban Swansea involved, of course, the surrender of their native language; like the parents of other writers of his generation – Glyn Jones, Alun Lewis, Rhys Davies – Thomas's parents did not pass on their language to their children. To get a good job and advance socially in that generation, one spoke English. But at the same time the presence of that other language, still spoken by parents and, in Thomas's case, relatives in west Wales, subtly affects these young writers' attitude to English. It sensitises them to the qualities of English words, their shape and sound and colour, to a degree defamiliarises them. However, in Thomas's case, this was heightened to the extent that he frequently treated words as objects in and of themselves. A friend, Charles Fisher, recalled him 'collecting words,

they were rare butterflies, and pleased him. He . . . had a notebook
there and he would put down fine words, word combinations'.[7] Glyn
Jones – who himself kept notebooks in which to record words and
phrases he heard – also noticed Thomas's fascination. On a visit to
Laugharne together in the mid 1930s, Jones happened in conversation
to use the word 'huddled':

> [Dylan] stopped and began repeating it over to himself, remarking on its
> *strangeness*, savouring it as though it were as outlandish as 'Chimborazo'
> or 'Cotopaxi' and not an ordinary English vocable in common use. This
> was not the first indication I had had that Dylan was not just interested
> in words but was obsessed by them.[8]

Walford Davies has appositely suggested that this hypersensitivity
to words, this sense of their almost having their own autonomous
life, is indicative of a 'certain sense of externality to the English language' that has its origins in the writer's cultural situation.[9] Indeed, for
Davies, 'Thomas's poetry represents a kind of no man's land between
two languages'.[10] Yet I would argue that the effects of this cultural
situation are far reaching, and inevitably affect not only Thomas's
verse, but the short stories too, where its marks and the directly-
related anxieties of identity are a powerful presence.

Glyn Jones recalled that Thomas's 'short stories in the early
days . . . were almost as important to him as his poetry . . . those
stories obviously come out of the same world as the early poems'.[11]
Indeed, in the early years of their friendship, Jones writes, 'Dylan . . .
urged me to write short stories'.[12] It was in many ways sound advice
for a young writer keen to get into print, for the 1930s and 1940s
were one of the boom periods for the short story in Britain; the sheer
number of magazines that were publishing short stories suggests a
substantial readership, one that grew after 1939, despite restrictions
on paper during the war years. One might suggest that the dis-
rupted lives of readers, both civilians and those in the forces, was
conducive to the reading of shorter fiction. Between 1934 and 1946,
Jones and Thomas contributed stories to virtually all of the London
magazines that published short stories: these included *English Story*
(edited by Woodrow Wyatt and published by Collins); H. E. Bates's
New Stories; *The Adelphi* (where Richard Rees had taken over the
editorship from Middleton Murry in 1930); Robert Herring's *Life
and Letters To-day*;[13] T. S. Eliot's *The Criterion*; A. R. Orage's *New

English Weekly; John Lehmann's *New Writing*; *Contemporary Poetry and Prose*; and *Penguin Parade.* In addition, there were anthologies that reprinted selections of the best published stories, such as E. J. O'Brien's *Best Short Stories* series, published by Cape.

Other Welsh short story writers – including Alun Lewis, Nigel Heseltine, Rhys Davies and Margiad Evans – were, of course, publishing in some of the same magazines. Thus, when Faber published *Welsh Short Stories* in 1937, the list of contributors was a rich one, including Thomas and Jones as well as Rhys Davies, Dorothy Edwards, Caradoc Evans, Margiad Evans, Geraint Goodwin, Richard Hughes and Gwyn Jones.[14] The same year saw the publication of the first issue of Keidrych Rhys's *Wales*, its cover bearing the opening of Thomas's 'Prologue to an Adventure'; Thomas was to publish three more stories in *Wales* in 1937–9, alongside stories by Rhys Davies, Caradoc Evans, James Hanley, Nigel Heseltine and Glyn Jones.

It goes without saying that not all of these magazines and journals had the same readership, a fact of which Thomas shows his awareness when advising Dent as to where to send review copies of *The Map of Love*: '*Seven* . . . has an important circulation in Oxford and Cambridge and other university towns' (*CL* 395). Moreover, while magazines with a smaller, more high-brow readership might accept surrealist stories and take a liberal attitude to content, Thomas was aware that in order to publish them as a collection he would need to find 'some innocent publisher who doesn't mind losing money on twenty difficult and violent tales' (*CL* 227). In the event, when he sought in 1936 to publish a collection of his early stories as *The Burning Baby*, the immediate problem was not difficulty or violence but their sexual references.[15] At the same time it seems that Richard Church at Dent was attempting to get Thomas to write less 'difficult' – and thus more marketable – fictions about his 'earlier world' (*CL* 227). Thomas evidently took his advice, 'A Visit to Grandpa's' being published in *New English Weekly* in early 1938, and 'The Peaches' in *Life and Letters To-day* later that year. In May of 1939, Thomas reported to Henry Treece that he had been 'working on . . . straightforward stories, sold now for large (to me) sums to Life & Letters and Story' (*CL* 373). At a time when Thomas was desperately short of money, the financial factor in his shift from the surrealist techniques of his earlier stories to the more 'straightforward' technique of the stories in *Portrait of the Artist as a Young Dog* should not be ignored.[16]

II

When Glyn Jones returned to Cardiff after one of his first visits to Dylan Thomas in 1934, he brought with him a bundle of Thomas's early stories, which Thomas had asked him to read. These stories, so 'new, vital, *strange*' for Jones, were being copied into the same notebooks that Thomas was transcribing his poetry; they are filled, like the poetry, with a young man's anxieties about sexuality, about the processes of the body and, frequently, with a sense of isolation and alienation.[17] Thomas himself seems to have been aware of their subjective origins, describing them as 'dream stories, very mixed, very violent'.[18] Many of them are set in an area which he calls the Jarvis Hills, a re-imagined version of rural west Wales, that 'strange Wales' beyond Swansea. The world of the Jarvis Hills is an elemental world, full of ambiguous, violent energy, a landscape that is always disturbingly 'other' to the disorientated, frequently lonely figures who wander through it. In the story entitled 'The Enemies' (1934), Mr Owen had been 'walking lonely through the country' (*CS*, 16) when he came upon the isolated Jarvis Valley. Now, some time later, he and his wife have built their little house in the valley, set apart from any community and seemingly at the mercy of the elements: 'The valley roared around it, the wind leapt at it like a boxer' (*CS*, 18). Indeed, as Mr Owen tends his garden, the natural world is disturbingly, nightmarishly alive: 'Not only a mandrake screams; torn roots have their cries; each weed Mr Owen pulled out of the ground screamed like a baby. In the village behind the hill the wind would be raging, the clothes on the garden lines would be set to strange dances' (*CS*, 17). As in Thomas's early poems, the rhythms of human life in these stories are part of much larger natural processes; while Owen uproots the weeds/babies,

> women with shapes in their wombs would feel a new knocking as they bent over the steamy tubs. Life would go on in the veins, in the bones, the binding flesh, that had their seasons and their weathers even as the valley binding the house about with the flesh of the green grass. (*CS*, 17)

Into this teeming, violent landscape comes another wanderer: the Reverend Mr Davies has 'lost his way' (*CS*, 17). In fact, his loss of direction is not just a matter of his having taken a wrong path:

'wherever he sought to hide from the wind he was frightened by the darkness. The farther he walked, the *stranger* was the scenery around him' (*CS*, 17, my emphasis). He is experiencing a profound sense of disorientation: 'the hills had given under his feet or plunged him into the air' (*CS*, 20). While the Owens' house offers him shelter, his sense of disturbance continues; Mrs Owen's eyes are green, 'the *strangest* he had even seen' (*CS*, 18, my emphasis). In fact, she is a *swynwraig*, a sort of witch, and her mysterious ways of knowing seem much more attuned to the energies abroad in the countryside than the Christian orthodoxies of Revd Davies. At the end, Davies can only kneel and stare in bewilderment, 'frightened of the worm in the earth, of the copulation of the tree, of the living grease in the soil' (*CS*, 20).

The loneliness experienced initially by Owen and later by Revd Davies, a loneliness that can reach beyond the merely social to the metaphysical in its power to disorientate the individual's sense of who s/he is, haunts many of these stories. The protagonist of 'The Visitor' (1934) is, as it were, isolated at the edge of life; Peter, a widowed poet, is dying of heart disease, his time measured out by the 'busy-voiced clock . . . the voice of an old enemy', which echoes through his silent bedroom (*CS*, 24). Isolated in his bed, which he occasionally pictures as a remote island (*CS*, 26), Peter is gradually becoming dislocated even from familiar things: 'His room around him was a vast place. From their frames the lying likenesses of women looked down on him' (*CS*, 25). He is becoming uncannily disconnected from his own body (the heart 'under the ribs' armour was not his, not his the beating of a vein in the foot'), from his own identity ('There was nothing more remote under the sun than his own name'), and from the words with which he has shaped his life (*CS*, 25). Language itself has become defamiliarised into a set of enigmatic objects, ambiguously related to that which they signify: '. . . poetry was a string of words, stringed on a beanstick . . . the tree was a tree of words, and the lake rhymed with another word' (*CS*, 25, 27). When Peter supposedly does go out into the dark, wooded world of the Jarvis Valley, carried by the mysterious Callaghan (is he a friend? is he death?) for whom Peter has been waiting, that world is suffused with the smell of death, evoked by Thomas in characteristically physical terms:

Now the sheep fell and the flies were at them. The rats and the weasels, fighting over the flesh, dropped one by one with a wound for the sheep's fleas staring out of their hair . . . Now the worm and the death-beetle

undid the fibres of the animal bones, worked at them brightly and
minutely . . . (*CS*, 29–30)

And then, equally characteristically, from decay new life mysteriously
emerges:

> . . . and the weeds through the sockets and the flowers on the vanished
> breasts sprouted up with the colours of the dead life fresh on their leaves.
> And the blood that had flowed flowed over the ground, strengthening the
> blades of the grass, fulfilling the wind-planted seed in its course. (*CS*, 30)

But though Peter may imagine crying out for joy, his isolation
becomes complete; he is unable even to communicate with Rhianon
who has nursed him and now, in the story's final line, pulls the sheet
over Peter's face.

In fact, we realise that the episode in the woods, in which Peter is
carried in the arms of the naked, muscular Callaghan, is the product of Peter's lonely, dreaming mind. Moreover, events in the 'real'
world of these Jarvis Valley stories move according to the arbitrary,
disconnected logic of dream, vividly and disturbingly recreated by
Thomas. Indeed – and sometimes without any signal to the reader –
the narratives repeatedly slide across the border between this already
strange 'real' world into the protagonist's own private dream world.
'The Orchards' (1936) begins with Marlais's vivid dream: 'He had
dreamed that a hundred orchards on the road to the sea village had
broken into flame; and all the windless afternoon tongues of fire shot
through the blossom' (*CS*, 42). The sexual undertone of this powerfully suggestive scene, beautiful yet threatening, becomes focused on
a young woman, sensually twining her hair, who kisses Marlais and
at this point he wakes up. Marlais shares not only Thomas's name but
is also a writer. When he gets to his writing table, Marlais finds that,
disturbed by his dream, he is unable to write; the sense of restless,
frustrated creative isolation here is one with which the author would,
presumably, have been all too familiar. Marlais's pencil becomes defamiliarised as a tower, an image of isolation which recurs in several
of the stories, and there is, again, a sense of the otherness of his own
body and of what he is writing: '[H]e fingered the pencil tower, the
half-moon of his thumb-nail rising and setting behind the leaden
spire. The tower fell, down fell the city of words, the walls of a poem,
the symmetrical letters' (*CS*, 44). The morning has become 'foreign'.

Thereafter, as he gazes through his window at the town and landscape below, he moves, dream or imaginative flight, into a journey across a visionary version of south Wales, seeking to regain the place of the orchards and the young woman. The journey in his imagination takes on an epic, Homeric dimension ('I am walking towards the sea', says Marlais. '"The wine-coloured sea," said Dai Twice', whom he meets on the way; *CS*, 46). Marlais becomes 'a legendary walker, a folk-man walking, with a cricket for a heart; he walked by Aberbabel's chapel, cut through the graveyard over the unstill headstones' (*CS*, 47). Here he is less the Classical hero than something closer to home. As M. Wynn Thomas has pointed out, Thomas 'may well be viewing him as a figure from pre-Nonconformist, "Celtic" Wales', a figure from the fantastic world of the *Mabinogion*, and suggests that Marlais's journey represents Dylan Thomas's perception of his own plight as a writer 'caught between fear of the old Wales and hope of the new, experiencing both the trauma of disorientation and the exhilaration of adventure'.[19] Certainly, the story engages the variety and complexity of south Wales and its culture more fully than any other of the early stories. For once the protagonist wanders not in the isolated and ambiguous freedom of the Jarvis Valley but crosses a nightmarish version of industrial south Wales, the 'strange . . . coal-pitted Wales':

> Marlais strode . . . down behind the circle of the town to the rim of Whippet valley where the trees, for ever twisted between smoke and slag, tore at the sky and the black ground . . . Whippet's trees were the long dead of the stacked south of the country; who had vanished under the hacked land pointed, thumb-to-hill, these black leaf-nailed and warning fingers. Death in Wales had twisted the Welsh dead into those valley cripples. (*CS*, 46)

After this sterile world and the implicit threat of 'Aberbabel's chapel' and its graveyard, 'Marlais the poet' battles on, 'over the brink into ruin, up the side of doom, over hell in bed to the red left' (*CS*, 48), until he regains the vision of the orchards, and the girl he dreamed of at the beginning. The story does indeed seem, in its surreal, nightmarish imagery and the syntactical disjunctions, to indicate 'the trauma of disorientation'. The 'exhilaration of adventure' that Wynn Thomas points out is endorsed by the sheer energy of the writing, the imaginative vitality. But there is little sense of release at the end, no sense of lyric freedom: 'A dream that was no dream skulked there; the real world's wind came up to kill the fires; a scarecrow pointed to the extinguished trees' (*CS*, 49). What one is aware of above all is Marlais's isolation and the effort he has to make; Marlais can only remain 'Brave in his desolation' (*CS*, 44).

'The Lemon' (1936) is altogether more darkly claustrophobic, set in a house of endless shadowy corridors, haunted by ghost-like strangers. This time, it seems we enter entirely into the nightmare world of the narrator. The house itself, isolated on a high hill, is where a mysterious doctor carries out grotesque experiments: a cat's head is grafted onto a chicken's trunk, a glass hand is grafted onto flesh 'and the glass nails grew long' (*CS*, 57). In this monstrous place, the narrator's sense of identity is uncannily unstable. He becomes an alter ego of Nant, the boy isolated in the house, taking on Nant's consciousness:

> I was that boy in a dream, and I stood stock still, knowing myself to be alone, knowing that the voice was mine and the dark not the death of the sun but the dark light thrown back by the walls of the windowless corridors. I put out my arm and it turned into a tree. (*CS*, 57)

The disturbing, claustrophobic world of dream is convincingly recreated by Thomas; he catches that familiar panic of half awareness – 'I knew that I was dreaming' (*CS*, 58) – but incapacity to escape. In the logic of dream, the narrator is both alone – 'There was nobody to guide me' – *as* Nant, and at the same time he is *with* Nant; almost inevitably, they run to the doctor's tower, again an image of separateness: 'he climbed in my image, I in his, and we were two brothers climbing' (*CS*, 58). With the discovery of the doctor's body – there is no explanation of what has happened – the story climaxes in a grotesque, sexually-charged dance of death:

> There was a corridor leading to the tower of ten days' death, and there a woman danced alone, with the hands of a man upon her shoulders. And soon the virgins joined her, bared to the waist . . . In the long hall they danced in celebration of the dead. This was the dance of the halt, the blind, and the half dead, this the dance of the abnegation of the dead . . . the grave girls bared to the waist. (*CS*, 59)

Ultimately the consciousness of the narrator parts from that of Nant, but escape from the house does not result in security or a waking into

community: 'I parted from him, leaving a half ache and a half terror, going my own way, the way of the light breaking over Cathmarw
hill and the Black Valley' (*CS*, 60). Given those ominous names
('Cathmarw' means 'dead cat') and his continued aloneness, the dawn
seems less than reassuring. He is still the alienated outsider.

The irrationality of these dream worlds is echoed by the way in
which the wild landscape of the Jarvis Valley is haunted by actual
human insanity, frequently associated with the unpredictability and
potential for violence of the natural world: the lonely wandering
'idiot' is crucified in 'The Tree'; the vicar's son walks howling in the
hills in 'The Burning Baby', 'holding a dead animal up to the light of
the stars' (*CS*, 36); Marlais is aware of 'the reverend madmen in the
Black Book of Llareggub' in 'The Orchards'; there is 'a prison for
mad women' at the beginning of 'The School for Witches' (*CS*, 67)
and 'The Mouse and the Woman' opens with another 'lunatic asylum'
and a madman 'howling like a dog' (*CS*, 74). The unnamed protagonist of 'The Dress' is a madman who has escaped from an asylum
– '. . . he stole a knife from the kitchen and slashed his keeper and
broke out into the wild valleys' (*CS*, 23) – and has eluded his armed
pursuers for two days. As he runs, hunted, through the mist-shrouded
woods, where owls swoop on mice and hares are at the mercy of weasels, his irrationality links him to this dangerous instinctive world:
he smiles 'like a cat', he is as 'crafty as a fox' (*CS*, 21, 22). Like so
many of the characters in these stories – Annie in 'After the Fair',
Revd Davies in 'The Enemies', the 'idiot' in 'The Tree', the travelling
tinkers in 'The School for Witches', even the violent protagonist in
'The Vest' who 'cried aloud in a panic of loneliness' (*CS*, 34) – the
madman in 'The Dress' is another outsider, estranged from the security of home and community. Fascinated by such figures, it seems that
Thomas is compulsively and imaginatively responsive to states of
separateness and disorientation.[20]

III

When *The Map of Love* was published by Dent in 1939, it contained,
alongside sixteen poems, five of the stories from the 'Red Notebook'
(as well as 'The Mouse and the Woman' and the title story).[21] Other
stories originally planned for inclusion in the aborted Europa Press
collection *The Burning Baby* remained unpublished. As it was,
Dent's editor, Richard Church, refused to include in the collection

'A Prospect of the Sea', described by Thomas as one of his favourite stories, on the grounds that it contained 'moments of sensuality without purpose [and it] brings us near the danger zone' (*CL*, 363, 374).

By March 1938, in fact, Thomas had heeded Church's earlier advice to draw on his 'earlier world'. Thomas wrote to Vernon Watkins that he was 'working on a series of short, straightforward stories about Swansea' (*CL*, 279), and a year later Thomas told his agent, David Higham that 'my Welsh book, a sort of provincial autobiography, is coming on well' (*CL*, 375).

In contrast to the surrealism of the earlier work, these stories are certainly more 'straightforward' in terms of narrative accessibility, and several have become as well known and as popular with readers as some of the major poems. However, care should be exercised in considering these stories as pieces of autobiography. Thomas clearly uses locations, characters and even episodes from the years in which he was growing up in Swansea; but what is significant, and rewarding of study, is what Thomas does with this autobiographical material, what the result is of his having shaped it into fiction. One might also argue that the intensity of his looking back on his early years in his fiction (and in the broadcasts of the 1940s) is itself a manifestation of a concern with identity, with the cultural situations which have contributed to the making of who he is. Indeed the whole process of looking backwards, occasionally with nostalgia, might suggest an unease with his present situation. In other words, for all the manifest differences in style and concern between the early stories and the 'autobiographical' stories collected in *Portrait of the Artist as a Young Dog* in 1940, there are real continuities of concern. Beneath the domestic/suburban adventures of Thomas's young dog, as a boy and as a youth, there is again a recurring sense of isolation and unease.

The first story in *Portrait*, 'The Peaches' (1938), is once again manifestly set in that 'strange' rural Wales to the west. The young narrator, being taken by his Uncle Jim in a horse-drawn cart to stay with relatives at Gorsehill, is left alone on the cart in the dark alley outside a pub while Jim goes in for a drink. As he sits alone in the dark, staring into the pub window at the unfamiliar sight of the men playing cards, the boy becomes increasingly anxious and disorientated:

> The passage grew dark too suddenly, the walls crowded in, and the roofs crouched down. To me, staring timidly there in the dark passage in a strange town, the swarthy man appeared like a giant in a cage surrounded

by clouds, and the bald old man withered into a black hump with a white top; two white hands darted out of the corner with invisible cards . . . a hand clawed up the pane to the tassel of the blind; in the little, packed space between me on the cobbles and the card-players at the table, I could not tell which side of the glass was the hand that dragged the blind down slowly. (*CS*, 127–8)

The fact that the boy is fanciful and imaginative – indeed, he is a storyteller and recalls for reassurance 'A story I had made in the warm, safe island of my bed, with sleepy midnight Swansea flowing and rolling round outside the house' (*CS*, 128) – only exacerbates the anxiety with which he looks at this 'strange' (in every sense) new Wales. When Jim emerges and they drive on, the young boy's mood is hardly calmed by Jim's mention that a hangman had lived nearby, and when Jim lights his pipe in the dark, the description is a measure of the boy's anxiety: he 'set the darkness on fire and show[ed] his long, red, drunken fox's face to me, with its bristling side-bushes and wet, sensitive nose' (*CS*, 129). When the boy is later told by his cousin that Uncle Jim sells off a farm animal to pay for each visit to the pub, the Uncle takes on an even more surrealist appearance, anticipating the world of *Under Milk Wood*: 'We knew where uncle was; he was sitting in a public house with a heifer over his shoulder and two pigs nosing out of his pockets, and his lips wet with bull's blood' (*CS*, 134).

The boy's sense of alienation from his surroundings is again manifested in the surreal way in which he sees the farm house at Gorsehill as he approaches it: 'The front of the house was the single side of a black shell, and the arched door was the listening ear' (*CS*, 129). His anxiety is alleviated only when he leaves the dark entrance passage of the house and enters the living room and the warm welcome of his Aunt Annie. The actual terms in which Thomas expresses this shift, however, are revealing:

One minute I was small and cold, skulking dead-scared down a black passage in my stiff, best suit . . . clutching my grammar school cap, *unfamiliar to myself*, a snub-nosed story-teller lost in his own adventures and *longing to be home*; the next I was a royal nephew in smart town clothes, embraced and welcomed, standing in the snug centre of my stories and listening to the clock announcing me. (*CS*, 130, my emphases)

Not for the last time in this collection, the narrator/protagonist experiences a moment of uncanny doubleness, seeing himself from the outside, defamiliarised. However, even after his welcome, a bath and supper, as he goes to bed we get a somewhat surprising hint that this imaginative boy is no stranger to the sense of vulnerability and isolation in which we see him at the opening of the story, that home is perhaps less a place than a state of mind: 'I climbed the stairs; each had a different voice . . . I thought that I had been walking long, damp passages all my life, and climbing stairs in the dark, alone' (*CS*, 131). It is an odd moment, one that has a maturity of perspective that we might associate less with the young boy and more with the author. However, later in the story, settled at Gorsehill, running wild in the warm fields, the boy is ecstatically at one with the natural landscape and the rhythms of his own body, at home in his sense of who he is:

> I felt all my young body like an excited animal surrounding me, the torn knees bent, the bumping heart . . . the blood racing, the memory around and within flying, jumping, swimming, and waiting to pounce. There, playing Indians in the evening, I was aware of me myself in the exact middle of a living story, and my body was my adventure and my name. (*CS*, 137–8)

'The Peaches', perhaps even more than the other stories in *Portrait*, has at its centre a concern with what we have seen as one of the sources of Thomas's unease in his Swansea years: social class. Mrs Williams, the mother of Jack who is to stay at Gorsehill with the narrator, is a former mayoress and, according to the narrator, 'the richest woman in Wales' (*CS*, 134); she sweeps into the down-at-heel farmyard in her Daimler like a visitor from another world. Alongside Auntie Annie's clumsy, good-natured welcome, Mrs Williams's chill condescension is seen in all its insensitivity. Conducted into the *parlwr*, the 'best room', kept only for important visitors like the minister or the doctor, the narrator notes that Mrs Williams 'dusted the seat of a chair with a lace handkerchief from her bag before sitting down' (*CS*, 136). The proffered tinned peaches, a luxury carefully saved by Annie for such a special occasion, are casually dismissed: 'I don't mind pears or chunks, but I can't bear peaches' (*CS*, 137).

More subtle, however, is the way in which the social status of the narrator is registered. He too is a visitor from another world, as he himself is well aware: after the disorientation of the journey, his aunt embraces him: 'I was a royal nephew in smart town clothes, embraced and welcomed' (*CS*, 130); she fusses and clucks over him throughout, concerned about his food, concerned about his clothes staying clean in the farmyard. But, however much he is welcomed, he is aware of himself as an incomer to a place that does not observe the same codes of bourgeois respectability that define his life at home. At one level, he is all too happy to embrace this excursion from suburban cleanliness and decorum, to create a new, rural identity for himself. Urged back into his good suit to welcome Jack and his mother, the boy is disappointed; he wants to 'look like a proper farm boy and have manure in my shoes and hear it squelch as I walked, to see a cow have calves and a bull on top of a cow . . . to go out and shout, "Come on, you b----," and pelt the hens and talk in a proper voice' (*CS*, 135), a natural voice, as opposed to the modulated tones and approved registers of the Uplands. But he is still in a liminal situation: he is the bourgeois suburban boy – and treated as such by the family – and, however much he is drawn to the farm, his rural family and their unfamiliar ways, it is still essentially a 'strange' place. As well as the unfamiliarity of the farm itself, with its smells and unaccustomed physicality, this is a world of *eisteddfodau* – Uncle Jim's special chair is 'the broken throne of a bankrupt bard' (*CS*, 130) – and Welsh-speaking chapels. Thomas, during his childhood visits to west Wales, himself sat amongst the Welsh-speaking congregation; here the narrator sits and stares at his older cousin Gwilym's version of these unfamiliar rituals, including his breaking into 'singing and Welsh', poised on his pulpit cart in the shadowy barn: 'Gwilym was no longer my cousin in a Sunday suit, but a tall *stranger* shaped like a spade in a cloak' (*CS*, 139, my emphasis). The angular Gwilym is defamiliarised to the point of becoming surreal. Earlier, on his first morning on the farm, as the boy looks with Gwilym at the animals in the ramshackle farmyard, there is once more a moment in which the narrator, removed from the familiarity of the decorous codes of home, looks at himself from the outside: 'Now a young man and a curly boy stood staring and sniffing over a wall at a sow, with its tits on the mud, giving suck' (*CS*, 132).

In 'The Fight' (1939), Thomas's young narrator is in his teens. Already ambitious to be a writer, perhaps in London, he resents the constraints of the bourgeois world in which he lives. Walking to a friend's house one summer evening, past the neighbouring suburban villas, he literally kicks out at the gates of 'The Elms', throws gravel at 'The Croft' and vows to one night 'paint "Bum" all over the front gate of "Kia-ora"' (*CS*, 162). More interesting as a measure of his alienation, however, is yet another example of the narrator seeing himself from the outside, estranged, and hearing an uncanny double:

> Walking . . . in the early dusk through solid, deserted professional avenues lined with trees, I recited pieces of my poems and heard my voice, like a stranger's voice in Park Drive . . . rise very thinly up through the respectable autumn evening. . . . If I looked through a window onto the road, I would see a scarlet-capped boy with big boots striding down the middle, and would wonder who it could be. If I were a young girl watching, my face like Mona Lisa's . . . I'd see beneath the 'Boys' Department' suit a manly body with hair and sun tan, and call him and ask, 'Will you have tea or cocktails'? (*CS*, 161)

The alienation is at one level genuine, born of his antipathy for the life of the respectable villas. However, at the same time his disaffection is romanticised into the pose of the alienated poet: the poem he recites portrays 'the lone genius' to whom the frost 'has spake in visionary tears' (*CS*, 162), before the narrator slides into adolescent fantasy, itself coloured by the aspirational values he initially rejects.

Unlike the pretensions of the other villa names we have heard, the actual name of his friend Daniel Jones's home, 'Warmley', is retained, presumably because of the connotations of the word.[22] The family at 'Warmley' seems to take a more relaxed attitude to the codes of suburbia: Mrs Jones answers the door with a ball of wool in her hand, while Dan's own room is 'splendidly untidy, full of wool and paper and open cupboards . . . all the expensive furniture had been kicked; a waistcoat hung on the chandelier' (*CS*, 163). For the young narrator, it is a creative haven: 'I thought I could live for ever in that room'; this 'still room', he thinks, 'had never been strange to me' (*CS*, 164), and again we register that adjective. 'Warmley' is an escape from alienation into creative friendship; it is a homely place ('There, that's more homely', says Dan's mother when she switches on their light (*CS*, 164)). Social formality is reasserted with the arrival of Revd and Mrs Bevan for supper, though that is subverted by the behaviour of Mrs Bevan who 'didn't look all there' (*CS*, 166). She seems confused throughout the meal and, while this amuses the boys ('This was better than home, and there was a woman off her head, too'; *CS*, 166), her evident instability ultimately adds a darker tone to the story; in a way reminiscent of the early stories, insanity registers the essential arbitrariness of society's codes and their constraints of natural impulse. Dan has heard of a previous suicide attempt and asserts that 'She's terribly mad, she doesn't know who she is' (*CS*, 168). In a series of stories that seem repeatedly to engage issues of identity and disorientation, this is a resonant comment. As the wife of a minister of religion, Mrs Bevan has a social identity that is firmly defined by the community in which she lives, but the suggestion is, surely, that she pays a price for her social position. The final vision we have of her, as the boys go out into the dark street and look back at the lighted drawing-room window, is of a woman imprisoned in her suburban life: 'Mrs βevan's face was pressed against the glass, her hook nose flattened, her lips pressed tight . . .' (*CS*, 169).

Thus, ultimately, these slightly later, more realistic, more accessible and often ostensibly comic stories are marked by a similar sense of being 'out-of-home', of uncanny estrangement as the earlier dream-like stories; certainly, we frequently get the same tones of aloneness. In 'Just Like Little Dogs' (1939), the narrator is probably in his late teens and is again an aspiring young writer. Self-consciously standing apart from the mundane world of the domestic and the suburban, he has a romantic taste for walking alone:

> I was a lonely nightwalker and a steady stander-at-corners. I liked to walk through the wet town after midnight, when the streets were deserted and the window lights out, alone and alive on the glistening tramlines in dead and empty High Street under the moon, gigantically sad in the damp street by ghostly Ebenezer Chapel. (*CS*, 182)

His night wanderings take him into derelict houses, which are no longer homes, and he thinks as he stands in the dark, 'alone under a railway arch out of the wind', of those who are out in the night with – unlike himself – no homes to go to: the tramps, 'tucked up in sacks, asleep in a siding . . . their beards in straw, in coal-trucks think-ing of fires' (*CS*, 179). But the tramps are at this stage little more to him than images in his romantic, adolescent imaginings. However, when he hears the story of precisely why the two men that he meets, the brothers Tom and Walter, are also here out in the dark under the railway arch, and about the bleak isolation of Tom in his unhappy marriage, the result of a forced marriage when his girl got pregnant, the narrator confronts something altogether more authentic and dis-concerting. Tom is never going to be at ease in his own life: 'It is a sad life, without a home', he says, 'It's warm at home' (*CS*, 182), and the word echoes through the story. At the end, the young narrator can run home to Cwmdonkin Drive: 'it would take me ten minutes' (*CS*, 185). Tom, attended by his brother, remains out in the cold and the dark till the early morning, as he does every night.

The young man in 'One Warm Saturday' (1938) is yet one more aspiring writer self-consciously seeking to be alone with his imagination: he refuses his friends' invitations to go off for the day, and he condescendingly sees the noisy fun of the families around him at the seaside on this holiday Saturday as 'false and pretty, as a flat picture under the vulgar sun' (*CS*, 224). At the same time he is naggingly aware of the inauthenticity of his own 'loneliness' (*CS*, 226):

> He thought: Poets live and walk with their poems; a man with visions needs no other company; Saturday is a crude day . . . But he was not a poet living and walking, he was a young man in a sea town on a warm bank holiday . . . he had no visions, only two pounds and a small body with its feet on the littered sand. (*CS*, 226–7)

The awareness of the true nature of his situation seems to be the young man's own, not just that of the third person narrator; once again insecurity manifests itself in self-consciousness, in an external perspective on the self. The uncanny sense of disorientation is repeated as, having failed to pluck up the courage to respond to the gesture of a pretty girl on the sea front, he enters a pub; what we get is the sudden and disconcerting glimpse of the mirror-reflected self to which Freud refers in his essay:

> And what shall the terrified prig of a love-mad young man do next? he asked his reflection silently in the distorting mirror of the empty 'Victoria' saloon. His ape-like hanging face, with 'Bass' across his forehead, gave back a cracked sneer. (*CS*, 228)

The silent dialogue with this mocking other self – 'You saw a queer tart in a park' – culminates in an uncertain assertion of his identity: in the beer froth, he 'wrote his name on the edge of the table and watched the letters dry and fade' (*CS*, 228).

The entrance of the girl, Lou, and her friends into the pub, her receptivity to his attentions, and the ensuing party at her bedsit, shot through with his impatience at the presence of Lou's friends, has something of the tone of a sexual fantasy or dream. The promise of sleeping with Lou seems endlessly and frustratingly deferred by the presence of the others; indeed the promise itself is, for this presumably inexperienced young man, coloured by his own anxiety: 'He and Lou could go down together, one cool body weighted with a boiling stone, onto the falling, blank white, entirely empty sea, and never rise' (*CS*, 238). Dream slides into a nightmare of disorientation as the protagonist, seeking a lavatory in Lou's house, stumbles through darkened corridors, unable to find his way back to her: 'Down the stairs, clinging to the sticky, shaking rails, rocking on see-saw floorboards . . . he put out his hand, but the rail was broken and nothing there prevented a long drop to the ground down a twisted shaft that would echo and double his cry' (*CS*, 241–2). There is no escape back to security and romance from this Escher-like vision; at the end of the story, the final paragraph of *Portrait of the Artist as a Young Dog*, the young man can only go out into the derelict darkness; his sense of isolation is now no longer merely a pose; it sensitises him to the possibility of a more universal unhomedness:

> The light of the one weak lamp in a rusty circle fell across the brick-heaps and the broken wood and the dust that had been houses once, where the small and the hardly known and never-to-be-forgotten people of the dirty town had lived and loved and died and, always, lost. (*CS*, 243)

IV

The sense of insecurity of identity and, indeed, intimations of 'homelessness' as a more universal human condition persist in Dylan Thomas's prose writing in the 1940s, in *Adventures in the Skin Trade* and in some of the radio broadcasts. *Adventures in the Skin Trade* was planned as a novel but never completed; the first three chapters were published in the 1940s and 1950s as discrete narratives. The central concern of the novel was evidently to be with the evolution of the protagonist, Samuel Bennet, and the divisions within his own sense of identity; according to Vernon Watkins, the book was to be 'not strictly autobiographical, but bearing a relation to the two parts of [Thomas's] experience, his own actions and the actions of his dramatised self'.[23]

The first section, 'A Fine Beginning', starts with Samuel's leaving the family home in the suburbs of a town clearly based on Swansea, and his escape to London. There is a new strength of feeling in the cutting of family ties: on the morning of his flight, while his family still sleeps, Samuel breaks his mother's cherished tea service, vandalises the essays that his schoolmaster father has been marking, and rips up family photographs. But this vigorous tearing of family ties is accompanied by deep inner division: beneath his anger he feels 'guilt and shame' and, as tears run down his face, this inner division is dramatised by (the motif recurs) his catching sight of 'his round soft face in the mirror' (*CS*, 251), and the weakness of the guilty self is mocked by the rebellious mirror self. By now, however, the house is no longer 'home' but 'his parents' house' (*CS*, 250), and his family merely 'strangers . . . he had known since he could remember' (*CS*, 248).

When Samuel reaches London, his sense of estrangement is captured by the ways in which the narrative pushes disturbingly towards a dream-like unreality. In the second section, 'Plenty of Furniture', the house to which he is taken by Mr Allingham, whom he meets while hovering uncertainly at the railway station, is stacked high with furniture:

> Chairs stood on couches that lay on tables; mirrors nearly the height of the door were propped, back to back, against the walls, reflecting and making endless the hills of desks and chairs with their legs in the air, sideboards, dressing tables, chests-of-draws, more mirrors, empty bookcases, washbasins, clothes cupboards. (*CS*, 266)

Allingham is supposedly a furniture dealer, but he and his wife live and sleep amongst this chaotic parody of a suburban house, with its endlessly reflecting mirrors. Samuel had earlier got his finger stuck in a bottle, and he is still unable to remove it: Allingham makes apposite comment that it is 'like a kind of nightmare . . . one of those nightmares when you're playing billiards and the cue's made of elastic' (*CS*, 274). The sense of having entered a disturbing, dislocated Alice-in-Wonderland world continues: at the cafe they visit, the proprietor's daughter asks his name:

> 'Sam.'
> 'Mine's Mary. But they call me Polly for short.'
> 'It isn't much shorter, is it?'
> 'No, it's exactly the same length.' (*CS*, 276)

With names and identities becoming unstable, as Sam walks with his new friends in the final piece, 'Four Lost Souls', he shares the self-dislocating experience of those earlier Thomas protagonists, seeing himself from the outside: 'Look at London flying by me, buses . . . umbrellas and lamp posts . . . I am dancing with three strangers down Edgware Road in the rain, cried Samuel to the gliding boy around him' (*CS*, 286). The piece ends, however, not with freedom but with alienation and insecurity. In the night-club he visits with his new friends, Sam experiences a sexual anxiety familiar from earlier stories as Mrs Dacey's attentions become more pressing, her hand grasping his arm: '"Once I take a fancy I never let go" . . . If he struggled and ran she would catch him in a corner and open her umbrella inside his nose' (*CS*, 298). The nightmarish sense of entrapment is exacerbated as he gazes at the crowd of drinkers and dancers in the artificial half-light of the night club: his new London world has become a surreal phantasmagoria of alienation and disgust:

> There were deep green faces, dipped in a sea dye, with painted cockles for mouths and lichenous hair, sealed on the cheeks; red and purple, slate-grey, tide-marked, rat-brown and stickily whitewashed, with violet inked eyes or lips the colour of Stilton; pink chopped, pink lidded, pink as the belly of a newborn monkey, nicotine yellow with mustard flecked eyes . . . (*CS*, 298)

Earlier, as they sit in a pub, Allingham sighs, 'Here we are . . . four lost souls. What a place to put a man in' (*CS*, 287). But he isn't referring merely to the bar; he voices a sudden awareness that seems to reach beneath the usual drink-fuelled banter: 'I mean the world. This is only a little tiny bit in it. This is all right, it's got regular hours . . . But look at the world . . . No sense, no order, no nothing" (*CS*, 287–8).

Thus, the 'homesicknesses' which the young Dylan Thomas expressed in his letter from Ireland in 1935 was not merely a matter of his missing Cwmdonkin Drive. As he himself perceptively realised, 'I wouldn't be at home if I were at home'. What he detects is some more fundamental alienation from the world around him and – something that has not been discussed in previous critical comments on Thomas's fiction – his short stories are profoundly coloured by that alienation. Indeed, I should want to argue that it is one of the central themes of the stories. The early stories constantly express a vision of a world that is 'strange', inhabited by protagonists who struggle to make sense of the mysterious, even hostile landscapes in which they find themselves. Indeed in a number of the stories – 'The Tree', 'The

Dress', 'The Vest' – those protagonists, wandering the Jarvis Hills, are disturbed to the point of insanity, even violence.

While the later stories collected in *Portrait of the Artist as a Young Dog* are set in a Swansea and west Wales which is more recognisable, more 'straightforward', these stories are still shot through, as the protagonists grow, by a profound sense of unease and estrangement, for all of these stories' humour and nostalgia. It is perhaps not unexpected, then, when in a BBC radio broadcast in 1949 entitled 'Living in Wales', we again hear the tones of personal unhomedness and insecurity of identity with which we have become familiar in the stories:

> Lost and blown about in London town, a barrel-shaped leaf, am I still the same, I said to myself, as that safe and sound loller at the corners of Wales who, to my memory, was happy as a sandman . . .
> And now that I am back in Wales, am I the same person, sadly staring over the flat, sad, estuary sands . . . hearing the gab of gulls, alone and lost in a soft kangaroo pocket of the sad, salt West . . .
> I know that I am home again because I feel just as I felt when I was not at home, only more so.[24]

Notes

[1] Thomas had been taken to Ireland by Geoffrey Grigson to enable him to recover his health. See Paul Ferris, *Dylan Thomas* (London: Hodder and Stoughton, new edn 1999), pp. 118–19 and Andrew Lycett, *Dylan Thomas: A New Life* (London: Weidenfeld & Nicolson, 2003), pp. 115–16.

[2] Sigmund Freud, *The Uncanny*, trans. David McLintock (Harmondsworth: Penguin, 2003)

[3] Nicholas Royle, *The Uncanny* (Manchester: Manchester University Press, 2003), p. 1.

[4] Royle, *The Uncanny*, p. 1.

[5] Chris Wigginton, '"Birth and copulation and death": Gothic Modernism and Surrealism in the Poetry of Dylan Thomas', in John Goodby and Chris Wigginton (eds), *Dylan Thomas: New Casebook* (London: Palgrave, 2001), p. 91.

[6] Dylan Thomas, 'Reminiscences of Childhood', in Dylan Thomas, *The Broadcasts*, ed. Ralph Maud (London: Dent, 1991), p. 3. 'Strange' is italicised in Thomas's text.

[7] David N. Thomas (ed.), *Dylan Remembered, Vol. 1: 1914–1934* (Bridgend: Seren/NLW, 2003), p. 73.

[8] Glyn Jones, *The Dragon has Two Tongues*, ed. Tony Brown (1968; Cardiff: University of Wales Press, 2001), pp. 182–3; my italics. Cf. Thomas's letter to Pamela Hansford Johnson, 21 December 1933: 'The greatest single word

I know is "drome" which, for some reason, nearly opens the doors of heaven for me.' He goes on to list other 'favourite words' (*CL*, 73).

9   Walford Davies, *Dylan Thomas* (Milton Keynes: Open University Press, 1986), p. 99.

10   Walford Davies, 'The Poetry of Dylan Thomas', in John Goodby and Chris Wigginton (eds), *Dylan Thomas: New Casebook* (London: Palgrave, 2001), p. 110.

11   David N. Thomas (ed.), *Dylan Remembered, Vol. II: 1935–53* (Bridgend: Seren/NLW, 2004), p. 45. Most of the early stories were copied into the 'Red Notebook'; see *CS*, pp. 368–9. Not insignificantly, in the first letter that Thomas sent to Jones, he writes, 'I am a writer of poems and stories' (March 1934; *CL*, 96).

12   *The Dragon has Two Tongues*, p. 180. It seems likely that Jones was already doing so, since his diary records that by November 1934, he had sent two stories to the magazine *English Story*, edited by Woodrow Wyatt. See *The Collected Stories of Glyn Jones*, ed. Tony Brown (Cardiff: University of Wales Press, 1999), p. 359.

13   *Life and Letters To-day* under the editorship of Robert Herring was especially receptive to writing from Wales and, indeed, between March 1940 and September 1948 Herring published five issues partly or wholly devoted to the work of writers from Wales. See Meic Stephens, 'The Third Man: Robert Herring and *Life and Letters To-day*', *Welsh Writing in English: A Yearbook of Critical Essays*, vol. 3 (1997), pp. 157–69.

14   *Welsh Short Stories* (London: Faber 1937). There was not a single editor but a selection panel, which included Elizabeth Inglis Jones, Llewelyn Wyn Griffith, James Hanley (who was by this point living in mid-Wales) and Arthur Jones. The collection included translations of Welsh-language stories by E. Tegla Davies, Kate Roberts, D. J. Williams and Richard Williams.

15   After failing to place the collection with Dent or Faber (*CL* 245), Thomas attempted to publish them with George Reavey's Europa Press; but when Reavey sent him a 'lawyer's list of the objectionable words, phrases, passages and whole chunks in my short stories', rather than attempt to revise the stories Thomas dropped the project, writing to John Davenport in August 1938: 'I'd rather tickle the cock of the English public than lick its arse' (*CL*, 322).

16   In August 1939, Thomas writes to Desmond Hawkins: 'I'm trying to make my living out of straight stories now' (*CL*, 395).

17   Jones, *The Dragon has Two Tongues*, p. 166. My italics. Most of the early stories were copied into the 'Red Notebook'; see *CS*, pp. 368–9.

18   Walford Davies, *Dylan Thomas: Early Prose Writings* (London: Dent, 1971), p. ix.

19   M. Wynn Thomas, *Corresponding Cultures: The Two Literatures of Wales* (Cardiff: University of Wales Press, 1999), pp. 92–3.

20   Paul Ferris notes that, in 1932, 'A psychiatric hospital (lunatic asylum in those days) was being built above Sketty', to which Thomas refers in a poem of 25 June 1932, where 'The new asylum on the hill /Leers down the valley like a fool' (Ferris, *Dylan Thomas*, p. 70; see Dylan Thomas, *The Notebook Poems 1930–1934*, ed. Ralph Maud (London: Dent/Everyman, 1999), p. 112.) The image is echoed directly in a letter to Trevor Hughes a year later (*CL*, 18).

21 The five short stories are: 'The Tree', 'The Enemies', 'Dress', 'The Visitor' and
    'The Orchards'. 'The Mouse and the Woman' and 'The Map of Love' had
    been published in periodicals in 1936 and 1937 respectively; see *CS*, p. 369.
22 On 'Warmley' and the friendship between Dylan Thomas and Daniel Jones,
    see Lycett, *Dylan Thomas*, pp. 35–9, and Ferris, *Dylan Thomas*, pp. 41–6.
23 Vernon Watkins, Foreword to *Adventures in the Skin Trade* (London: Dent,
    1955), p. 9. Further references to *Adventures in the Skin Trade* are to the sec-
    tions of the text included in *CS*.
24 Dylan Thomas, *The Broadcasts*, pp. 205–6.

4

'TAWE PRESSED IN UPON HIM':
DYLAN THOMAS, MODERNITY AND
THE RURAL-URBAN DIVIDE

Andrew Webb

Over the last fifty years, the Welshness of Dylan Thomas's work has been explored and questioned from a number of angles.[1] While poems and stories have been linked to various locations in south-west Wales, the extent to which they engage with the particular circumstances of Swansea and its hinterland in the 1920s and 30s has, by comparison, received little critical attention.[2] This chapter aims to fill this gap by examining Thomas's late-1930s short stories through the prism of the townscape and its surrounding rural area. In particular, it holds a magnifying glass to the idea of a cultural 'frontier' between the expanding urban space of Swansea and its hinterland in the 1920s and 1930s. It demonstrates the way in which the area underwent specific changes in relation to this frontier, and how these changes are central to the stories in Thomas's *Portrait of the Artist as a Young Dog*, published in 1940.

Swansea's 'frontier' status – as a mainly English-speaking urban port pushing up against a Welsh-speaking, predominantly rural Carmarthenshire – has been pointed out by historians, as we shall see, and has also been registered in the literature of the area. It is important, for example, in the work of Lynette Roberts, one of Thomas's modernist contemporaries, writing out of rural Carmarthenshire during the Second World War.[3] The specific ways in which this frontier has shifted over time has not been considered in relation to Thomas's writing. This chapter contends that the frontiers between Swansea and its rural hinterland changed dramatically in the second and third decades of the twentieth century, altering the character both of the agricultural communities in the hinterland, and of their relation to the town. The short stories at the beginning of *Portrait* not only depict this cultural frontier; their characters' negotiation of this border is the central concern of these tales. Later stories in Thomas's collection shine a light on the ways in which this border shifts in location, and the subsequent pressures brought to bear on the hinterland. For example, they register its shift from agricultural community to tourist destination, and they question whether the countryside fulfils its emerging role as a recreational space for the inhabitants of Swansea's expanding suburbia. In some of the stories in *Portrait*, the frontier between Swansea and its hinterland is effectively dissolved in the fictional space of 'Tawe'. A key aspect of Thomas's prose style – his focus on moments of the gothic-surreal within a broadly realist narrative – emerges as an answer to the 'problem' of how to write about this border, and how to write the 'provincial Swansea novel', a text about the town within its broader region.

'The Peaches', the first story in *Portrait*, begins with an image of the grammar-schoolboy narrator waiting anxiously for his uncle in the cart outside The Pure Drop pub in Carmarthen, before travelling on to his aunt and uncle's farmhouse in rural Carmarthenshire.[4] The town of Carmarthen, it soon becomes clear, is midpoint on the boy's journey, with the narrator already in a state of alienation, 'unfamiliar' to himself, at a point between his longed-for Swansea 'home' and his destination (*CS*, 130). An invisible, but significant, frontier has already been crossed between urban, English-speaking Swansea and its rural, Welsh-speaking hinterland.

> One minute I was small and cold . . . clutching my grammar school cap, unfamiliar to myself, a snub-nosed story-teller lost in his own adventures and longing to be home; the next I was a royal nephew in smart town clothes, embraced and welcomed, standing in the snug centre of my stories and listening to the clock announcing me. (*CS*, 130)

The text portrays the boy's arrival at the farmhouse as his sudden transformation into a 'royal nephew', no longer 'lost' but now comfortably positioned at the 'centre of [his] stories', a home where he is 'embraced and welcomed'. His arrival also heralds a different mode of time: the 'clock announcing me' suggests that time now revolves around him in a way that it had not before. In this way, the opening of 'The Peaches' subtly registers the crossing of a frontier between the modernity of Swansea and the rural, Welsh-language hinterland as experienced by the upwardly-mobile grammar school boy. However, while the boy is conscious of experiencing the different modes of self and time associated with the farmhouse, it is significant that, even at this point, he does not completely belong to these new surroundings: he is, after all still dressed in 'smart town clothes'. Here the reader is confronted with another kind of alienation: that of the boy brought up in modernity who crosses a frontier into the not-quite-modern culture from which his family hails, but into which he does not quite now fit. For the child raised in modernity, there is no way back.

The idea of a cultural frontier between urban, English-speaking Swansea and its rural Welsh hinterland is a familiar one. Historian Kenneth O. Morgan, for example, describes Swansea in the 1920s and 1930s as 'a kind of frontier town, hard against the Welsh-speaking country areas of Carmarthenshire', a town with a 'complex relationship to its hinterland'.[5] Morgan downplays the existence of Welsh-speaking communities within urban Swansea. Nonetheless, read in these terms, 'The Peaches' is an exploration of the manifestations of this frontier in the daily lives of the characters. The story is set at a time in which the spread of modernity has placed existential pressure on the economic and religious culture of the hinterland. The Carmarthenshire farmhouse no longer seems an economically viable place: the uncle has taken to selling animals to fund his drinking, Aunt Annie is forced to augment her income by taking in her Swansea nephew's friend Dylan Williams as a lodger, and their son Gwilym does not work for a living. The infrastructure of nonconformist culture is similarly breaking down: Gwilym is an aspiring minister, but he preaches only to an empty barn. Meanwhile, the paraphernalia of modernity that turn up from time to time at the farmhouse remind its inhabitants of their 'backward' status in this brave new world. The motor car that brings Dylan for his stay contrasts with the horse and cart driven by the uncle, and feeds his resentment. But it is the tin of peaches that epitomises the uneasy relation between the two worldviews associated with each culture. On the one hand, it is seen by Annie as an exotic foodstuff, to be opened on a special occasion for visitors; for Mrs Williams, on the other hand, it is nothing special, a product of a globalising modernity that she takes for granted; she asserts her superiority over her hosts by letting them know that she prefers 'pears or [pineapple] chunks' (*CS*, 137). This modern food, then, is given a heightened status by those in the pre-modern culture, while its value is diminished by those modern people for whom it is an everyday choice of nourishment. The two cultures are separated by their relation to modernity, and its attendant values: Mrs Williams is oblivious to her own rudeness, not only in rejecting the peaches, but also in the manner in which she receives the hospitality. Annie welcomes her visitor into the parlour, her 'best room' (*CS*, 136), opened only for valued guests, yet Mrs Williams dusts her chair with a lace handkerchief before sitting down. The two cultures exist alongside each other in the space of the same geographical region. Yet they see the world in very different ways, and each seems unable to understand the other's perspective.

The child narrator in 'The Peaches' enables Thomas to establish a narrative perspective from which to explore both sides of the cultural frontier, a feat that the other characters fail to achieve. Mrs Williams makes a brief foray across the cultural frontier, but quickly retreats, full of disdain, back into the aspirational bourgeois culture with which she is familiar, taking her son with her. The narrator's uncle and aunt cross in the other direction in the sense that they enter a modern, commodified relation with Mrs Williams in which they are paid for looking after her son. They also try to show their 'modern' credentials by sharing the tin of peaches. But they too retreat back to their side of the border, having been put in their place by Mrs Williams. It is only the child narrator who successfully straddles the border, and only then because he is made to: he is brought out of Swansea to stay with his uncle and aunt in the school holidays for reasons that are never clear. From the start of the story, therefore, the narrator is already positioned on both sides of the cultural frontier. It is from this position, straddling the two cultures, that Thomas's child narrator questions and destabilises the border between the two.[6]

The same child perspective is present in *Portrait*'s second story, 'A Visit to Grandpa's'. Once again, the opening suggests a crossing that has already taken place. Readers encounter the narrator for the first time in his grandfather's Llansteffan house in the middle of the night, surroundings from which he is alienated by virtue of his upbringing in modern Swansea. His dreams on his first night are informed by modernity: the 'runaway coaches on mountain passes, and wide, windy gallops over cactus fields' recall Westerns (*CS*, 143). Yet his grandfather, even more than the uncle and aunt in 'The Peaches', is from another, not-quite-modern time: he dresses in nonconformist 'deep black' and is obsessed with his likely burial place after death; he drives a horse and cart, and is part of a community of villagers who know him well, and who look after him in old age (*CS*, 144–8). The difference between the two is more than a generational one; between them, the shadow of modernity has fallen, and a cultural frontier has emerged which – in the course of the short story – the boy alone straddles. This position informs the surreal imagery of his dream on the last night of his stay: modernity is fused with images from a residual Welsh culture; he has 'dreams where the Llanstephan sea carried bright sailing-boats as long as liners; and heavenly choirs in the Sticks [a local wooded area], dressed in bards' robes and brass-buttoned waistcoats, sang in strange Welsh to the departing sailors' (*CS*, 145). If we think of the child narrator here as a thinly disguised representation of the author, we might consider these stories as narratives in which Thomas articulates his own genesis as a writer who first finds his voice in destabilising the imagery of the cultures on either side of the border.

It is hardly surprising that the sense of a cultural frontier between urban Swansea and its rural hinterland operates as a central principle in these short stories. It is famously present in Thomas's immediate family history. Although Thomas's upbringing was through the medium of English, his Swansea Grammar School teacher father was Welsh-speaking, and the family often visited Welsh-speaking relatives in the town and further afield in rural Carmarthenshire and beyond.[7] The frontier is also present in the immediate geography in which Thomas grew up. His childhood home in Cwmdonkin Drive, Uplands, in which he was born in 1914, was newly built when his parents moved in, and represented then the suburban edge of Swansea. The pattern of the predominantly anglophone city pushing into its Welsh-language hinterland was reinforced through Thomas's childhood. In 1918, when Thomas was four, the boundaries of Swansea County Borough were changed, with the result that Swansea grew in size fourfold. For the first time, areas like Oystermouth on the edge of the Gower were included within its remit. Townhill, adjacent to Uplands, was acquired in 1913 and built upon in the 1920s. It was during this decade, some of Thomas's formative years that according to D. T. Herbert 'a rapid and more universal suburban expansion took place'.[8] Swansea's population grew from 143,000 to 165,000 between 1911 and 1931, the year when Thomas turned seventeen.[9]

The expanding townscape, its shifting frontier with its hinterland, and the importance of both to the stories' characters are registered on numerous occasions in *Portrait*. As Swansea expanded, some of its rural hinterland changed in character, nowhere more so than Gower, an area that of course features in several of the short stories. D. T. Herbert notes Gower's growing tourist trade in the years after the First World War, as well as the shift in character of some of its villages from agricultural community to dormitory suburb and tourist destination.[10] Gower became 'a place of nature' where Swansea's suburban dwellers could recharge their batteries. This change is explored in two of the stories in *Portrait*: in 'Who Do You Wish Was With Us?' particularly, and in 'Extraordinary Little Cough'.

'Who Do You Wish Was With Us' portrays the suburban teenage narrator and his friend Raymond Price taking a hike into Gower. It begins in the suburban 'square of the residential Uplands' from where the pair set off on foot past 'semi-detached houses, with a tin-roofed garage each and a kennel in the back plot and a mowed lawn' into 'wild Wales' (*CS*, 201). Their destination is Worm's Head, the long, narrow tidal island at the end of the Gower peninsula that stretches out into the Irish Sea (*CS*, 201–2). The short story subverts this idea of 'wild Wales', acknowledging instead the extent to which 1930s Gower, as C. C. Harris notes, had become 'a recreational area for the whole [Swansea] region'.[11] But the story also questions the idea that a visit to this new recreational hinterland was in any way as therapeutic for Swansea's suburban inhabitants as its supposed new status would suggest. In these two ways, the text registers a shifting cultural frontier, and a changed relation between Swansea and part of its hinterland.

The George Borrow-inspired idea of the two boys as 'a couple of wanderers in wild Wales' is subverted from the outset of the story. As soon as the idea of wild Wales is introduced, 'a lorry carrying cement drove past' to the golf course (*CS*, 202). Even in the Uplands, the boys walk past 'a crowd of day-trippers who waited at the stop of the Gower-bound buses', suggesting that this part of Swansea's hinterland had become a place of leisure for the town's middle classes (*CS*, 201). This impression is confirmed by the boys' experiences on their day out: they do not encounter any local Gower culture, instead meeting only cyclists and other day-trippers from Swansea in buses and charabancs. They have visitors' eyes for the countryside's natural features – its rolling hills, beaches and, of course, Worm's Head (*CS*, 203–4). This is Gower as a recreational space for Swansea's leisured classes.

'Who Do You Wish Was With Us?' also questions the idea that leisure trips into the countryside enable suburban dwellers to recharge their batteries, and work through the alienation of their urban existence. This is certainly Raymond's aim as he sets off in search of 'a different air', declaring 'God, I like this!' and 'This is the life!' (*CS*, 202–3). But Raymond and the narrator soon stop walking and catch the Rhossili bus, giving up any pretence of believing in the therapeutic benefits of hiking. As J. A. Edwards notes in his history of transport in the Swansea region, the Swansea–Rhossili bus, introduced in 1910, is the main vehicle – literally – through which the villages of Gower were turned into tourist destinations and commuter belt, so the boys' decision to take the bus suggests a complicity, unwitting or otherwise, in this process.[12] Moreover, the young narrator compares the village of Rhossili unfavourably to suburban Swansea: 'pretty pink cottages – horrible, I thought, to live in, for grass and trees would imprison me more securely than any jungle of packed and swarming streets and chimney-roosting roofs' (*CS*, 205). Walking in Gower, with its 'different air', is supposedly a way for Raymond to exorcise the ghosts of his dead father and his brother who had both died of tuberculosis. But, if anything, the trip to Worm's Head causes Raymond to revisit the trauma, to return to the nightmare of 'ghastly bedrooms' in which he attends to his dying father and brother (*CS*, 207). These extended reminiscences cause the boys to forget about their immediate surroundings, and lead to the story's cliffhanger ending in which they become trapped by the rising tide as night falls on Worm's Head. It is this treatment of the countryside as a therapeutic, benevolent place, then, which leads to the boys' further alienation from their rural surroundings and which ironically places them in greater danger (*CS*, 210). In this sense, the text reflects the impact of recent, modernity-driven changes onto the relation between Swansea and its hinterland, and is concerned to critique emergent middle-class perceptions of the latter as a recreational space.

If we compare the short stories discussed thus far with the 'Jarvis Hills' stories, all written a few years earlier in the mid-1930s, the extent to which the later stories in *Portrait* offer a more focused view of the shifting cultural relation between Swansea and its hinterland

becomes clear. 'The Tree', 'The Enemies' and 'The Visitor' are all
set in the Jarvis Hills, which are described as 'twenty miles of up-
and-down country', a fictional location somewhere in west Wales
(*CS*, 5). But while they might be thought of as a hinterland space,
these stories contain no mention of Swansea or modernity. Neither
do they seriously engage with the nonconformist agricultural community of west Wales. Rather, the Jarvis Hills take on the status of
a mythical, pagan space – 'Hills which have been from the beginning' (*CS*, 10) – a place governed by elemental forces of nature
where 'creation sweat[ed] out of the pores of the trees' (*CS*, 19). As
this image suggests, the Jarvis Hills stand for the physical processes
of creation, reproduction and death. Each of the stories portrays
these Hills as the site of an epic conflict between the pagan idea of
creation and other narratives, especially the Christian story. The
former always prevails: in 'The Tree', the boy protagonist adapts the
crucifixion story in macabre ways by nailing the 'idiot' to a tree; in
'The Enemies', the Reverend Davies fails to see the witchcraft before
his eyes even as he succumbs to it; and in 'The Visitor', Peter has a
shroud pulled over his face before he realises that he has died. The
Jarvis Hills, then, are a displaced setting for a metaphysical exploration of the relation between the embodied processes of reproduction
and death and a more abstract Christian consciousness, which, however it tries, cannot change them. In this sense, the 'Jarvis Hills'
stories address similar themes to the process poetry that Thomas
developed in the mid-1930s, as John Goodby has pointed out.[13] The
displacement of these concerns to a fictional space in west Wales is
premised on the ignorance of Thomas's readership about the west-
Walian setting. It is hard to imagine a similar displacement to the
English Home Counties, an area with which many of Thomas's
readers would arguably have been more familiar. For the purposes
of this chapter, then, the 'Jarvis Hills' stories offer a point of contrast to Thomas's later, sustained engagement with Swansea and its
hinterland in *Portrait*.

   If we think of the stories considered thus far – 'The Peaches',
'A Visit to Grandpa's' and 'Who Do You Wish Was With Us?' – as
texts that explore a shifting cultural frontier with a focus on the pressures and changes upon Swansea's hinterland wrought by the growing
town, we might think of some of the other stories in *Portrait* as texts
that focus on how Swansea changes in light of its hinterland. These
changes are registered, for example, in 'One Warm Saturday', the

last story in *Portrait*, when the narrator describes the journey back to Lou's bedsit in one of those overcrowded slums:

> they tore past black houses and bridges, a station in a smoke cloud, and drove up a steep side street with one weak lamp in a circle of railings at the top, and swerved into a space where a tall tenement house stood surrounded by cranes, standing ladders, poles and girders, barrows, brick-heaps. (*CS*, 237)

Here, the presence of the tall tenement house suggests buildings in the process of demolition. The proximity to the station, moreover, suggests that the story refers to one of the slum clearance areas in the town centre. Along with the expansion of Swansea in the 1930s went a reorganisation of its centre: as D. T. Herbert points out, there was a great effort to clear slums in 'a triangular area north-west of the railway station bounded by High Street, Dyfatty, New Orchard Street and Mariner Street'.[14] This clearance had not been completed by the start of the Second World War, when 'there remained 1771 overcrowded dwellings occupied by 8972 people.'[15] In this way, the text registers urban Swansea at a particular moment in its history before the Luftwaffe's bombers engaged in a clearance of their own.

The narrator, of course, is not quite at home in these urban surroundings. It is implied in the opening paragraphs that he is a 'sailor', a reminder that Swansea is a port town, who like many of the people on that warm Saturday afternoon has come into the town from outside (*CS*, 224). Indeed, the title draws our attention to that time in the week – Saturday afternoon – when the town's population was temporarily boosted by people from beyond its immediate perimeters coming to spend their leisure time and money. They literally bring the hinterland into the urban centre, and in doing so, they transform it into a cultural melting pot, a place where the frontier between the town and its hinterland – for a time – disappears. It becomes 'Tawe'.

The semi-fictional name 'Tawe' suggests a geographical space in which the border between the hinterland and the town is unclear. The name 'Tawe' is repeated across several stories: 'One Warm Saturday', 'Where Tawe Flows', and 'Old Garbo'. In the latter, the young reporter writes his location as 'Reporters' Room, *Tawe News*, Tawe, South Wales, England, Europe, The Earth' (*CS*, 215). While a lot of attention has been paid to the provocative placement of south Wales in England, less attention has been focused on the earlier places in the list: 'Reporters' Room, *Tawe News*, Tawe'. Here, the act of writing is linked to the power of writing (in this case, journalism) to name a place, and even conjure it into existence. The name 'Tawe' is also repeated, of course, in 'Where Tawe Flows', another short story that concerns itself with writing about a particular place. This odd title invites readers to dwell on the word 'Tawe', and manages to suggest the word 'inspiration' (for which it is a replacement). The river Tawe, which literally flows from the Welsh interior into the town, might be seen as a symbol of that journey from the hinterland into Swansea, or even a literal transporting of water from the surrounding area into the town, a physical linking of the two spaces. In this way, 'Tawe' also suggests a broader geographical space which is part-real, part-fictional. It is distinct from but related to 'Abertawe', the name for Swansea in Welsh. It also alludes to the Welsh-speaking area, the Swansea Valley or 'Cwm Tawe', beyond the town's perimeter. The Swansea Valley is a different hinterland to the more rural spaces of Gower and Carmarthenshire: it is more industrial, but culturally and linguistically distinct, and still, crucially, a hinterland to urban Swansea. 'Tawe' thereby suggests a larger area which includes the town, but also the hinterland within the town's gravitational pull. In this sense, 'Tawe' is a name for a space that straddles a border, bringing together the hinterland/town and the Welsh/English languages into one space. So, in 'One Warm Saturday', when the narrator describes how 'Tawe pressed in upon him', we are invited to see the town and the hinterland through the same lens, not as two separate domains, but as a new space and time in which the provincial town is enriched by its environs:

> He sat sad and content in the plain room of the undistinguished hotel at the sea-end of the shabby, spreading town where everything was happening. He had no need of the dark interior world when Tawe pressed in upon him and the eccentric ordinary people came bursting and crawling, with noise and colours, out of their houses, out of the graceless buildings, the factories and avenues, the shining shops and blaspheming chapels, the terminuses and the meeting-halls, the falling alleys and brick lanes, from the arches and shelters and holes behind the hoarding, out of the common wild intelligence of the town. (*CS*, 230)

This is Swansea as a carnival town, impossible to contain – literally 'spreading' but also teeming with the irrepressible life that comes from the list of institutions that feature in the extract. These instances of the 'wild', 'eccentric' and carnivalesque are not conjured by the speaker's individual imagination; they come from the 'eccentric ordinary people', from the 'common wild intelligence' of the people of Tawe. Thomas is here reaching towards an understanding of the distinctiveness of Tawe – a place in which the artist's aesthetic emerges from the 'common', 'ordinary' people living in places that are 'plain' and 'undistinguished' – the everyday, communal life – of the 'shabby, spreading town where everything was happening'. Because he has access to this already-surreal resource, he has 'no need' of 'the dark interior world' of his individual consciousness. The two cultures either side of the cultural frontier that the child narrator alone straddles in 'The Peaches' and 'A Visit to Grandpa's' has been transformed into the distinctive, enriching feature of 'Tawe'.

What follows for the narrator of 'One Warm Saturday' is that 'Tawe pressed in upon him'. The result in the remainder of the short story is a series of tableaux whose gothic-surrealism sits within the realist style in which they are couched. A few paragraphs on, for example, the narrator Jack, having been accosted by a drunkard, is invited to feel for the drunk man's bottom, only to find out that he doesn't have one: 'That's right. Nothing. Nothing. There's nothing to feel', laments the drunkard, before regaling Jack with his story (*CS*, 230). He had been a miner 'working underground in Dowlais [in the south Wales Valleys], and the end of the world came down on me', an accident for which he had received only 'two and three ha'pence a cheek . . . cheaper than a pig' (*CS*, 230). There are many similar examples of the gothic-surreal in 'One Warm Saturday'. Catching his reflection in the saloon window, the narrator tells us that 'his ape-like hanging face, with "Bass" across the forehead, gave back a cracked sneer' (*CS*, 228). On one level, of course, this is a realist depiction of what he sees, but it is also a distortion that is experienced, a description that draws readers' attention to the gothic-surrealism of modernity. It is a reminder that the dead and macabre surface at surprising moments across the stories. In 'One Warm Saturday', we see the speaker chatting up Lou, the girl of his dreams, at the saloon bar, while on the floor beneath their encounter, a drunkard 'rolled in his sleep, and his head lay in the spittoon' (*CS*, 234). The exuberance of the narrative voice, as the opening paragraph suggests, takes the description beyond the strictly realist, and into the gothic-surreal. On learning, after several rounds, that Lou is waiting for Mr O'Brien, we learn that '[t]he young man clenched his fist on the table covered with dead, and sheltered her in the warm strength of his fist' (*CS*, 235). The 'dead' refers to used and empty glasses, while the image of Jack sheltering Lou 'in the warm strength of his fist' suggests his desire to aggressively protect her, but both phrases are meant metaphorically. They depart from classic realist narrative. Here, the gothic surrealism does not come from the narrator's observations of the everyday, so much as it driven by the internal dynamic or the 'process' of language, in this case the associations of the word 'dead'.[16]

At the end of 'Who Do You Wish Was With Us', when the speaker and his friend Raymond are stuck at twilight on Worm's Head, there is a similar metaphorical reference to the dead: 'the sea began to cover our rock quickly, our rock already covered with friends, with living and dead, racing against the darkness' (*CS*, 210). Again, the language moves without warning from the literal ('the sea began to cover our rock quickly') to the surreal ('our rock already covered with friends, with living and dead'). To whom does the term 'dead' refer? The marooned boys, Raymond's dead father and brother about whom he has been speaking, or someone else? The language's resistance to literal interpretation unsettles our confidence in what it describes, drawing our attention to the act of perception. Just as the characters are marooned, literally cut off from the familiar, not quite 'at home' in this Worm's Head hinterland, so too are we, as readers, unsettled: relieved of the reassuring idea that language offers an objective grasp on the physical world.

The gothic-surrealism that is employed to describe the boys' situation in 'Who Do You Wish Was With Us?' echoes the language used to portray the narrator's alienation right back in 'The Peaches', the first story of the collection, and it occurs at the very moment when the child finally crosses the cultural 'frontier', when the cart pulls up at the farmhouse.

> We drove into the farm-yard of Gorsehill, where the cobbles rang and the black, empty stables took up the ringing and hollowed it so that we drew up in a hollow circle of darkness and the mare was a hollow animal and nothing lived in the hollow house at the end of the yard but two sticks with faces scooped out of turnips (*CS*, 129)

This narrative moves mid-sentence from realist description of a recognisable time, place and event – the arrival of the boy and his uncle at night into the farmyard – to a scene that has been transformed by the boy's fearful, gothic imagination. It is significant, I would suggest, that at the crossing of a cultural frontier between the modernity of Swansea and the agricultural community of its hinterland, we encounter the gothic-surreal for the first time.

But it is in 'One Warm Saturday', 'Where Tawe Flows' and 'Old Garbo' – praise prose-poems for 'Tawe' or a Swansea that has been written into its hinterland – where the gothic-surreal is employed more frequently. Thomas's development of gothic-surrealism within a broadly realist prose style is a way of writing that is adequate to the task of representing this imagined space.[17] '[L]et's get our realism straight', says Mr Humphries in 'Where Tawe Flows', one of the characters who is trying to write 'a Novel of Provincial Life' (*CS*, 191–2). In a way, the collaborative authors in this short story, one of whom is named Thomas, have something in common with the author of *Portrait*: both are searching for the way of writing adequate to the task of creating the provincial Swansea novel. Thomas, the young journalist in 'Old Garbo', similarly wants to write 'a Provincial Autobiography' (*CS*, 215). We might think of these 'provincial' genres not in a pejorative sense as weak versions of their metropolitan equivalents, but as prose texts that aim to register social life in a particular geographic setting. In order to write the provincial Swansea novel, Thomas needs to find a style that writes the town into its 'province' or hinterland. I want to suggest that this is exactly what Thomas achieves in *Portrait*. But in order to do so, like Mr Humphries, Thomas needs to get his 'realism straight'. He does so by creating a highly refined form of realism that is in effect surreal, full of features that we would normally associate with modernism. The text is stringently realist, but repeatedly homes in on examples of the macabre, bizarre and surreal, none of which are fully explained. For example, 'Old Garbo' opens with Mr Farr, senior reporter on *Tawe News*, walking along a dark passage to the lavatory, recalling another visit when he had discovered a sink 'full of blood' and 'Mr Farr, no father' scrawled in brown on the wall' (*CS*, 211). He recalls how 'once Ted Williams found a lip outside the Mission to Seamen. It had a small moustache' (*CS*, 215). In 'Old Garbo', Thomas takes every opportunity to challenge the conventions of classic realism:

> Two small men, Mr Farr and his twin brother, led me on an ice-rink to the door, and the night air slapped me down. The evening happened

suddenly. A wall slumped over and knocked off my trilby; Mr Farr's brother disappeared under the cobbles. Here came a wall like a buffalo; dodge him, son. (*CS*, 220)

Here, the language strains the bounds of conventional realism: identical twins appear out of nowhere, and disappear as quickly, a floor becomes an ice-rink, there is a speeding-up of time, and walls suddenly collapse. The speaker is, of course, drunk, and in this sense, the narrated events are rooted in the 'real', but the way the evening is described is not classic realism. The text instead draws our attention to the presence of the surreal in everyday perception. It is the stylistic development which enables Thomas to write his own 'provincial autobiography'.

This chapter has argued that the changing 'frontier' between a mainly English-speaking Swansea and the Welsh-speaking, nonconformist, agricultural communities of its hinterland in the second and third decades of the twentieth century is a central concern of *Portrait*. The early stories dramatise their characters' negotiation of this border and suggest that, for the young Thomas depicted in these stories, the ability to write about life spilling over the cultural divide was a key factor in his development. We can read these stories for the light they shed on the ways in which this border shifts in location, on the subsequent pressures brought to bear on the hinterland, and as an intervention in contemporary debates about the new role for the countryside as a recreational space for the inhabitants of Swansea's expanding suburbia. But we can also read these stories as Thomas's attempt to find a form of expression that is adequate to the task of writing Swansea into its hinterland, of imaginatively disrupting the border that he straddled as a child. Through the creation of the fictional space of 'Tawe', and through the creation of a new style – the gothic-surreal within a broadly realist narrative – we see how, in *Portrait of the Artist as a Young Dog*, Thomas effectively solved the 'problem' of how to write about this border, and write his own 'provincial autobiography'.

Notes

[1]   See, for example, Walford Davies's recently reprinted *Dylan Thomas* (Cardiff: University of Wales Press, 2014 [1972]) in the *Writers of Wales* series; John Ackerman's *Welsh Dylan: Dylan Thomas's Life, Writing and his Wales*

(Bridgend: Seren, 1979); M. Wynn Thomas's essay 'Portraits of the Artist as a Young Welshman', in M. Wynn Thomas, *Corresponding Cultures: the Two Literatures of Wales* (Cardiff: University of Wales Press, 1999); and, more recently, John Goodby's magisterial *The Poetry of Dylan Thomas: Under the Spelling Wall* (Liverpool: Liverpool University Press, 2013).

2   For a critical text that makes connections between the poems, stories, biography and specific locations in the Swansea region, see James A. Davies, *Dylan Thomas's Swansea, Gower and Laugharne* (Cardiff: University of Wales Press, 2000).

3   See, for example, Lynette Roberts's poem 'Swansea Raid', in which the speaker describes the Luftwaffe's night time bombing of Swansea in February 1942, as witnessed from a farm on the Llansteffan peninsula in Carmarthenshire. The poem is well introduced by Patrick McGuinness in his introduction to his edition of *Lynette Roberts: Collected Poems* (Manchester: Carcanet, 2005), pp. xix–xx.

4   Dylan Thomas, *Collected Stories* (London: Phoenix, 1983), p. 127. All subsequent references to this text are included in parentheses after the quotation.

5   Kenneth O. Morgan, *Rebirth of a Nation: Wales 1880–1980* (Oxford, Oxford University Press, 1982), p. 263.

6   In many ways, the narrator's destabilisation of the border between an aspirational, bourgeois English-speaking culture in Swansea, and that of a rural, Welsh-language hinterland anticipates Thomas's later position as a disruptive presence within the canons of English and Welsh literatures, as Rhian Barfoot has pointed out in *Liberating Dylan Thomas: Rescuing a Poet from Psycho-Sexual Servitude* (Cardiff: University of Wales Press, 2015).

7   For further biographical detail, see Paul Ferris, *Dylan Thomas: The Biography* (London: Dent, 1999); or the more recent Andrew Lycett, *Dylan Thomas: A New Life* (London: Phoenix, 2004).

8   D. T. Herbert, 'The Twentieth Century', in W. G. V. Balchin (ed.), *Swansea and its Region* (Swansea: University College of Swansea, 1971), 179–94 (p. 188).

9   Herbert, 'The Twentieth Century', p. 183.

10   Herbert, 'The Twentieth Century', p. 189.

11   C. C. Harris, 'Social Structures', in W. G. V. Balchin (ed.), *Swansea and its Region* (Swansea: University College of Swansea, 1971), 305–17 (p. 305).

12   J. A. Edwards, 'Transport and Communication', in W. G. V. Balchin (ed.), *Swansea and its Region* (Swansea: University College of Swansea, 1971), 273–87 (p. 275).

13   Goodby, *Under the Spelling Wall*, p. 240.

14   Herbert, 'The Twentieth Century', p. 186.

15   Herbert, 'The Twentieth Century', p. 186.

16   This use of language echoes the textual strategies of the early process poems.

17   This gothic realism gestures towards the kind of heightened photographic naturalism epitomised by Zola.

5

THE COMIC VOICES OF DYLAN THOMAS

M. Wynn Thomas

> A drummer is a man we know who has to do with drums,
> But I've never met a plumber yet who had to do with plums,
> A cheerful man who sells you hats would be a cheerful hatter,
> But is a serious man who sells you mats a serious matter? (*CL*, 5)

This, the second 'poem' recorded in Dylan Thomas's *Collected Letters*, is reckoned by the editor Paul Ferris to have been written by the poet when he was still little more than a child. And it is immediately preceded by another childish rhyme that runs as follows:

> It was a lonely spot
> With desolation spread,
> An eerie, solemn silence reigned,
> Around the sleeping dead. (*CL*, 5)

Comedy, then, here follows hot on the heels of a verse already hinting at that camp relish for the gothic and the ghoulish that was to be one of the signature features of the imagination of both the adolescent and the adult poet. And it leads one to speculate: could there perhaps be a causal connection between the one and the other? Could one of the many dazzlingly diverse uses Dylan Thomas found for his native comic genius throughout his career have been to control those terrors towards which he was inexorably drawn and by which he was chronically haunted? He certainly described his poetry much in these terms in a letter of 16 May 1938, baldly stating that 'very much of my poetry is, I know, an enquiry and a terror of fearful expectation, a discovery and facing of fear' (*CL*, 297).

Few critics have allowed themselves to be detained for very long by a careful, thorough and thoughtful consideration of Thomas's comic writings. And yet it could be reasonably claimed, I think, that he may have been naturally gifted with a greater talent for comedy than for poetry. Poetry involved for him the serious, determined and willed practising of a laboured craft and wrestling with a stubbornly sullen art. Comic writing on the other hand came to him entirely unbidden, spontaneously, in garrulous improvisatory profusion – or so at least it would seem, until one begins to notice the cunning uses to which it was so often put.

For me, his case calls to mind the famously provocative comment Dr Johnson made in his *Preface to Shakespeare*, that the great Tragedies were the products of skill, the great Comedies the products of instinct. The minute one starts investigating Thomas's comic writings one is struck by the virtuosic diversity of his lavish inventiveness – ranging from manic verbal pyrotechnics, through fantastic characterisations and mockingly astute depictions of social mores and human relations to satiric sketches. It is as if a comic perspective were for him a reflex action of his engagement with life. The outrageous, the hilarious, the pathetic, the camp – his talent for comedy is seemingly at ease with all of these. At once dazzling, calculated and compulsive, this carnivalesque display sets one wondering where exactly it comes from, and where it is all going? What precisely are its implications and purposes? What might perhaps be the psychosocial drivers of such theatrical excess? Such questions lead us back, of course, to such clues as the intriguingly suggestive juxtaposition, in that first, very early letter in Thomas's hand, of the gothic and the comic. But they also encourage us to examine the occasion and context of any given comic exercise. That first letter, for instance, was addressed to Thomas's older sister Nancy, and so the comedy in it was obviously designed to impress on her the precocious sophistication of her little brother. And this was to be a recurrent feature of Thomas's comic writing – much of it was consciously performative in character, designed to project a carefully constructed, beautifully calibrated persona and composed very much with an eye to making a certain kind of impression.

*   *   *

Where, then, to start exploring Thomas's career as a comedy writer? We could do worse, I think, than begin by attending to that period in his early life to which he himself remained magnetically drawn after he had moved away from Swansea. In a marvellous letter that he sent from Ireland in 1935 to his old chum Daniel Jones, then based in Harrow, Thomas vividly conjured memories of the fantasy world they had invented together in early adolescence in the front room of Warmley, the Jones family's bourgeois villa in the cosy Swansea suburb of Sketty:

> I never can believe that the Warmley days are over – ('just a song at twilight when the lights Marlowe and the Flecker Beddoes Bailey Donne and Poe') – that there should be no more twittering, no more nose-on-window-pressing and howling at the streets, no more walks with vampire cries and standing over the world, no more hold-a-writing-table for the longest, and wrong adjectives; I can't believe that Percy, who droppeth gently, can have dropped out of the world, that the 'Badger Beneath my Vest,' and 'Homage to Admiral Beatty' are a song and a boat of the past, that Miguel-y-Bradshaw, Waldo Carpet, Xmas Pulpit, Paul America, Winter Vaux, Tonenbach, and Bram, and all that miscellaneous colony of geniuses, our little men, can have died on us; that the one-legged grandmother – remember the panama-hat-shaped birds, from the Suez Canal, who pecked at her atlas-bone – doesn't still take photographs of Birmingham, that the queer, Swansea world, a world, thank Christ that was self-sufficient, can't stand on its bow legs in a smoky city full of snobs and quacks. (*CL*, 196)

The passage is a brilliant display of Thomas the verbal contortionist's gleefully anarchic way with words, a demonstration of his subversive ability to bend them all-ways to his own will, evidence of the wilful arbitrariness of his irrepressible fantastications. It is a triumphant affirmation of his complete youthful mastery of his medium, of the mercurial shape-changing transformations effected by his fertile imagination, often in response to social situations to whose challenges and opportunities he was always preternaturally sensitive.

And that last point leads us to notice that, in this most intimately convivial of letters to his oldest and closest friend, Thomas admits that for him such a manically comical world as he and Jones had between them created did actually serve a variety of important functions: it had been the protectively permissive nursery of their vital but vulnerable creative talents, the playground of their secret inner beings, and a defence against the incursions of the grim tyrannical Reality Principle of the established social order. And at this very early stage of his development, when he was still affecting a Leftish politics much influenced by his friend Bert Trick's Communist sympathies, Thomas was even prone to adventitiously describe his comic writing as a revolutionary act: fascinated by the malleability of the word, he toyed with the idea that it advertised the malleability of the world. Rather than risking life and limb fighting Franco and fascism in Spain, he implied, he preferred to prepare the way for revolution through his revolutionary writing.

Percy's world in Warmley 'was, and still is, the only one that has any claims to permanence', Thomas accordingly insisted to Daniel Jones, 'a world of our own – from which we can interpret nearly everything that's worth'. Fiercely denying that it was 'escapism', he asserted it was 'the only contact there is between yourself and yourselves' (*CL*, 197). It is a fascinating admission by Thomas of the many multiple beings of which his singular social self, his fixed public persona, was actually composed. Comedy, he implies, came naturally to him because it enabled him to speak his turbulent inner world in the different voices of its inhabitants. And, as this long, remarkable letter also makes clear before it ends, Thomas was fully aware that his extravagant comic improvisations and the 'surrealist' images of his poetry were part of a single spectrum of bizarre imagining. So, resuming writing to Daniel Jones the morning following the previous night's rapturous recollections of Warmley, he picks up the 'night threads' to find 'they lead, quite impossibly, into the socket of a one-eyed woman, the rectums of crucified sparrows, the tunnels of coloured badgers reading morbid literature in the dark, and very small bulls, the size of thimbles, mooing in a clavichord' (*CL*, 198). Recalling what Thomas reveals here about the continuity between his comic and his 'serious' writing, helps us register the archness with which he deploys the hyperbolic extravagances of some of his poetic images: they often knowingly teeter on the dangerous edge of comic absurdity, while defying us to push them over the brink.

As has already been implied, it would be a mistake to treat Thomas's comedy solely as the product of the urgent promptings of his inner needs. As often as not, it had the most shamelessly calculated designs on its readers or listeners. Think, for instance, of those innumerable delicious comic riffs in his early letters to Pamela Hansford Johnson, when he is so anxious to play to perfection the part of the callow provincial wannabe-sophisticate to her ironically imagined metropolitan poise and glamour: 'perhaps you are sitting in the bus, passing Chelsea or Kronsky, and wondering what the hell rhymes with piano. And here *I* lie, in a lukewarm bath of half-slumber, with the unpolished taps of words turned full on' (*CL*, 121).

'The mouse is released, the cheesy bandits have nibbled off, there are squeaks of jubilation, and whiskers glint in the sun' (*CL*, 287): to receive a letter that began like that – as did Vernon Watkins in April 1938 – was obviously a tonic, so it is no wonder that Thomas the 'comic turn' could endear himself to so many. Reading the letters, one can only marvel at the wild, prodigal inventiveness of his writing. In his case the cliché 'hysterically funny' would seem to have a literal application, as one senses always a sharp, nervous edge to the comedy. Affable or genial it rarely is. Rather, it is highly flavoured with anarchic aggression or indeed with malice, as when characterising the publisher George Reavey, who doesn't 'know how to sell anything except a false personality. He's tucked up under his own armpits & looks at the world around him through a moist clump of ginger hair' (*CL*, 294). Nor do the admirers of Thomas's poetry fare any better. Approached for advice by the secretary of a verse-speaking London choir preparing to record 'And Death shall have no Dominion' for HMV, he had to endure a recitation of it down the phone: 'Picked voices picking the rhythm to bits, chosen elocutionists choosing their own meanings, ten virgins weeping slowly over a quick line, matrons mooing the refrain, a conductor with all his vowels planed to the last e' (*CL*, 344). His theatre of the absurd ran easily to black humour – 'Mr [Neville] Chamberlain is crazy about modern verse, and I shall send a photograph of myself, in bowler and gasmask, rhyming womb with tomb' (*CL*, 325). It is an image worthy of Magritte. And Thomas's comic vision included the world of objects much as did that of Dickens, so that he can describe the Laugharne house to which he has newly moved in May 1938, as 'a small, damp fisherman's cottage – green rot sprouts through the florid scarlet forests of the wallpaper, sneeze and the chairs crack, the double-bed is a swing band with coffin, oompah, slush-pump, gob-stick, and almost wakes the deaf, syphilitic neighbours – by the side of an estuary in a remote village' (*CL*, 296).

When riled – as he was when Henry Treece accused his poetry of a lack of social awareness – he was stirred to display the prodigious, omnivorous appetite of an astonishing creative imagination whose natural overflow was comedy. 'You are right,' he tartly comments to Treece, 'when you suggest that I think a squirrel stumbling at least of equal importance as Hitler's invasions, murder in Spain, the Garbo-Stokowski romance, royalty, Horlick's, lynchlaw, pit disasters, Joe Louis, wicked capitalists, saintly communists, democracy, the Ashes, the Church of England, birthcontrol, Yeats's voice.' And so the mad, serendipitous listing continues, unedited, uncensored and unstemmed, to its crazy ending in 'means tests, the fascist anger, the daily, momentary lightnings, eruptions, farts, dampsquibs, barrelorgans, tinwhistles, howitzers, tiny death-rattles, volcanic whimpers'. Such, he concludes, is the crazy paving of bric-a-brac – the consequential and inconsequential all mixed up higgledy-piggledy – that make up 'the world I eat, drink, love, work, hate and delight in' (*CL*, 310). And his comedy was the very spitting image of that world that resembled 'a chapter of accidents written in a dream by a professor of mathematics who has forgotten all formulas but the wrong one that 2 & 2 make 5', as he himself put it in a completely different context (*CL*, 528).

But Thomas was also shrewdly aware that his comic genius could allow him to get away with murder. Perhaps the most egregious, most remarkable, and most unsavoury example of his use of his talents to such nefarious ends was the extraordinary letter of ostensible 'apology' he wrote to one of his oldest and closest friends, Vernon Wakins, twenty-six full days after having failed to turn up to act as best man at the latter's London wedding. It opens with a floridly comic piece of scene-setting:

> Rocking and rocking back from a whirled London, where nothing went right, all duties were left, and my name spun rank in the whole old smoky nose, I try, to a rhythm of Manchester pocket-handkerchers, and Conk him on the mousetrap, Conk him on the mousetrap, from the London-leaving wheels, to explain to you both, clearly and sincerely, why I never arrived, in black overcoat & shiny suit, rose-lapelled, breathing cachous & great good will, at lunch and church. (*CL*, 527)

Having characterised his cowering writing self as hemmed in by 'soldiers, all twelve foot high & commando-trained to the last lunge of the bayonet' (*CL*, 528), he proceeded to a virtuosic string of excuses, involving a trip to Coventry, a failure to catch the only available train on to London, which necessitated the risk of travelling there on the morning of the wedding itself, due arrival in the capital only for

Thomas to forget the name of the church that was his destination, and a consequently abortive cab trip to the wrong venue, followed by a failed subsequent attempt to phone the newly married couple with an abject apology. The whole letter is a shameless, hilarious 'fruity farrago' (his phrase from elsewhere, *CL*, 763) of nonsense leading to the tendentious conclusion that Thomas had been nothing but the hapless victim of a 'somersaulting and backspinning of circumstance against my being where I most wanted to be: at your wedding' (*CL*, 529). After which he still had the gall to conclude his letter with a 'God bless you both, & do try to forgive me' – which, of course, the gentle, otherworldly Watkins duly did. What chance did this honourable, soft-hearted character have of withstanding the seductively comic blandishments of the worldly, unscrupulously selfish rogue who professed to be his 'bosom friend'?

Thomas tries on a range of personae for size in his correspondence with Pamela Hansford Johnson, and particularly productive of comedy is his fine line in world-weary misanthropic gloom. 'The worms are doing very nicely today. Sunday in Wales. The Sunday-walkers have slunk out of the warrens in which they sleep and breed all the unholy week, have put on their black suits, reddest eyes, & meanest expressions, and are now marching up the hill past my window. Fathers are pointing out the view to their stiff-collared whelps' (*CL*, 110). And so on and so miserably forth for six more pages of the *Collected Letters*, brimful of what he elsewhere called 'stagey melancholia' (*CL*, 130). Indeed, his correspondence with Johnson repeatedly offers classic examples of his humour at its most addictively sour, not to mention the casual cruelties in which it also abounds, as when he characterises Glyn Jones, the talented, sweet-natured writer who had been one of his earliest friends, with cutting condescension as 'a nice, handsome young man with no vices. He neither smokes, drinks, nor whores. He looks very nastily at me down his aristocratic nose if I have more than one Guinness at lunch' (*CL*, 135). Nice Thomas never was in his early letters, when his youthful comedy was at its most dangerously uninhibited and scandalously productive.

* * *

A study of comedy in the letters, then, exposes for us that ceaseless dialectic between the spontaneous and the calculated, the compulsive and theatrically performative, that was also a core feature of Thomas's compellingly complex personality. When, however, we turn our attention to the stories, as eventually to *Under Milk Wood*, the balance between these two conflicting elements seems to me to tilt decisively away from the involuntary and towards the artfully contrived. The comic instinct that in the letters repeatedly drives him willy-nilly to risk a walk on the wild side becomes increasingly tamed and domesticated in such works – demurely house-trained, so to speak, as he himself never fully was. This impressively achieved body of comic writing is understandably much-loved and comfortably well-travelled precisely because it amuses and titillates without ever threatening to startle the horses. It is often suffused with geniality, which is not true of the humour of his letters, wickedly subversive to the very end – sending a letter about 'the best bone-boys' to Irene Jones (Daniel Jones's wife) a few months before his death, he signed off, 'Yours, with love, bottom' (*CL*, 943). And of course, later circumstances – his wartime work as fluent scriptwriter of morale-boosting propagandist documentaries, his increasing fame as a supreme broadcaster, the chronic financial crises that turned the eternally impecunious, sponging poet into a journalistic hack ever ready to capitalise on his uncanny knack for turning out highly marketable products – all conspired to effect this transformation. To reach such a conclusion is not snootily to despise his later comic achievements at all, but simply to clarify (and perhaps mildly regret) the limited terms of their enjoyable successfulness.

In his set-piece exercises in comedy, Thomas is almost always operating from deep within the comfort zone of his imagination, and he does so by locating that comedy securely within the place – or places – with which he was himself most comfortably familiar, namely those regions of the Wales of his time that were home to his family, friends and relations. There were two such regions in particular; that of the industrial society of south Wales centred on the beloved town of Swansea where his upwardly mobile parents had settled into bourgeois suburban comfort and he had grown up, and the adjacent yet entirely different Welsh-speaking region of the religiose and rural south-West, centred on Carmarthen, from which his father's and mother's people had actually come and where his maternal relatives continued to live. 'Peasants' and 'townies', Welsh-speakers and English-speakers: Thomas made the comically bizarre interplay between their two worlds the subject of such marvellous fictions as 'The Peaches', the opening story in *Portrait of the Artist as a Young Dog*.

Nowhere is the exquisite social ballet resulting captured with more painful exactness than in the scene where the mother of little Dylan's

towny friend Jack – the stately Mrs Williams from Swansea, ostenta-
tiously bejewelled and bedecked – pays a visit to humble Annie Jones
down on the farm. The matron 'was tall and stout, with a jutting
bosom and thick legs, her ankles swollen over her pointed shoes;
she was fitted out like a mayoress or a ship, and she swayed after
Annie into the best room' (*CS*, 136). The fussing, flustered, Annie,
on the other hand, 'wore a black, shining dress that smelt of moth
balls, like the chair covers in the best room' (*CS*, 135). The contrast
between the two is registered with deadly social accuracy, with the
author's sympathy clearly resting with the anxious 'peasant woman'
whose elaborate attempts to impress her visitor with the rare proffered delicacy of tinned peaches is brusquely rebuffed. The innate
courtesy of poor Annie, however awkwardly expressed, here offsets
the unfeeling, arrogant manner of her guest. And no detail in the
scene is more touchingly telling than the sight of Annie 'opening the
china cupboard, upsetting the Bible on the floor, picking it up, dust-
ing it hurriedly with her sleeve' (*CS*, 136). A pious chapel-goer, Annie
endeavours to live by 'the good book', but knows her visitor will have
eyes only for whether or not it has a clean cover – having no doubt
at home a maid delegated to look after such domestic matters (as
indeed had the Thomas family). The crassly blundering Mrs Williams
upsets more than an apple cart when she enters the front parlour; she
heedlessly overturns a whole way of life by showing such a callous
contempt for its values, courtesies and customs.

As 'The Peaches' clearly shows, Thomas's Welsh society featured
several prominent pressure points, and from the resulting fractures
– that ran directly through his own imagination as well as through
his surrounding world – issued some of his comic writing. What he
is exploring in that story, albeit in a comic key, are several aspects
of what might be termed the typical experience of the Welsh people
during the second half of the nineteenth-century and on into the
twentieth; that of the physical migration, radical social dislocation,
language rupture, and culture shift that was resultant upon the explo-
sively rapid development of a new, cosmopolitan industrial society in
the south-east of the country. For most of the population, this process
had led to proletarianisation and a new class identity. But Thomas's
own family experience had been rather different.

Thomas's mother's parents had moved from the Carmarthenshire
countryside to Swansea, and she was born and raised in the working-
class area around the great docklands area to the east of the town.

This large port had been home to the legendary 'Cape Horners', but by the time she was a girl it was serving the heavy industries crammed into the hinterland of a town that had become renowned the world over as a great 'Copperopolis' and centre of the metallurgical industry. Thomas's father's background was in the rural west, where the family had for generations been farmers until D.J.'s father (Dylan's paternal grandfather) succeeded in advancing to the eminently superior position of railway guard at Carmarthen. This no doubt assisted his son to gain a rare place as one of the extremely small cohort of undergraduates admitted to study at University College, Aberystwyth, where he gained an outstanding degree in English. Although ever resentful of his failure thereafter to secure a lecturing post at a university, he went on to enjoy a socially prestigious career at the renowned Swansea Grammar School. This was one of the network of state schools newly established to provide a tiny percentage of students (selected on the basis of a fiercely competitive exam) with educational opportunities designed to prepare them to become productive members of the professional English middle-class. And D.J. was accordingly very anxious that his only son be clearly separated at birth from the family's lowly Welsh-speaking background and raised instead to speak Shakespeare's own tongue. One of the few concessions he made to the Welsh language was to name the boy 'Dylan' – a bow to the contemporary renaissance of Welsh-language culture that had seen the unearthing of that great medieval classic, *The Mabinogion*, from one of whose most obscure characters the pointedly learned and exotic name was taken (no doubt prompted by the recent stage success of Lord Howard de Walden's play, *Dylan: Son of the Wave*).

Social dislocation is treated lightly, yet affectingly, in 'A Visit to Grandpa's', another story from *Portrait of the Artist as a Young Dog*. The journey grandpa had undertaken during the closing years of the nineteenth century from Llangadog to the Carmarthen area may have been a mere twenty miles, but in his experience it constituted the momentous shift that is enacted in reverse in the old man's failing mind half a century and more later, as he sinks into dementia. Llangadog was a rural village nestling in the very heart of Welsh-language chapel culture. But in Carmarthen, an administrative centre that was home to a professional class as well as being a market town for the Welsh-speaking area by which it was surrounded, it was English that had long ruled the roost, and Llanstephan, the neighbouring village in which Grandpa had actually settled, was also heavily anglicised compared to his native district. A telling detail in the story therefore comes in the form of an aside about the reaction of Griff the barber – one of the old man's cronies – to the news of mental and physical strayings. 'He hurried indoors and I heard him talking in Welsh' (*CS*, 146). In this locality, the place of Welsh is in the back kitchen with the servants. In public, it is spoken, if at all, only *sotto voce*. This is the context in which Grandpa's fantasy of returning to Llangadog to be buried is set.

And in the opening paragraph of the story, Thomas sets this fantasy in a context that comically highlights its anachronistic character even further. The little boy is woken in the middle of the night 'from a dream full of whips and lariats as long as serpents, and runaway coaches on mountain passes, and wide, windy gallops over cactus fields', by the sound of the old man 'crying "Gee-up!" and "Whoa!" and trotting his tongue on the roof of his mouth' (*CS*, 143). The American Westerns the little boy has been avidly devouring in Swansea cinemas and that are busily colouring his imaginative development are here juxtaposed with Grandpa's poignantly involuntary recollections of the bygone world of his rural youth. Social dislocation is here piled on social dislocation, and the medium Thomas skilfully uses to dissect the consequences of this collision between several disparate worlds is that of comedy, albeit a comedy redolent of a genuine pathos.

Having heard Grandpa shout 'Gee-up!' as loudly as a bull with a megaphone, the boy ventures to enter his bedroom, where he sees the old man sitting up in bed: 'Over a white flannel nightshirt he was wearing a red waistcoat with walnut-sized brass buttons. The overfilled bowl of his pipe smouldered among his whiskers like a little, burning hayrick on a stick' (*CS*, 143). Slowly, the fantasies subside and he adjusts again to the realities of contemporary experience. As we know, Thomas wasn't just partial to the comic grotesque, he was positively addicted to it. And this is just a mild, gentle, friendly example. For examples of a more sinister kind, one needs to turn to those evocations of the mental and physical world of Thomas's late adolescence and early adulthood found in the seedy stories that conclude *Portrait of the Artist as a Young Dog*, which feature such moments as that when 'a drunk man weave[s] towards him on wilful feet, carrying his dignity as a man might carry a full glass around a quaking ship' (*CS*, 230), and invites him to touch him on the seat of his trousers where nothing is to be felt because he has lost his bottom working underground in Dowlais when 'the end of the world came down on me. Do you know what I got for losing my bottom? Four and three. Two and three ha'pence a cheek. That's cheaper than a pig' (*CS*, 230). Just for the very briefest of tantalising moments, Thomas here allows the hazards of that world of mining and heavy industry by which Swansea was surrounded to stimulate him to produce a promising new line in black comedy it would have been so interesting to see him develop very much further.

* * *

Thomas began a radio broadcast entitled 'A Dearth of Comic Writers' by celebrating the true comic writer's defiant ability to create 'a great comic world of his own out of the tragic catastrophe of this' (*QEOM*, 123). His own need to perform this particular form of alchemy seems to have been much intensified following the inauguration, at Hiroshima and Nagasaki, of the nuclear age that so terrified him. That might be one explanation for his repeated creation, in some of his later comedy, of a charmed circle of events, circumstances and asexual characters all miraculously innocent of the enormously powerful passions, ambivalent at best, by which the fully adult world is inescapably animated. These texts proffer ingeniously contrived instances of arrested development, in which fully-grown men (women seem always to play a peripheral part) indulge companionably in kindergarten high-jinks. And one of the most memorable examples of this is the story of a group of friends who band together for a boozy trip to the popular seaside town of Porthcawl (a destination never reached, of course), which is witnessed and subsequently recalled by a young boy.

'A Story' (also known as 'The Outing') opens with an incident that sees Thomas eliminate sex by almost literally knocking it on the head. The uncle in whose house the little boy is staying is so large, and his wife so little, that 'every Saturday night at half past ten he would lift her up, under his arm, on to a chair in the kitchen so that she could hit him on the head with whatever was handy, which was always a china dog' (*CS*, 128). Saturday night, after closing time at the pub, was the time stereotypically given over to conjugal sexuality in popular tales of working-class life. And the china dog is also taken directly from life, as no working-class Welsh home was complete without at least one sitting smugly on the mantelpiece above the kitchen fire. Part of the charm of Thomas's period piece comes from the way it is credibly grounded in a lovingly faithful attention to all the quirks and peculiarities of its particular place and time. The uncle 'breathing like a brass band' memorably evokes the popular musical culture of the south Wales valleys, and local details like this beautifully set off and set up Thomas's brilliant hyperbolic riffs, as when describing his uncle as 'so big and trumpeting and red-hairy' that he 'used to fill every inch of the hot little house like an old buffalo squeezed into an airing cupboard' (the buffalo again comes straight out of the Westerns for which the young Thomas had a passion); as for his physical appearance, 'the forest fire of his hair crackled among the hooked hams from the ceiling' (*CS*, 127). Thomas seems, instinctively if unconsciously, in such instances to tap deep into Welsh time; to link all the way back with the tradition of the fantastic and the comically grotesque found in popular Welsh tall-tale and legend, as in the descriptions of the unkempt giant Ysbaddaden Bencawr in *The Mabinogion*.

And oral story-telling left its mark on Thomas's stories, as they did on *The Mabinogion*. Characters are rendered instantly memorable by being nailed in a few deadly phrases – 'Jenkins Loughor. Keep him off economics. It cost us a plate-glass window' (*CS*, 130) – or condemned to repeat their catch-phrases to all eternity, 'Stop the bus, I'm dying of breath!' (*CS*, 135). The homely is easily mixed with the surrealistic, as when they pull up at a 'small, unhappy public-house with a thatched roof like a wig with ringworm'. And that isn't all: 'From a flagpole by the Gents fluttered the flag of Siam, I knew it was the flag of Siam because of cigarette cards' (*CS*, 133). How typical of Thomas's highly unorthodox, creatively transgressive imagination that it should instinctively yoke together the exotic and the demotic, the high and the low, mysterious Eastern allure and the trashy mass products of Western popular culture.

W. H. Auden was surely right when, in a brilliantly eccentric essay on Dickens's *Pickwick Papers* entitled 'Dingley Dell & The Fleet', he classified the kind of comedy we find in 'A Story' as 'Arcadian' or 'Edenic'. 'The four great English experts on Eden,' he wrote, 'are Dickens, Oscar Wilde, Ronald Firbank and P. G. Wodehouse'[1] – and the great Welsh expert on Eden, I would venture to add, was Dylan Thomas. Edenic settings are populated entirely by overgrown innocents – adults whose natures have remained essentially childish. And, Auden points out, one way that a writer can portray such innocents is 'to show an adult behaving in a way which his society considers outrageous without showing the slightest awareness of public opinion' (*SE*, 174). The outrageous actions of the group of grown men in 'A Story' are witnessed by an innocent little boy who finds them entertainingly odd, but they are recalled and narrated by an adult who views it all with elegiac indulgence. Elegiac because, by the end, the 'make-believe' of such an impossible world of adult innocence is over, as Auden predicted it had to be by the end of any Edenic fiction: 'players and spectators alike must now return to reality. What you have heard was but a tall story' (*SE*, 189).

That 'A Story' is to be precisely such a fiction – a tall-tale that is also a shaggy-dog story – is actually signalled in the very opening sentences where what follows is described as 'A Story . . . If you can call it a story. There is no real beginning or end and there's very little in the middle' (*CS*, 117). And yet, there *is* a very definite end – an unforgettably plangent end that puts an unignorable full stop to all the adults' childlike nonsense. 'And dusk came down warm and gentle on thirty wild, wet, pickled, splashing men without a care in the world at the end of the world in the west of Wales. And "Who goes there?" called Will Sentry to a wild duck flying' (*CS*, 136). As in Shakespeare, the voice and vision of a simpleton are used to convey the deepest intuitions about the human condition – here the recognition that interludes of idyll are rare and precarious and fugitive indeed as the flight of that wild duck in adult life.

By 1953 – the date the story was actually published in *The Listener* – the west of Wales had become an important place of refuge for the imagination of a Thomas increasingly troubled by all the cares that had newly entered a world permanently altered by the catastrophic arrival of the nuclear age. Consequently, as the great post-nuclear poem 'Fern Hill' so movingly confirms, Thomas sought in the rural west Wales where he had spent many of his childhood holidays a bolt-hole to which to retreat to the comfort of the memories of his pre-nuclear childhood. Yet, even as he compulsively did so, he was of course aware that time insisted on taking him by the shadow of his hand and showing him how tragically steeped in adult knowingness his idyllic recreations of childhood really were. Both 'Fern Hill' and 'A Story' accordingly end by poignantly exposing the illusion that lies at the very core of every idyll.

Humour was, then, for the later Thomas, an indispensable instrument for coping with the dark absurdities of the nuclear age. It was to 'the amiably comic eccentricity of individual beings', he emphasised in that broadcast on comic writers, and to 'the ludicrous, the *gauche*, the maximless gawky, the dear and the daft and the droll, the runcible Booby, the Toby, the Pickwick, the barmy old Adam', that he looked when daily confronted 'by the delt and the peeve and the minge and the bully,' and above all by 'the maniac new Atom' (*QEOM*, 122). But any old comedy wouldn't do, he added, taking for example the fiction of P. G. Wodehouse, which he abhorred because it was so narrowly class-based, so artificial, so transparently stylised. For him, '[a] truly comic, invented world must live *at the same time* as the world we live in' (*QEOM*, 124). And such a generously inclusive, expansive alternative world, he insisted, could not be created in essays; it was the jealous preserve of stories (*QEOM*, 126).

* * *

In keeping with his comments on the need for a mode and style of comedy attuned to the age of the 'maniac new Atom', Thomas ends 'A Story' on a note in which humour blends with nostalgia to produce a new, wistful, kind of elegy we also encounter so memorably in that other late work 'Fern Hill'. It is an elegy that mourns the passing of Edenic innocence. And Thomas tended to associate that innocence either with the age of childhood (as in 'A Story') or with that later period of early adolescence when incipient knowingness was still touchingly, comically callow, and adult sexuality no more than a dirty rumour and a hopeful, titillating promise. This is the world evoked in 'The Followers', a story full of encounters between two would-be louche youngsters and much more precociously experienced and assured young women:

> Leslie said, in a low voice: 'Think she'll let us have one on tick?'
> 'Wait a bit, boy,' I murmured. 'Wait for her to thaw.'
> But the barmaid heard me, and looked up. She looked through me, back to my small history to the bed I was born in, then shook her gold head. (*CS*, 119)

In the rain, they wander the streets of a dingy provincial where nothing ever happens, their heads full of the exciting romantic adventures of popular cinema, randomly pursuing young women about whom they weave their wistful and lustful regressive fantasies, such as being welcomed into a room full of music and whispering girls lounging on divans who'll 'chatter round us like starlings and put us in kimonos too, and we'll never leave the house until we die' (*CS*, 123).

One such young woman is Hermione, a spinster approaching thirty, who on closer acquaintance (they follow her home and spy through the window) turns out to wear 'horn-rimmed spectacles and a sensible tweed costume, and a white shirt with a trim bow-tie' (*CS*, 122). Undeterred by such drab banalities, they linger outside the window, peering in surreptitiously in hopes of some melodramatic turn. And they are indeed eventually rewarded by a surprising turn of events as Hermione and her 'round, friendly, owlish' mother in a pinafore start turning the pages of a photograph album. When they come to images of the mother's exotically named sister Katinka, who presumably died young, they start smiling secretly at each other, whereupon Katinka's own voice seems to make itself heard recalling the striking outfit she'd worn long ago on a choir outing to the Welsh seaside town of Aberystwyth.

No explanation is offered in the story of this supernatural intervention, which ends with the snooping boys, detected at the window by mother and daughter, having to make a rapid escape before parting company without a word being spoken about what they've seen and heard as they re-enter 'normal' life. Interpret the story, then, as you will, but one possible reading obviously is that it is about the power of fantasy, in the hands of a born story-teller such as Dylan Thomas, to take on such a life of its own that it ends up establishing its own reality. A reality that, as Thomas points out in that broadcast on comic writing, has the power and authority to co-exist credibly alongside that of the ordinary, familiar world. It is the same understanding of the power of story that Thomas celebrates with such poignantly ambivalent exhilaration in 'The Peaches', when the little boy playing Indians down by the stream with his cousin Gwilym suddenly becomes aware of himself 'in the exact middle of a living story, and my body was my adventure and my name' (*CS*, 132).

Thomas knew with every fibre of his being that he was born to be a story-teller; that, for better and for worse, it was his true essential identity; that to be such was destined to be the precarious adventure of his whole life. And interestingly enough, he reverts in 'The Followers' to the image of flying wildfowl when evoking the mad adventures to which his comic narratives are irresistibly drawn. Recalling Saturday night at a pub, he tells how

[m]en from the valleys dropped in for nine or ten; sometimes there were
fights; and always there was something doing, some argie-bargie, giggle
and bluster, horror or folly, affection, explosion, nonsense, peace, some
wild goose flying in the boozy air of that comfortless, humdrum nowhere
in the dizzy, ditchwater town at the end of the railway lines. (*CS*, 341)

And, as was the case with the wild duck in 'A Story', the flight in 'The
Followers' of that wild goose – the phrase surely alludes in part to the
'wild goose chases' that for Thomas all humorous stories inevitably
were – signifies again the elegiacally fugitive nature of all such comic
respites from reality.

*   *   *

Despite Thomas's confident assertion that it was only story that could
provide space and opportunity hospitably sufficient to accommodate the alternative reality of a comic world, it was, of course, in
the different genre of radio drama that his own comic vision was
to find its most ample, highly developed form. *Under Milk Wood* is
from charmed beginning to end such an extravagantly light souf-
flé of absurdly extravagant imaginative invention and verbal excess
that it is bound to collapse under even the most delicate of critical
comment – and the past half century has seen a superabundance
of solemn analysis. The radio – for which it was after all intended
– seems to be not only ideally suited to its performance, but also to
be the metaphorically apt medium for a text designed to be at once
as life-sustaining and as mortally ephemeral as breath. So many of
its passages are just that – passing improvisations, random flights of
fantasy, virtuosic verbal cadenzas. And if there is a sweet poignancy
to it all, it is because the text urgently and repeatedly confesses itself
to be haunted by the darkest of passages – the passage of time itself.
From the very beginning, this is a work that knows it is racing against
the clock and it is that knowledge that lends the relentless comedy its
hectic, reckless, headlong quality and that propels all its promiscuous verbiage.

    And since it is undoubtedly Thomas's supreme achievement in the
Edenic genre, *Under Milk Wood* is naturally condemned by its willed
innocence to be denied access to the malice and related feelings of
mature adulthood that gives some of the humour in Thomas's early
letters its exhilarating edge. Which is perhaps, sadly, why the comedy
in this renowned and globally beloved radio play can begin to pall

after repeated hearings or readings. But then it was never intended to be more than the brief bravery [finery] of a night, to borrow a phrase from Ben Jonson. It features Thomas in his role as Lord of Misrule and Master of the Revels, and it allows him to display at least some of his extensive gifts for comedy.

After all, as he had himself prophetically reflected in his broadcast, 'society to a comic writer is always funny, even, or especially, on its death-bed' (*QEOM*, 122). Substitute 'his' for 'its' and this remark may perhaps be applied to the circumstances of his own sadly premature passing. Thomas's own last known words were, at least in popular memory, reported to have been 'I've had 18 straight whiskies; I think that's the record.' And whether they are purely apocryphal (as scholars suppose) or not, these 'final' words seem, in the black humour of their evident sardonic exaggeration, to provide an apt epitaph for a writer who thus died as what he had been born to be: a writer of true comic genius.

Note

[1] W. H. Auden, 'Dingley Dell and the Fleet', in *The Dyer's Hand and Other Essays* (London: Faber, 1975), p. 411.

6

'As long as he is all cucumber and hooves': Dylan Thomas's Comedy of the Unconscious

Rhian Barfoot

Under Milk Wood is perhaps the best known and best loved of all Thomas's work; riotously funny, deeply moving, and much more easily digestible than the early verse, it has managed to reach a far wider audience than his poetry. Since receiving its first public readings with actors at the Poetry Center of the Young Men's and Young Women's Hebrew Association in New York, in May and then October 1953, the play has managed to capture public imagination and has enjoyed a virtually uninterrupted history of performance. Originally commissioned by Douglas Cleverdon as a short radio feature for the BBC's home service, Thomas's new 'Play for Voices' was first broadcast on the Third Programme on 25 January 1954 (just two months after his premature death). Since then, the prose drama has been successfully adapted for stage, screen and the music industry; it has been translated into more than thirty languages winning international acclaim and delighting audiences worldwide.

Under Milk Wood's popularity stems, in part, from the fact of its immediate posthumous publication – since first released by J. M. Dent in 1954 it has never been out of print – and, because of its indisputable success and unignorable popularity, critics have, on the whole, been quite generous if slightly dismissive in their response to this comparatively light hearted work.[1] Of course, the work of critical assessment, particularly in its more traditional and conventional modes, has been complicated by the remarkable paradox of the play's success: 'quite obviously it has little or no dramatic development, no characters with any depth, and of course no action for the audience to appreciate. Yet despite these handicaps, which ought to be crippling, it has played successfully ever since its initial reading'.[2] Read in the light of Thomas's own belated and marginal modernism, the apparent shortcomings of the text, however, point to a wider questioning and further radicalisation of modernism's challenge towards realist modes of representation that posits a challenge to linearity, narration, self-referentiality, and character portrayal. Like his modernist precursors, a generation earlier, Thomas's modernism was crucially concerned with issues of representation. For in the foregrounding of its heteroglossic aspect – an exuberant miscegnatory montage of sound sense and music that includes but is not limited to its lyric descriptive passages, drinking songs, schoolyard rhymes, guidebook parody, poetry, prayer, 'jolly rogered' *double entendres*, bawdy humour, nostalgic lament, dialect and local gossip – the text calls into question and contests its own mode of construction. The obvious antecedent to his polyphonic evocation of the cycle of a day within a small seaside town is quite clearly Joyce's *Ulysses*. Although the work does not claim to invite comparison, like Joyce's novel, Thomas's carnivalesque re-imagining flaunts and displays a number of psychic structures; and like the Circe episode of *Ulysses*, in particular, it might well be described as a comedy of the unconscious. Thomas is known to have been an assiduous reader of the surrealist journal *transition*, a publication in which Joyce had published extensively, and one whose output was richly informed by contemporary developments of Freud, in particular the work of Jung and Lacan.[3] Yet critics have hitherto failed to recognise a valid, if not paradigmatic, psychosocial impulse in Thomas's work. This chapter will close that gap by placing Thomas in dialogue with Freudian and post-Freudian discourse. It will be argued that *Under Milk Wood* is particularly receptive to a psychoanalytic approach because it explores and transgresses boundaries while at the same time playing with the fusion of a variety of worlds, staging both transformations and dissolutions, and as such poses a constant challenge to representation.

'WHATEVER IS HIDDEN SHOULD BE MADE NAKED'

When I set myself the task of bringing to light what human beings keep hidden within them . . . by what they say and what they show, I thought the task was a harder one than it really is. He that has eyes to see and ears to hear may convince himself that no mortal can keep a secret. If his lips are silent, he chatters with his finger-tips; betrayal oozes out of him at every pore. And thus the task of making conscious the most hidden recesses of the mind is one which is quite possible to accomplish.[4]

Thus wrote Freud in 1905, with the authoritative tone of one assured of his own penetrating gaze. But the speaker of this passage might just as easily have been the author of *Under Milk Wood*: Thomas's comic masterpiece certainly accomplishes the task of making conscious the most hidden recesses of the mind, 'of bringing to light, as Freud put it 'what human beings keep hidden within them'. In a letter to Madame Caetini, the editor of the Rome-based magazine *Botteghe Oscure*, where the first half of an early version of the work appeared in print, Thomas outlined his disarming poetic psychology:

And the first voice is really a kind of conscience, a guardian angel. Through him you will learn about Mr Edwards, the draper, and miss Price the sempstress [*sic*], and their odd and, once it is made clear, most natural love. Every day of the week they write love letters to each other, he from the top, she from the bottom, of the town: all their lives they have known of each other's existence, and of their mutual love: they have seen each other a thousand times, and have never spoken; easily they could have been together, married, had children; but that is not the life for them; their passionate love, at just this distance, is all they need. And Dai Bread the baker, who has two wives: one is loving and mothering, sacklike and jolly; the other is gypsy slatternly and, all in love, hating: all three enjoy it. And Mrs Ogmore-Pritchard who, although a boarding house keeper, will keep no boarders because they cannot live up to the scrupulous and godlike tidiness of her house and because death can be the only boarder in the end. And Mr Pugh, the schoolmaster, who is always nagged by his wife and who is always plotting her murder. This is well known to the town, and to Mrs Pugh. She likes nagging; he likes plotting, in supposed secrecy, against her. He would always like plotting, whoever he lived with; she would like nagging, whoever she lived with. How lucky they are to be married. (*CL*, 813)

Significantly, earlier in that same letter, Thomas referred specifically to the way in which the comedy or 'entertainment' would develop directly from the 'darkness of the town'. Read in the light of his old adage that 'whatever is hidden should be made naked' – a remarkable echo of the terms used by Freud himself – this seems to acquire a specific thematic and structural significance, that reflects interestingly on the status of the prose drama as a comically inflected staging and re-imagining of the unconscious.[5]

Of course, strictly speaking, the unconscious cannot be known directly; 'its presence, force, and operations can only be inferred from the phenomena Freud had been the first to single out for analytic inspection'.[6] And it is important to realise that despite its common coinage, which actually points more to the substratum of subconscious thought, in psychoanalytic terms, the unconscious is properly understood not so much as background thought or perception but as a 'mind within a mind', as Juliet Flower MacCannell puts it, a reservoir of repressed material, the *terra incognita*, as it were, that has become encrypted within the psyche. It is only 'given away', as MacCannell goes on to state, 'through slips-of the tongue, unsuitable gestures or compulsive acts. These alone are how the Unconscious indirectly manifests itself'.[7] But the very notion of presenting the fact that there is something unpresentable, something that remains inexpressible, or something that in normal terms would seem to resist symbolisation, is, as I have argued elsewhere, a key feature of Thomas's writing, and offers a further radicalisation of modernism's challenge to realist modes of expression that is registered in *Under Milk Wood*.

John Goodby has been keen to note how the play's surtitle crucially declares that it is 'not a play or a drama for radio, but a "play for voices" and also *of* "voices"', creating a purely aural dimension that (he quite rightly concludes) has more in common with sound poetry and the kind of radio comedy that was popularised by the *Goons* and *ITMA*. And as such, the work depends to an unusual degree on both sound effects and the imaginative engagement of the listener, making the medium very much the message here.[8] According to Goodby's incisive reading, it is the medium of the play that actually facilitates Thomas's carnivalesque inscription of the body, and this reflects interestingly on his staging of the unconscious. For, like his grotesque exaggeration of the body, and the sexual body in particular, it is precisely that same parallel gesture of 'not having to present it in visual terms' that ultimately enables the text's riotously funny, and often deeply moving, unveiling of the town's psychic landscape.[9] Thus, the dark subcontinent of the unconscious is evoked by virtue of a 'complex layered polyphony' of independent and unmerged voices and consciousness, and is articulated primarily, though not exclusively (a point to which we shall return in due course), through the diegetic framing of the first and second voices and Blind Captain Cat – 'an eavesdropper on the living and the dead' – as well as in the dreams and frustrations, dismays and desires of Llareggub's eccentric townsfolk.[10]

Before turning to specific examples from the text, it is important to consider that, to some extent at least, Thomas was both embodying and responding to something of a more general, periodic concern with issues of presentation. As Marjorie Perloff has noted:

> The shift that takes place at the turn of the decade [1930s] is one from the modernist preoccupation with form – in the sense of imagistic or symbolist structure, dominated by a lyric 'I' – to the questioning of representation itself. Discourse now becomes increasingly referential, but reference does not go hand in hand with the expected mimesis. Rather, the boundaries between the 'real' and the 'fantastic' become oddly blurred. The taste for the 'natural', as in Pound's insistence that 'the natural object is always the adequate symbol', gives way to artifice and a marked taste for abstraction and conceptualisation. In the same vein, irony – so central to modernist poetics – gives way to the parodic, but even parody is not often sustained, with abrupt tonal shifts and reversals in mood becoming quite usual. Indeed, this 'time of tension' . . . exhibits a mannerist style as distinct from its modernist antecedents as from the social realism to come.[11]

Given the genuine polyphony of independent voices and unmerged consciousness that seems to enact something of a postmodern awareness of difference and heterogeneity in *Under Milk Wood*, this can, with qualification, be applied to Thomas. For although her references are specifically transatlantic, Perloff is referring to a similarly imploded improvisation of high modernism when she speaks of a 'mannerist modernism'. Moreover, the blurring of the worlds of fantasy and reality coupled with the privileging of parody, and the abrupt tonal shifts that she identifies as defining features of this 'simulacrum' modernism resonate quite remarkably with Thomas's mid-century masterpiece.

'A WALES THAT NEVER WAS'

Writing to A. G. Prys Jones in 1952, Thomas described *Under Milk Wood* as an extravagant play 'about a day's life in a small town in a never-never Wales' (*CL*, 848). The phrase itself, 'a never-never Wales', immediately suggests a blurring of the boundaries of fantasy and reality, and it is fair to say that the work was a product of both fact and imagination, though perhaps not in equal measure. The twenty-four hour parabola is set in the fictionalised Llareggub, a small Welsh fishing village populated by a cast of eccentric townsfolk; it includes a curious, but largely genial co-mingling of drunks, prostitutes, a poet-preacher, a potential poisoner in the shape of retired schoolmaster, a bigamist, a couple of ghosts and a group of peculiarly garrulous spectral presences. Bracketed off from the rest of society, both spatially and temporally, Llareggub functions as an entirely subjective and autonomous space, a place that knows no outside, and remains blissfully and almost childishly unhindered by any kind of external influence. The clock in the local pub has been stuck at half past eleven for fifty years, a remarkable stroke of luck for the town soak Mr Cherry Owen for 'it is always opening time in the Sailors' (*UMW*, 27). It is as if the cycle of life has been placed on repeat play, thus generating a sense of almost mythic timelessness that unites old age and infancy in a kind of continuous present as 'babies and old men are cleaned and put into their broken prams'; echoing a baby's cries with more than a hint of oral fixation, an Old Man announces 'I want my pipe and he wants his bottle' (*UMW*, 27)!

Superficially, at least, this is a relatively painless idyll, where there is no real sense of judgement, and no consequences to suffer. There is no plot to speak of and virtually no character development, and as the name of the town itself mischievously indicates ('bugger all' spelt backwards) it seems that nothing ever really happens here. Llareggub's less 'fantastic' inhabitants – the tradespeople, chattering wives and retirees – all go about their daily routines with little interruption, behaving much like characters, or perhaps more precisely *caricatures*, in a kind of live action *Camberwick Green* (even the town's genial and habitual drunk Cherry Owen bears a certain resemblance to the iconic children's television character Windy Miller, who falls asleep after drinking too much cider).[12] But despite the cartoon like quality of the work – think, for instance, of the peculiarly 'Disneyesque' feel of a phrase like 'bridesmaided by glow-worms down the aisles of the organplaying wood' (*UMW*, 1) – this is not to say that there are no darker forces at play beneath its surface. This is certainly not a 'quaint or pious Welsh heritage vision of life in a small 1950s seaside town'.[13] Beneath its thin toy-town veneer, a seething cauldron of erotic and even murderous impulses, obsessions, frustrations and anxieties

bubbles – an ever-present reminder, as it were, of Llareggub's nomina-
tion as the 'capital of dusk' (*UMW*, 56). There is certainly a darker
and more malign aspect to the comedy that Walford Davies reads in
terms of the grotesque, gothicised modernism that had dominated
Thomas's early work – the Jarvis Valley stories in particular – and its
negotiations of Welshness.

According to Davies, the play distils 'a particular brand of Welsh
gothic too often unrecognised'. The comedy 'retains a residual darkness', he insists, 'because of the degree of its instinctive investment
in spectral presences, psychological anxieties and the misrule of the
carnivalesque.[14] Interestingly, it is in these early stories that the name
Llareggub first appeared. In the 1930s, Thomas had applied it variously to a village (in 'The Holy Six' and 'The Orchards'), and to a
'sowfaced woman' in 'The Burning Baby' ('Death took hold of his
sister's legs as she walked through the calf-high heather up the hill . . .
She was to him as ugly as the sowfaced woman Llareggub who had
taught him the terrors of the flesh' (*CS*, 36)), a deeply disturbing
and semi-surrealist tale of incest, in which a preacher has sex with
his daughter and then incinerates the fruit of her womb. So, when
Thomas chose to revive the palingram for the 'Play for Voices' it was,
in his mind at least, already heavily freighted with those associations
of religion, death, sexuality and transgression, that would become
the subject matter of his drama.[15] Significantly, then, this ongoing
concern with the interrelationship between a repressive and puritanical religious creed and an open and uninhibited sexuality reaches its
climax in *Under Milk Wood*, which, as Linden Peach has commented,
provided the 'perfect vehicle' for continuing the exploration of these
two themes that had begun in the early stories.[16]

The town itself seems to acquire its own personality divided
roughly, though certainly not strictly, along Freudian lines into a
conscious world of relatively mundane daily activity narrated by the
First Voice, and a subconscious or unconscious world of repressed,
and often highly eroticised thoughts and feelings that are revealed in
the diegetic framing of the Second Voice. Hence, The Second Voice
exposes the secret fantasies of the publicly prim and proper school-
mistress Gossamer Beynon, who feels Sinbad Sailors's 'goatbeard
tickle her in the middle of the world' and doesn't mind 'if he does
drop his aitches . . . so long as he's all cucumber and hooves' (*UMW*,
45). In a similar manner, the Second Voice reveals the murderous but
repressed designs of Mr Pugh, who imagines concocting 'a fricassee

of deadly nightshade, nicotine, hot frog, cyanide and bat-spit for his needling stalactite hag and bednag of a pokerbacked nutcracker wife' (*UMW*, 50). In his seminal *The Psychopathology of Everyday Life* (1901), Freud propounded his conviction that, as individuals, we all develop an unconscious that affects our behaviour – a conviction that paralleled modernism's intense interest in the way in which we as individuals find ourselves vitally compelled by our obsessions, drives and instincts, and which acquires specific thematic significance within the context of Thomas's prose drama. From 1923 on, Freud's second tripartite map of the psyche postulated a primal and pleasure seeking id, a repressive authoritarian superego, and an embattled ego – part conscious, part unconscious – whose job it was to mediate between the poles of wilful exuberance and authoritarian prohibition.[17] This tension, which is often central to the negotiation of passion and convention in modernist texts, can, as I have indicated above, be discerned in the competing and contradictory forces of the unbridled sexuality and the repressive religious code of the community, a contradistinction that both underscores and haunts the text of *Under Milk Wood*.

These tensions are highlighted throughout the work by its repeated juxtapositions of promiscuity and propriety. Think, for instance, of the positioning of the punitive and puritanical Jack Black in the text; his introduction follows on immediately from the highly erotic fantasies of Myfanwy Price and Mog Edwards. This underlines and accentuates Jack Black's life-denying and excessive morality and repressive outlook: 'Come now . . . to the bible-black airless attic over Jack Black the cobbler's shop where alone and savagely Jack Black sleeps in a nightshirt tied to his ankles with elastic' (*UMW*, 6). But, even though these tensions are held in opposition throughout the text, things are rarely that simple or straightforward for Thomas. It is important to understand that these opposing forces do not exert an equal pressure on the town, or its inhabitants. Within what Goodby reads as the carnivalesque space of the text, it is in fact the demanding and rebellious id that appears to finally hold sway:

> The life of the town, libidinous in dreams and under the trees of Milk Wood, is, in daytime, a relatively painless idyll. Llareggub's web of unconsummated relationships form a genially repressive structure, charged to an unusual degree, if not animated by, the libidinous night-time id. The punitive superego, at least, is not much in evidence, and the reality principle is defied without too much suffering, because Llareggub is autonomous

and timeless; its 'symbolic practices and textual forms' establish a 'life
[. . .] subject only to its own laws' and form an 'entire world'.[18]

Goodby's reading is informed by a Bakhtinian understanding of
Llareggub as a site of subversive potentialities and transgressive misrule. And this appropriation of the 'carnivalesque' certainly seems
to complement and confirm a more specifically psychoanalytically-
inflected approach to the staging of the unconscious. As the 'capital
of dusk', the town is explicitly presented and consciously constructed
as a liminal and transitional space – a space where boundaries are
blurred and borders are at their weakest. It continues to exist in a
state of 'betwixt and between', hovering uneasily though relatively
happily between darkness and light; childlike innocence and bawdy
adult humour. Importantly, according to Freud, it is precisely in those
places and times where repression and restraint are relaxed that unde-
cidability occurs, and thus facilitates and enables the emergence of
the unconscious. These moments can occur at times of unusual stress,
but also in the normal condition of sleep, for there is little likelihood
of any kind of unconscious impulse being carried through and translated into 'dangerous action'.[19] Hence Freud's assertion that dreams
are the 'royal road' to the unconscious; it is in those moments when
the censor of repression is lowered, so to speak, and all inhibitions
are lost, that the id is allowed to roam free. For the alcohol-fuelled
Cherry Owen, it is drink that proves the great and indeed regular
disinhibitor: '[He] likes getting drunk every night; & his wife likes
living with two men, one sober in the day, one drunk at night' (*CL*,
814). Remarkably, it seems that Mrs Cherry Owen loves both equally.
For her unfortunate husband seems to be the subject of a kind of
psychic tug of war enacted on a daily – and nightly – basis between a
rebellious and pleasure-seeking id, and a restraining and prohibitive
superego. When the affable but 'worse-for-wear' Cherry Owen returns
from the Sailors Arms, he announces that, 'God has come home!' –
before removing his trousers; throwing sago at the picture of Aunt
Bessie, and missing (both the picture and his wife-by an inch); picking
a fight (with no one in particular); singing 'Aberystwyth' – tenor *and*
bass; and finally declaring himself 'King Cherry Owen', and his wife
'Mrs Sheba' (*UMW*, 24–5). The slapstick comedy of his drunken
antics certainly highlights the id's defiance of social convention, and
in this context it is certainly worth noting the specific reference to
Joseph Parry's 'Aberystwyth' – the preferred vocal for Cherry Owen's

alcohol initiated recitals – 'I *always* sing "Aberystwyth"' (*UMW*, 25). 'Aberystwyth' is a hymn tune composed by Parry in 1876, and first published in 1879 in Edward Stephen's *Ail Lyfr Tonau ac Emynau* (Second Book of Tunes and Hymns). It has been the most popular setting for Charles Wesley's hymn 'Jesus, Lover of My Soul', and the reference would not have been lost on the mid-century audiences in Wales; they would have immediately recognised the comic inappropriateness of this drunken rendition of one of the nation's favourite hymns. But perhaps this is where we notice the most obvious contrast with the poetry. The humorous irreverence of Cherry Owen's vocal is strikingly at odds with Thomas's blasphemous reinterpretation of a castrated and feminised Christ; for example, in the early stories we see hints of a feminised reinterpretation of Christ as 'Mrs Jesus' ('The Orchards'). However, it is in the poetry that this is pushed to its limits in what I have referred to elsewhere as 'Thomas's obscene object'. The obscenity of this image is saved by the genial comedy and emotional economy of childhood that sustains his 'Play for Voices'.[20]

DREAMS AND STRATEGIES OF DESIRE

In Thomas's later work especially, the ability to dream is inextricably linked to a sense of personal freedom. As an expression of the unconscious, and founded on desire, dreams are central to *Under Milk Wood*, and play as important a role in revealing character as the monologues. In keeping with both Freudian and Jungian dream analysis, the dreams of the townsfolk are invested with symbols from each individual's personal visual lexicon. Jack Black, the puritanical cobbler, dreams, joyfully, of catching the 'naughty couples'. Blind Captain Cat dreams of his long-dead sea-faring comrades, aboard the S.S. Kidwelly. Evans Death, the undertaker, dreams of a childhood day, stealing currants from his mother. Mister Waldo, now Widow Waldo, is haunted by dreams of the three repressive forces in his life: his mother, his wife and the neighbours. Gossamer Beynon dreams of Sinbad Sailors, her 'small rough ready man'. Butcher Beynon's teasing extends into his wife's nightmare dreams, as he is charged with selling illegal varieties of meat. The Reverend Eli Jenkins dreams of *eisteddfodau*, poetry and beer tents black with *parcheds*. Mr Pugh dreams he is pretending to be asleep, and able to satisfy his homicidal urge to murder his nagging wife. Mrs Organ Morgan, a 'martyr to music' takes refuge in the silence of her dreams. Mary Ann Sailors dreams of the Garden of Eden. Dai Bread dreams of harems; Polly Garter of babies; Nogood Boyo of nothing, and Lord Cut-Glass of clocks. But, in Llareggub, the worlds of dream and reality are blurred and merged, defined only by Reverend Eli Jenkins's poems at dawn and dusk that bracket off the waking hours, and there is, in fact, no clearly discernible difference between the lives of the townsfolk and the manifest content of their dreams. It is as if the text itself functions, a kind of complete dreamscape, where the minutiae of daily lives spill over undisguised and unmediated by the process of dream work. However, this does not preclude the possibility that the text itself is a function of the strategy of the desire of the First Voice, making this presiding consciousness a personification of Freud's process of secondary revision that knits together, and gives coherence to the disparate elements of Thomas's polyphonic dreamscape.

Given their shared emphasis on the role of language it is worth pausing at this point to consider Lacan's concept of desire, which lies at the heart of his claim that the unconscious is structured like a language, and bears interestingly on the web of frustrated and unconsummated relationships in *Under Milk Wood*. Lacan's elaboration of the concept is supported by, yet goes beyond, its Freudian origins. As Sean Homer indicates, it stresses the fact that desire can never be fulfilled:

Fantasy originates in 'auto-eroticism' and the hallucinatory satisfaction of the drive. In the absence of a real object the infant reproduces the experience of the original satisfaction in a hallucinated form. Thus, our most fundamental fantasies are linked to our very earliest experiences of the rise and fall of desire. The important point here is the nature of the relationship between fantasy and desire; fantasy is not the object of desire, but its setting. Fantasy is the way in which subjects structure or organise their desire; it is the support of desire . . . the subject is faced with the enigma of the desire of the Other and is forced to pose certain questions of itself, such as: 'What am I in the Other's desire?' Fantasy is a response to that question. It is through fantasy that we learn how to desire and we are constituted as desiring subjects. The space of fantasy . . . functions as a kind of screen for the projection of desires . . . [it] is not the object of desire, neither is it the desire for specific objects; it is the setting or the *mise-en-scène* of desire. The pleasure we derive from fantasy does not result from the achievement of its aim, its object, but rather from the staging of desire in the first place. The whole point of fantasy is that it should never be fulfilled or confused with reality. The crucial term that mediates between fantasy and the real is the objet petit à.[21]

Without wishing to overinflate any thematic correspondence, this account of desire does appear to chime remarkably with Thomas's staging of the unconscious. Mog Edwards and Myfanwy Price's epistolary love affair might well be understood as the discourse of desire writ large, in the most literal of ways. It continues to exist by virtue of the fact that their love is never consummated. It is suspended, constantly deferred along a chain of signifiers and is always postponed and always delayed in this lyric summation of frustrated desire. Significantly, this is echoed at a linguistic level in the piling up of signifiers structuring Mog Edwards's comic declaration of love: 'I love you more than all the flannelette and calico, candlewick, dimity, crash and merino, tussore, cretonne, crepon, muslin, poplin, ticking and twill in the whole Cloth Hall of the world' (*UMW*, 5). In a similar vein, Mrs Dai Bread Two becomes an overarching symbol of Nogood Boyo's desire, for she embodies and represents the discourse of the Other, and becomes a mobile and transient symbol of his desire for a sexual encounter as she 'gypsies up his minds slow eye', wearing only a bangle, before morphing into a geisha girl (*UMW*, 53), Sinbad Sailors is similarly constructed in terms of the eroticised gaze of the Other; in Gossamer Beynon's Eleusian fantasy, he becomes radically transformed into the archetypal Pagan goat-footed God, replete with 'cucumber and hooves', a crude and profoundly Freudian image of phallic power (*UMW*, 45). But desire is not exclusively linked with sexuality in Llareggub; it is a profound longing for a lost corporeality through which their desire speaks, and which propels the voices of the spectral presences who haunt the dreams and imagination of Captain Cat: 'How's it above? Is there rum and laverbread? Bosoms and robins? Concertinas? Ebenezer's bell? Fighting and onions?' (*UMW*, 4). Any thematic sense of nostalgic lament that emerges here, however, is immediately offset by the playful materiality of the language, that keeps the typical and uniquely 'Welsh' tension between mournfulness and the musicality of language in check.

'[L]OVE THE WORDS . . . *LOVE* THE WORDS'

Psychoanalytic literature, and indeed psychoanalysis in general, has tended to subsume the imagination within a rubric of phantasy. Like the arts, its problem has been to decide when and whether imagination is escapist or creative, defensive or adaptive. It is generally agreed that creative imaginative activity involves the participation of unconscious non-verbal phantasy. Thomas's genius lies in the verbal embodiment of his phantasies. It is perfectly apt then that the only stage direction he gave actors to read when the play was first staged in New York was 'love the words . . . *Love* the words.'[22] Thomas was an unashamed lover of words. His use of language has consistently been seen as the distinguishing feature of his work, the characteristic richness and verbal density of the mesmeric lyrics, which arise from his controlled and artificial use of language, having been, of course, recognised as the hallmark of the writing. The vision that his work articulates and embodies is one in which the authoritarian repression of discursive language is eclipsed by a radical linguistic materialism, the unconscious and feminine other of denotative meaning and that Julia Kristeva has called the semiotic.[23] This is a mode of language that exults in the multiplicity of sonorous meanings, which are often communicated before being understood, so the flavour, and colour, of words becomes an integral part of the way the language is being deployed. Think for instance of the opening lines of *Under Milk Wood*:

[Silence]

FIRST VOICE [very softly]

To begin at the beginning:

It is Spring, moonless night in the small town, starless and bible-black, the cobblestreets silent and the hunched, courters'-and-rabbits' wood limping invisible down to the sloeblack, slow, black, crowblack, fishingboat-bobbing sea. The houses are blind as moles (though moles see fine to-night in the snouting, velvet dingles) or blind as Captain Cat there in the muffled middle by the pump and the town clock, the shops in mourning, the Welfare Hall in widows' weeds. And all the people of the lulled and dumbfound town are sleeping now. (*UMW*, 1)

This principle creates a world that is physically exciting, sonorous and hypnotic in effect, intuitive as well as emotive and sensory in its communication, and gestures implicitly towards a pre-symbolic stage of symbiotic unity, theorised by Lacan as the 'imaginary'.[24] This is the time of absolute identification with the other that precedes the castrating effects of the symbolic order, reaching back to that almost 'Edenic' bliss and pre-Oedipal plenitude. And this is perfectly in keeping with the emotional economy of childhood innocence that sustains Llareggub. For beneath the 'jolly rogered' *double entendres*, saucy puns and sexual innuendos, Thomas's 'place of love' depends on the recognition of the innate imperfection of the self. But there is no sense of regret or lament here; rather, there is a humour and a delight, an open-armed embrace of the impossibility of perfection. It is perfectly apt that this 'promised land' and its 'chosen' people are watched over by Eli Jenkins – the archetypal *senex*, the wise old man, who himself seems to gesture back to an older Celticised fertility variant of Christianity. He is certainly not the punitive Oedipal father who interrupts the primary dyad of mother and child, but an endorsing and enabling presence; Kristeva's re-configuration of a *loving* third term, the pre-Oedipal father, who is, among other things, a conglomerate of both sexes.[25] An *affective* rather than a legislative father, this is not the punitive law-giver who regulates the symbolic, but is instead what she calls 'an archaic inscription of the father'.[26] Described variously by Kristeva as '[h]e', 'she' or 'it', her heretical notion of a loving third term is a 'father-mother' conglomerate, a kind of hybrid fusion of 'father-and-mother, man-and-woman',[27] who belongs to the prelapsarian id-saturated landscape. He functions as a symbolic representation that facilitates in a non-judgmental manner, and circumscribes the phonetic territory of Llareggub with his morning and evening prayers – a radical otherness that is pitted against Jack Black the punitive, prohibitive father writ large, who dreams of 'chasing the naughty couples . . . flogging the tosspots . . . driving out the bare, bold girls from the sixpenny hops of his nightmares' (*UMW*, 6). Black is the personification, we might say, of the threat of castration; the agent of a repressive puritanism who attempts to force the body, and the female body in particular, to the margins of the text. The Reverend Eli Jenkins, on the other hand, rejoices in both the body *and* the bodily materiality of song and verse: 'Praise the Lord for we are a musical nation!' he declares in response to the promiscuous Polly Garter's musical tribute to her many and varied lost paramours.

Given that Eli Jenkins is generally agreed to be a self-mocking parody of Thomas, it is interesting to note that Kristeva has written about this loving version of the third party specifically in terms of the dilemma of the creative artist:

> A hardy explorer of the same psychic landscape, the artist pours or spends the identificatory symptom into original discourse: into style. Neither subservient like the believer, nor subjected to somatic conversation like

the hysteric, but sometimes both of these, he constantly produces multiple identifications, but he speaks them. Hypothesis: because more than any other he is in the grip of the 'father in the individual prehistory'. Contrary to the widespread myth of the artist subject to the desire for his mother, or rather in order to defend himself against this desire, he takes himself . . . not for the phallus of the mother, but for this ghost, the third party to which the mother aspires, for the loving version of the third party, for a pre-Oedipal father 'who loved you first' (say the Gospels), a conglomerate of both sexes (suggests Freud) . . . 'God is Agape'.[28]

A kind of spectre of the double-nature of the artist's own pre-history, this loving third party is a ghostly reminder of the fact of the instabilities of the symbolic, of the fragile and unstable nature of its architecture. As a structure, Lacan's Symbolic order, like Llareggub, and indeed the text itself, is, to some extent at least, always haunted by the threat of the unconscious libidinal drive – a point that emerges quite clearly in the bodily materiality of Thomas's language that (re) captures something of our own pre-moral delight in the substance of words.

Notes

1 *Under Milk Wood* was first published in book form in by J. M. Dent in 1954; 13,000 copies were sold in the first month, 53,000 in the first year, and by 1956–7 it had generated an income of £16,043.
2 R. B. Kerschner, *The Poet and His Critics* (Chicago: American Library Association, 1976), p. 16.
3 Kerschner, *The Poet and His Critics*, pp. 136, 137, 145.
4 Sigmund Freud, 'Fragment of an Analysis of a Case of Hysteria (Dora)', trans. J. Strachey, in Sigmund Freud, *The Penguin Freud Library*, vols 1–15 (London: Penguin, 1990–3), p. 114.
5 Thomas committed himself to this position in his response to an 'Enquiry' sponsored by Grigson's *New Verse* (October 1934). When asked if he had been influenced by Freud, he replied: 'Yes. Whatever is hidden should be made naked . . . Freud cast light on a little of the darkness he had exposed . . . poetry must drag further into the clean nakedness of light more even of the hidden causes than Freud could realise.' Reprinted in Constantine Fitzgibbon, *The Life of Dylan Thomas* (London: J. M. Dent & Sons, 1965), pp. 142–3.
6 Juliet Flower MacCannell, 'Sigmund Freud', in Julian Wolfreys (ed.), *Modern European Criticism and Theory: A Critical Guide* (Edinburgh: Edinburgh University Press, 2006), pp. 59–60.
7 MacCannell, 'Sigmund Freud', p. 60.
8 See John Goodby, *The Poetry of Dylan Thomas: Under the Spelling Wall* (Liverpool: Liverpool University Press, 2013), p. 418.

9   Goodby, *The Poetry of Dylan Thomas*, pp. 418–19. For a properly contextual-
    ised discussion of the importance of the 'Play for Voices' in terms of its status
    as a radio feature, see also Peter Lewis, 'The Radio Road to Llareggub', in
    John Drakakis (ed.), *British Radio Drama* (Cambridge: Cambridge University
    Press, 1981), pp. 72–110.

10 Keith Williams, 'Post-war Radio Broadcast', in Laura Marcus (ed.), *The
    Cambridge History of Twentieth-Century English Literature*, vol. 1 (Cambridge:
    Cambridge University Press, 2005), p. 477.

11 Marjorie Perloff, '"Barbed-Wire Entanglements": The "New American
    Poetry", 1930–1932', in Marjorie Perloff, *Poetry On & Off the Page: Essays
    for Emergent Occasions* (Evanston: Northwestern University Press, 1998),
    pp. 53–4.

12 It may be difficult to believe, but in 1966 the not-quite-so politically correct
    BBC did actually broadcast an episode of *Watch With Mother* in which poor
    Windy had passed out after overdosing on an excess of home brew.

13 See *https://www.independent.co.uk/arts-entertainment/films/reviews/under-
    milk-wood-film-review-snobbery-and-spanking-in-rural-wales-a6714291.html*
    (accessed 9 August 2018).

14 Walford Davies, *Dylan Thomas*, Writers of Wales Series (Cardiff: University
    of Wales Press, 2014), p. 13.

15 By the summer of 1951, Thomas was calling the play *Llareggub Hill;* but by
    October 1951, when the play was sent to *Botteghe Oscure*, its title had become
    Llareggub. A piece for Radio Perhaps. See Douglas Cleverdon, *The Growth of
    Milk Wood* (New York: New Directions, 1969). By the summer of 1952, the
    title was changed to *Under Milk Wood*, apparently because John Brinnin felt
    Llareggub Hill would be too 'thick and forbidding' to attract a transatlantic
    audience. See John Malcolm Brinnin, *Dylan Thomas in America* (New York:
    Avon, 1955), p. 132.

16 Linden Peach, *The Prose Writing of Dylan Thomas* (London: Macmillan,
    1988), p. 38.

17 Peter Childs, *Modernism* (London: Routledge, 2000), pp. 53–4.

18 Goodby, *The Poetry of Dylan Thomas*, p. 419.

19 Elizabeth Wright, *Psychoanalytic Criticism: A Reappraisal* (Cambridge: Polity
    Press, 2006), p. 16.

20 For further discussion of this interesting motif, see Goodby, *Under the
    Spelling Wall*; and Barfoot, *Liberating Dylan Thomas*.

21 Sean Homer, *Jacques Lacan* (London: Routledge, 2005), pp. 86–7.

22 Walford Davies, 'Introduction', in Dylan Thomas, *Under Milk Wood* (London:
    Penguin, 2000), p. xxi.

23 Kristeva establishes and develops her concept of the semiotic in her pioneering
    text *Revolution in Poetic Language*. This is the only place where she actually
    theorises the distinction between the symbolic and the semiotic that was cen-
    tral to her thought. Julia Kristeva, *Revolution in Poetic Language* (New York:
    Columbia University Press, 1984).

24 For Lacan's explanation on the imaginary, see, in particular, his 1949
    paper 'The Mirror Stage as Formative of the *I* Function as Revealed in
    Psychoanalytic Experience'. This is reproduced in full in Jacques Lacan,
    Écrits: The First Complete Edition in English, trans. Bruce Fink (New York:

W. W. Norton and Company, 2006). Bruce Fink also provides a lucid and coherent introduction to Lacan's tripartite, topographical model of the psyche in *The Lacanian Subject: Between Language and Jouissance* (Princeton: Princeton University Press, 1995).

25 For a fine account of Julia Kristeva's heretical notion of this 'imaginary father', see Elizabeth Grosz, 'Julia Kristeva', in Elizabeth Wright (ed.), *Feminism and Psychoanalysis: A Critical Dictionary* (Oxford: Blackwell, 1992), p. 199.

26 Julia Kristeva, *Tales of Love*, trans. Leon S. Roudiez (New York: Columbia University Press, 1987), p. 44.

27 Kristeva, *Tales of Love*, pp. 43–6.

28 Julia Kristeva, cited Rainer Emig, *Modernism in Poetry: Motivations, Structures and Limits* (London: Longman, 1995), p. 144.

7

'THROWN BACK ON THE CUTTING FLOOR': DYLAN THOMAS AND FILM

John Goodby

I

In 'Spajma and Salnady or, Who Shot the Emu?', the 'one act play never to be presented' that Dylan Thomas sent to Pamela Hansford Johnson in a letter of January 1934, the two writers appear in ana-gramatised form as the characters 'Salnady Moth' and 'Spajma Oh-no-el'. The play opens with Spajma engaged in conversation with 'the Spirit of Poetry', but the arrival of Salnady and his demand for '[a] quick womb please, two milks, a hangman, a dash of sleep and a pint of wax' has the Spirit uttering a scream and making for the exit. Left alone, the two talk about their daily doings, and in response to learning that Spajma has recently seen a movie star-ring John Barrymore, Salnady launches into a denunciation of both Barrymore in particular ('a bunch of mannerisms and a profile') and mainstream film more generally ('atrociously bad'). He then lists a few alternatives: 'Among the few films I have enjoyed are: The Cabinet of Dr Caligari, Atalanta, Student of Prague, Edge of the World, Vaudeville, Waxworks, The Street, M, & Blue Angel (all German); Sur lest Toits de Paris; Potemkin (Russian); The Gold Rush, the Three Little Pigs, & the Marx Brothers (American)' (*CL*, 115).

Much has been written about Thomas's relationship to radio, naturally enough; but, as this illustrates, at the crucial moment in the forging of the process style that would inform everything he

subsequently wrote, the mass medium he was most concerned with,
and influenced by, was film. Thomas would spend over seven years
of his working life writing film-scripts, from 1941 until 1948, and
as Constantine Fitzgibbon has noted, Thomas 'probably put more
words on paper in this professional capacity than in any other'.[1] There
is something of the 'truculent, a shower-off, all plus-fours and no
breakfast' (*QEOM*, 45) about his list, of course – the young poet
from the sticks is trying to impress his London girlfriend, and laying
it on a bit thick. Nevertheless, it's an impressive one for a 19-year-
old, and the informed interest it bespeaks is apparent throughout his
early writing. A member of the first generation to grow up on film,
the quintessentially new and most thoroughly Modernist art form
of the twentieth century, as a boy he had been a regular attendee at
'the local flea-pit picture houses' of suburban Swansea, 'where [I]
whooped for the scalping Indians . . . and banged for the rustlers'
guns' (*QEOM*, 53). All his life he had an abiding love for film, not
only of European art movies, but its trashier genres too – comedies
(Charlie Chaplin and the Marx Brothers make his list), weepies, hor-
rors, thrillers and westerns. Revealingly, his taste in them blurred the
boundaries between 'high' and 'low', just as his writing mingled and
fused radically different kinds of literary material. For most of the
1940s, Thomas actually worked in film, as well as radio, and at one
point hoped for a career as a feature film script-writer. His script for
the then-unmade feature film, *The Doctor and the Devils*, was published in book form in 1952, the year before he died. Film, then, was
a lifelong passion, and it should come as no surprise that on his first
visit to the USA, in 1950, Thomas seems to have been more enthused
by his meeting with Chaplin than any literary figure. On his fatal, final
US visit, in October 1953, two of his last public appearances were at
symposia on film in New York City, one with Arthur Miller and Maya
Deren, the other, titled 'Poetry and the Film', with Robert Lowell.

It is important to note that Thomas's love of film was not merely
that of a fan, a merely superficial or impressionistic one. His childhood love of the 'tuppenny crush', as children's Saturday film matinees
were called, turned to a deeper appreciation in his teenage years. In
July 1930, at the age of fifteen, he published an essay, 'The Films', in
the *Swansea Grammar School Magazine*, in which he displayed a grasp
of film history and an appreciation of the technical problems facing
the then-new 'Talkies', one sufficiently detailed to suggest, as John
Ackerman claims, that he had read Paul Rotha's recently-published

The Film Till Now (1930).[2] By his late teens, a filmic sensibility was informing his most original poems and fictions in complex and fruit-ful ways, and to a degree that is still little appreciated. Those looking for allusions to Donne or Blake, say, in 'I see the boys of summer' or 'The force that through the green fuse' also need to be aware of a debt to film. Thus, the Expressionist films on his list contributed to the Germanic-gothic, noirish, and uncanny atmospheres of early poems and stories, while his experience of the defining Hollywood versions of classic Gothic and horror roles – Bela Lugosi's *Dracula* (1931) and Boris Karloff's *Frankenstein* (1931) and *The Mummy* (1932) – stocked his image-bank of mummies ('Should lanterns shine'), vampires ('My world is pyramid'), and mad scientists ('The Lemon'). Thomas's early taste for worms, graves and ghosts is traceable to Jacobean drama, Beddoes and Arthur Machen, of course; but it also owes much to film. Thomas was immersed in the culture of film, *au fait* with the spirit of its mass appeal; we know he read film journals, wept as he watched tear-jerkers, yearned (or feigned a yearning) for its hero-ines, and memorised sequences of dialogue, like favourite poems, by heart. In her recollection of their first meeting, in 1940, for example, Theodora Fitzgibbon recalled how she and Thomas realised that they shared a love for James Whales's *The Old Dark House* (1932), an early landmark horror movie, and that this led to them 're-enacting large parts of it, squabbling for the best bits, which Dylan insisted on doing'.

Film figures both directly and indirectly in Thomas's early poetry. An example of the former is part V of 'Altarwise by owl-light', in which conflicts within the Nonconformist imaginary are played out using the stock figures of the Hollywood Western. The archangel Gabriel, for example, is the 'two-gunned' gunslinger of the poem's opening line, Jesus is a card-sharp who 'trump[s] up the king of spots' from his sleeve ('trump' punning on its card game sense and the Last Trump, or Judgement), while a hellfire preacher of the kind Thomas had often heard in Swansea's 'black bethels' rants 'Black-tongued and tipsy from salvation's bottle' (*CP*, 84). 'I, in my intricate image' goes further still, alluding to a specific film – the notorious sequence in Salvador Dalí and Luis Buñuel's *Un chien andalou* (1928), in which a woman's eye is sliced open with a cut-throat razor, in the lines as 'Death instrumental / Splitting the long eye open' (*CP*, 72). Here, the slicing of the literal 'eye' punningly tells of the metaphorical slicing up of the speaker's 'intricate image', or 'I', which is the poem's subject.

Popular gangster movies of the time, like *Scarface* (1932), typically starring James Cagney and Humphrey Bogart, are evoked even more clearly in 'Our eunuch dreams':

> In this our age the gunman and his moll,
> Two one-dimensioned ghosts, love on a reel,
> Strange to our solid eye,
> And speak their midnight nothings as the swell:
> When cameras shut they hurry to their hole
> Down in the yard of day. (*CP*, 54)

This poem, above all others by Thomas, goes beyond simply using film as the vehicle of a conceit, delving into its deeper psycho-sexual and social effects. Films themselves are viewed as 'eunuch', offering a glamorised vision of sex, but in a de-sexed mode – that is, as simulacra or 'ghosts' that ultimately dissipate life energies, a claim elaborated and tested in a series of metaphysical conceits and images which punningly contrast 'real life' adolescent fantasies with the 'reel life' substitutes offered for them by the Hollywood 'dream' factory, asking which are the truest ('Which is the world?'). In 'Our eunuch dreams', we might say, Thomas interrogates his own love of film, demanding to know whether its exemplary ideological potency might outweigh its value as art and entertainment. Yet the 'real/reel' question cannot be an either/or choice in his dialectical vision of the wor(l)d, and the poem ends by linking film to social revolution: 'Of our two sleepings ['real' or 'reel' fantasy], which / Shall fall awake when cures and their itch / Raise up this red-eyed earth?' [the socialist masses] (*CP*, 54). For Thomas, in full apocalyptic anarcho-socialistic cry here, film (punningly present as the 'shots' fired against capitalism) must be recruited as a weapon of liberation in the struggle against 'the old dead', used to blast aside the 'one-sided' phantoms of repressive ideology: in this battle of one kind of ghost with another, he may have had in mind the *The Communist Manifesto*, which opens with the 'spectre' of revolution haunting the ghostly reality of the old order, threatening to overthrow it and body forth a new, classless society:

> our shots shall smack
> The image from the plates;
> And we shall be fit fellows for a life,
> And who remain shall flower as they love,
> Praise to our faring hearts. (*CP*, 55)

If film is ultimately viewed here as potentially revolutionary – and the reference in his list to Eisenstein's *Battleship Potemkin* shows that Thomas knew how it could be used in this way – a more psycho-genetic and fated appreciation of its ideological dimension can be traced in one of the more curious conceits of Thomas's early poetry, namely, that the unborn see, before birth, the events and chief per-sonae (mother, father, lovers, etc.) 'projected' as a film on the wall of the womb, the embryo being granted foreknowledge of its fate, which it loses after birth. In 'Then was my neophyte', for example, God appears as the cosmic director of the film of the neophyte/embryo's life-to-be, displayed on the 'tide-hoisted' womb-wall:

> He films my vanity.
> Shot by the wind, by tilted arcs . . .
> His reels and mystery
> The winder of the clockwise scene
> Wound like a ball of lakes
> Then threw on that tide-hoisted screen
> Love's image till my heartbone breaks
> By a dramatic sea. (*CP*, 90)

Still more strange, 'The tombstone told when she died' is in the voice of someone who claims, in his embryonic state, to have witnessed in such a 'life-film' the tragic story of a woman whose tombstone he has just now, as an adult, encountered. As the inscription on the tomb states, she died in the period between her marriage ceremony and its physical consummation, and the poem makes her the 'hero-ine' of a film which is a sexualised version of the medieval Dance of Death:

> I who saw in a hurried film
> Death and this mad heroine
> Meet once on a mortal wall . . . (*CP*, 105)

The best-known use of this conceit occurs in 'Altarwise by owl-light' IV, which concludes:

> Love's a reflection of the mushroom features,
> Stills snapped by night in the bread-sided field,
> Once close-up smiling in the wall of pictures,
> Ark-lamped thrown back upon the cutting flood. (*CP*, 83)

There is a note in Thomas's hand on these lines in Edith Sitwell's copy of *Twenty-five Poems* which reads: 'Love is a reflection of the features (the features of those you will know and love *after* the womb) which are photographed before birth on the wall of the womb – the womb being surrounded by food; a field being its own field, and the womb being its own food.' Love, that is, is based on the unconscious operation of precognition, a buried and forgotten familiarity with the 'features' of certain 'mushroom' (squashed) faces (punning on 'feature' films) asserting itself when we discover matches for them. 'Love' is 'Ark-lamped' because *arc*-lamps were the light source for film projectors (as in 'Then was my neophyte'), and because the embryo is a kind of 'ark', a vessel containing hope for the future, adrift on the 'flood' of history. 'The cutting flood' conflates the breaking of the amniotic waters which severs (cuts) the child from its mother, and the severing of the umbilical cord, viewing both as part of a process in which the child is edited, as it were, from the maternal body ('the cutting floor' is that of the room where a film is edited, but also of the birth-chamber). Typically fusing the meaty (Darwinian-biological) and metaphysical (Christian-religious), the organic and the mechanical, Thomas forges a poetic language based on film, which incorporates but tests the ability of different kinds of determinism to 'explain' the strength of the child-parent bond and our irrational-seeming choice of love-partners.

An appreciation of his immersion in film also allows us to see how it informed the stylistic aspects of Thomas's poetry. These are often a source of confusion to novice readers, but make better sense if it is understood at the outset that the paratactical image-leaps by which the poems so often proceed are indebted to filmic narrative techniques. Indeed, it is arguable that these owe more to filmic montage than the learned, literary-allusive form of montage we usually find in Modernist poetry. *The Waste Land* is the classic example of this, of course, but its lapidary, jerky switches of register and source material are very different from Thomas's subsuming of his varied materials within an appearance of a smooth narrative flow. A poem such as 'When, like a running grave' draws on an extremely wide range of allusion, from embalming to lipstick adverts, but it presents these within structures that are nominally grammatically 'correct' (often parodically so; there are thirty-five separate clauses in its opening sentence). It is the tension between impeccable behaviour and the 'revolution of the word' it can barely contain that is the essence of the poetry, of course, and it can be related to the way in which film plays off its strictly time-bound ('grammatical') nature tricks against its unrivalled potential for flashback, montage, dissolve and so on. Not for nothing had Thomas read Eisenstein's *The Film Sense*, in which these matters are explored at length. Film was thus more than a merely thematic issue for Thomas; in its continuous flows and disjunctions, it models his view of the universe as continuous change and simultaneity, or 'process', as he embodied it in his 'process poetic', which may be legitimately described as 'filmic'.

Thomas's habitual self-mockery became more pronounced as he grew older, and one can see the critique of his morbidity found in 'Salnady and Spajma' repeated in later send-ups of his earlier provincial bohemian pretentiousness. One that also uses film as a way of doing this occurs in *Portrait of the Artist as a Young Dog* (1940). *Portrait* in general offers a take-down of Thomas's intense modernist pretensions of just five years before, and it contains a specific, filmic instance in a characteristically sly aside in 'Old Garbo'. This is a story about the young Dylan-narrator, a cub reporter, being taken on a tour of the rough-and-tough pubs of Swansea docks by the seasoned older reporter whose nickname provides the story's title. While the primary meaning of 'Garbo' is the nickname, it is derived, as we are meant to notice, from the film star Greta Garbo, a Thomas favourite. All it means ostensibly is that the senior reporter is a bit of a prima donna. But it gestures towards the encounter with film within the story, when, trying to kill time and get out of the rain ahead of their rendezvous, the young narrator blags his way into the nearest cinema by flashing his press card:

> I went to the Plaza. 'Press', I said to the girl with the Tyrolean hat and skirt.
> 'There's been two reporters this week.'
> 'Special notice.'
> She showed me to a seat. During the educational film, with the rude seeds hugging and sprouting in front of my eyes and plants like arms and legs, I thought of the bob women and the pansy sailors in the dives. (*CS*, 215)

The point is that the 'educational film' – a short feature before the main offering – is one of those highly accelerated time-lapse photographic accounts of the life-cycle of a seedling; of almost instantaneous growth, maturity and decay, like the 'boys of summer', both ripe and rotten, 'seedy' as fecund and wasted. In other words, the spasmodic vegetable 'writhing' it depicts (a word just one letter away from 'writing', after all) serves as a glancing ironic comment on the imagery and urgency of poems such as 'I see the boys of summer', 'The force that through the green fuse', or such stories as 'The Map of Love'.[3] Presented as a glimpsed and barely noticed film sequence, it seems casual, but it is a farewell to the earlier form of his process poetic for all that.

II

From making film a basis of his poetic, Thomas moved, during the war years, to actually writing scripts for them and helping to make them. It was not, despite his fascination with and love of film, anything like the natural move it later seemed. He had reacted to the outbreak of war in September 1939 with strained insouciance – 'I [shall] declare myself a neutral state, or join as a small tank' – but his objections went beyond this to resistance to being 'told by the State to fight not my enemies', a phrase whose tortuous construction reflects his anguishing, and opposition to the 'fostering of hate against a bewildered, buggered people', the Germans. To his friend Desmond Hawkins, he wrote: 'What have we got to fight for or against? To prevent fascism coming here? It's come . . . To protect our incomes, bank balances, property, national reputations? I feel sick. All this flogged hate again.' (*CL*, p. 415) But whatever its ethical purity, his stance had reduced him and his young family to a peripatetic, hand-to-mouth existence, lodging with relatives and friends, relying on loans and handouts to get by, and it could not last. Fearing compulsory munitions work, in September 1941 he accepted a job as script-writer with Donald Taylor's company, Strand Films (renamed Gryphon Films after 1943).

Paradoxically, Strand, then the largest documentary-maker in the country, sold all of its output to the Ministry of Information (MoI); still more paradoxically, Thomas happened to be very good at his job of writing propaganda. In 1942, his first full year of work for them, Strand produced seventy-five films, six of which were scripted by Thomas. Despite the excesses he is associated with, Thomas had a professional approach to writing and usually made a good job of what he undertook to do. He was a valued Strand employee, by all accounts (his salary soon rose to £10 per week, and later to

£20, plus expenses), who enjoyed the company of film people, and who had a particular knack for creating realistic and humorous dialogue. Luckily, this matched official requirements. British propaganda in the Second World War differed greatly from the bellicose jingoism of the First World War, which it was understood had fostered disbelief in government claims. The population was felt to be too sophisticated and sceptical to accept outright demonisation of the enemy. Recalling the cynicism created by stories of Belgian babies on Prussian bayonets in 1914, the British press were actively discouraged from running atrocity stories, and the BBC refrained from stridency, opting for a tone that achieved the effect of sincerity through restraint.

This allowed scope for Thomas's talents. His first year at Strand saw him script a varied assortment of short information and documentary pieces – *This is Colour* (about the dyeing industry), *New Towns for Old* (urban redevelopment), *Battle for Freedom, Balloon Site 568, CEMA* (about the forerunner to the Arts Council) and *Young Farmers* – and his contribution gradually extended to other aspects of film-making, such as directing, compiling, producing and supplying voice-over commentary. *Balloon Site 568*, a recruitment film for the Women's Auxiliary Air Force (WAAF) shows, in its modest way, how effective he could be. The film is almost entirely in dialogue, thereby eliminating a potentially patronising external commentary; the women speak for themselves. The difficulty and importance of the job is stressed, but the women are distinct individuals and have a social dimension: they go dancing, they want to (but cannot) go to the cinema, while at one point Myfanwy Thomas – perhaps a self-reference? – begins a mocking song about 'a great fat, hefty sergeant. The review of this film in the July 1942 *Documentary Film Newsletter* praised the varied use of character ('A dress shop assistant [blonde sex-appeal], a domestic servant [practical-Scottish]'), the visual interest ('The weird flock of balloons going to bed makes a striking picture') and the construction ('The story flows naturally, usually by a dialogue reference to the next stage'). It concluded that 'The film should bring recruits to the Service'.

Balloon Site 568 was a sign of what was to come. This may surprise those who know of Thomas's beliefs. How could he bring himself to write propaganda, and such effective propaganda at that? The wartime poem 'A Refusal to Mourn the Death, by Fire, of a Child in London' (1945), after all, precisely refuses to harness the girl's death

to State and Church-sanctioned modes of mourning, and denies offi-
cialdom the right to use grief for its own ends:

> I shall not murder
> The mankind of her going with a grave truth,
> Or blaspheme down the stations of the breath
> With and further
> Elegy of innocence and youth . . .
>
> After the first death, there is no other. (*CP*, 172–3)

As we have seen, there was compulsion in Thomas's participation
in the war effort, and it is possible that a poem like this one was, in
part, his reaction against the work he was doing (or, also as some
have argued, a qualification of the more exultant tone of his previous
elegy, 'Ceremony After a Fire Raid'). Many intellectuals conscripted
for propaganda work were disgusted by it; some, like George Orwell,
resigned in protest. Thomas's poem does, after all, open with the
totemistic Churchillian word 'Never', familiar from his two most
celebrated wartime speeches ('We shall fight them on the beaches . . .
We shall never give in. We shall never surrender', and 'Never in the
field of human conflict . . .'), wrenching it away from the bombast of
public utterance in order to place it in a timeless apocalyptic limbo.
But there were other factors at work too. One that would have helped
reconcile Thomas to his labours had to do with the feeling, during
the early war years, that there must be no return to the terrible social
conditions of the 1930s. The Beveridge Report, the blueprint for what
became the Welfare State, was an unlikely best-seller in 1942, precisely
because most of the British population was unwilling to make the
sacrifices necessary for military victory unless the government also
promised social justice – an attitude less extreme than, but not totally
dissimilar to, Thomas's when he had complained that fascism was
'already here'. To mobilise the masses, the MoI itself articulated the
widespread sense that those who had suffered equally in Blitz and
battle would be rewarded with job security and decent social provi-
sion after the war was over.

Thomas was granted the opportunity to voice one element of this
mood, concerning housing, in two films, the shorts *New Towns for Old*
(1942) and *A City Re-Born* (1945), as well as contributing to a film
on the rebuilding of Coventry called *Building the Future* (1943). Set

in the northern city of 'Smokedale', the first of these features a visitor touring the sites of the city's pre-war slum clearance programme,
which has been halted by hostilities. The visitor has an RP accent,
and is evidently middle-class and from the south. The film's aim – to
persuade its viewers that the halt in building is temporary, and that the
government slogan of 'Homes fit for all' will not go the way of 1918's
promise of 'Homes fit for heroes' – is achieved by the puncturing of
his well-meaning but unconsidered comments ('Well, you can't say
the children are unhappy') by the blunt Smokedale councillor, Jack
Clem ('But they shouldn't be 'ere!'). Throughout the film, compla-
cent assumptions are undermined; the need for unity of the classes is
hinted at, but so too is the idea that for this to happen those at the top
learn from those lower down. At the end of the film, it is Clem who
turns to address viewers directly, in a democratic invitation to civic
reconstruction: 'For *your* town. Remember, it's *your* town!'

Another feature of the morale-boosting efforts of government
was its promotion of culture. The body responsible for this was the
Council for the Encouragement of Music and Art, CEMA, later to
become the Arts Council. In the film *CEMA*, Thomas contributed
only dialogue at an exhibition of art, and the comment of a soldier
at a harp recital. Most of the film, after a leaden introduction by the
President of the Board of Education, shows music, drama and the
visual arts being taken from their traditional venues to be performed
in factory canteens, billets, church halls and the like: what would
now be dubbed 'outreach' programmes. Thomas was probably present
when the Old Vic rehearsal of *The Merry Wives of Windsor*, shown
in the film, took place; Bolton was chosen as the location, as a letter of his notes, because the directors wanted 'smoking chimneys in
the background'. As the comment suggests, *CEMA* was another film
promoting Beveridgean principles of the best for all, the juxtaposition of 'culture' and grimy industrial northness intended to signal a
Britain united in being able to appreciate its artistic heritage. And, as
Ackerman notes, it also illustrates the contemporary spirit of 'social
idealism, harmony and cultural aspiration', showing how the use of
different locations for such events helped promote a 'war-time sense
of community'. However brief, Thomas's contributions lighten a film
which might easily have been purely didactic.

Given the creative constraints, Thomas's contributions could
not always be as successful. *Battle for Freedom*, for example, has no
humour or dialogue, just a single voice-over, and offers a hortatory,

self-interested justification of the British view of history, combined
with vague, paternalistic promise of future Indian freedom:

> To their colonies and protectorates, as well as their own drugged or
> chained people, the Axis Powers bring all the advantages of a new civi-
> lisation. 'Remember Hongkong!' [a reference to British provocation of
> the Opium Wars] but remember, too, Abyssinia, Guernica, Rotterdam.
> These men and women have been protected. Forever. And these people
> of the British Colonies, without the civilising influence of bayonet and
> gas-bomb, have been brought new weapons of science to fight against
> disease and suffering . . . They have been given new knowledge, new skill,
> new careers and professions, hospitals, maternity centres, schools and
> laboratories, a new sense of social responsibility, and a system of training
> by which . . . they may achieve full independence and self-government.

The war required such an assertion of imperial unity, of course,
but even allowing for this the irony at the expense of the Axis powers
('the civilising influence of bayonet and gas-bombs') backfires; much
of the Empire was ruled by 'bayonets', and the RAF had dropped
'gas-bombs' on Iraqi towns and villages in the 1920s. Something
of this contradiction surfaces in the reference to the fact that the
Congress Party of India had recently refused Foreign Secretary
Stafford Cripps's 'proposals' for something less than full independ-
ence. The stark contrast implied between Japanese 'slavery' and the
Raj is therefore a rather dubious one, since while there were obvious differences, to the average Indian these were not as absolute
as the film implies. Even so, the script at one point mentions 'the
Commonwealth of New Nations', an indication of the way 'Empire'
was being rebranded to give the appearance of a new dignity to its
component parts.

By contrast, *These Are the Men* (1943) shows how imaginatively
anti-Nazi Thomas could be when he was given more scope. It opens
with sequences contrasting men at work and on the battlefield, co-
operation in creation juxtaposed with its antithesis. The question of
the workers sent to fight is: 'Who sent us to kill, to be killed, to lose
what we love? . . . Who is to blame . . . Shout, shout, shout out their
name!' This cues the rest of the film, which uses sequences lifted from
Leni Riefenstahl's notorious *Triumph of the Will*, a eulogistic film
record of the Nazis' 1934 Nuremberg Rally. English voice-over 'translations', supplied by Thomas, are supplied for the film of speeches by
the Nazi leaders Hitler, Goebbels, Streicher, and Hess, so that each

supplies his own psychopathology and list of crimes. Hitler's rantings are rendered as

I was born of poor parents.
I grew into a discontented and neurotic child.
My lungs were bad, my mother spoilt me and secured my exemption
    from military service.
Consider my triumphant path to power:
I took up art.
I gave up art because I was incompetent.
I became a bricklayer's labourer,
A housepainter,
A paperhanger,
A peddler of pictures,
A lance-corporal,
A spy on socialists and communists,
A hater of Jews and Trade Unions . . .
Patriotic industrial magnates financed me.
Röhm and others supported me.
Later I betrayed Röhm and the others.
They had fulfilled their purpose.

(The crowd roars) Heil! Heil

I am a normal man.
I do not like meat, drink, or women.

If the list of Hitler's alleged failings is somewhat dubious by today's standards, the usurping of his voice is nevertheless a powerful deflating device, quasi-Brechtian in the cumulative effect of its laconic put-downs. As a reviewer in *Documentary News* declared, 'Dylan Thomas's verse frequently cuts like a knife into the pompously bestial affectations of this race of supermen.' It is not, in any case, the individual foibles that count most, but the collectivist nature of the condemnation: the film first establishes solidarity with 'the makers the workers . . . the farmers the sailors / The tailors the carpenters the colliers the fishermen' ('maker' also being an old Scottish word for 'poet'), before moving powerfully to link failure to fascism, neurosis to violence. In this it matches the collectivism and radical solidarities of other Thomas documentaries, such as *Wales – Green Mountain, Black Mountain* (1942), and *Our Country* (1944), the best of his wartime films, and his most celebrated at the time. The first of these shows

Thomas beginning to evolve his own version of the poetic style associated with Auden and the New Country poets, and found in pre-war
documentaries such as *Night Mail* – richly, at times lushly, descriptive and expansive, and displaying an 'ordinary, commonplace yet
heroic lyricism', in Ackerman's words.[4] Thomas had already sounded
out elements of this new mode in poems such as 'The hunchback in
the park' of mid-1941, and the recently-rediscovered 'A Dream of
Winter', dating from early 1942, but he would write no more poetry
until 1944. His lyric energies were channelled into the best of the
documentaries; the two mentioned allowed freer rein for his talents
than usual because they were among the few filmed according to his
script, rather than vice versa.

Wales – Green Mountain, Black Mountain offers a potted history
of Wales, using the visual overcoming of its geographic divisions –
through a montage of images of rural northern Wales (Snowdon and
uplands sheep-rearing) and industrial south Wales (Glamorganshire
steel plants and mines) – to suggest that Wales's rebelliously anti-
English past has been subsumed by the larger, contemporary struggle
against Germany. Images of social harmony and quaint but noble difference from an assumed British norm are conveyed via *eisteddfodau*,
hymn-singing Nonconformist congregations, and the like; amusingly,
at one point, Thomas, of all people, describes the chapels as 'never
grim or grey'. However, the film has a radical social edge that offsets its tourist board clichés and sentimentality. In particular, present
harmony is shown to be underwritten by full employment, and to be
haunted by recent austerity. At one point, older footage of closing
colliery gates, queues, and people grubbing for coal on a slag-heap,
derived from Donald Taylor's 1936 film *Today We Live*, is used. These
were iconic images of the 1930s socialist documentary movement,
and they are accompanied by an indictment of unemployment and
the government policies that created it:

> Remember the procession of the old-young men
> From dole queue to corner and back again,
> From the pinched, packed streets to the peak of slag
> In the bite of the winters with shovel and bag,
> With drooping fag and a turned-up collar,
> Stamping for the cold at the ill-lit corner
> Dragging through the squalor with their hearts like lead . . .
> Remember the procession of the old-young men.
> It shall never happen again.

The point is made so forcefully, in fact, that the script was rejected by the British Council, who had commissioned it, as unsuitable for overseas audiences. The MoI, however, had no such qualms, taking it over and releasing it for domestic consumption.

Our Country is focalised rather more coherently via a central fig-ure, a merchant seaman, who is shown travelling through England (London, Dover cliffs, Kent hopfields, a West Country harvest, indus-trial Sheffield), Wales (Rhondda mines, a choir, a Welsh-speaking village school) and Scotland (forestry camp, fishing port) in search of a new berth aboard a ship. The route of his quest links Britain's several national components, Northern Ireland excluded, and offers examples of collective labour, in what is an obvious metaphor for national soli-darity and unity of purpose (although it is not only national; one of the most surprising – and heartening – aspects of the film is an extended passage showing black US servicemen drinking, dancing and socialising with members of the white British population.). If the most memorable verse passage in *Wales – Green Mountain, Black Mountain* look back to a 1930s social realism, which Thomas chose not to use at the time, the more numerous successful lyric flights in *Our Country* closely echo the wartime elegies he did write; thus, the description of streets around St Paul's Cathedral in London recalls 'Among Those Killed in the Dawn Raid was a Man Aged a Hundred' and 'Ceremony After a Fire Raid':

> And all the stones remember and sing
> the cathedral of each blitzed dead body that lay or lies
> in the bomber-and-dove-flown-over cemeteries
> of the dumb heroic streets.

Equally, in its pastoral passages, the script anticipates 'Poem in October', 'Fern Hill' and the poems of the *In Country Heaven* project, such as 'In the White Giant's Thigh':

> By orchard and cottage cluster
> the drinking trough in the market square
> and the lovers' lanes
> they thundered through a hundred
> all over the country's strangely singing names . . .
>
> The journeying man from the sea may find some peace . . .
> breathing the smell of cattle and leather and straw

> on the clucking quacking whinnying mooing market day
> and going into the farmers' pubs
> that once were all haggling and cider
> and once a week news of the slow countryside.

Of course, the Blitz elegies differ from such scripts in problematising and resisting co-option within the 'war effort', dramatising Thomas's dilemmas concerning uncritical public mourning and celebration. While he did, in fact, occasionally attempt to resist incorporation in his film work – one spoof film project, called *Is Your Ernie Really Necessary?* (mocking the government slogan 'Is Your Journey Really Necessary?'), is said to have been made, although neither copy or script survives – his scripts had to conform to MoI requirements, and this meant a degree of simplification which erased finer moral discriminations and scruples.

Traditionally, most of Thomas's critical champions – John Ackerman and Walford Davies chief among them – applaud the fact that he turned to writing film (and radio) scripts during the war, viewing this as work that forced him to turn his back on a Modernist style whose density often makes them uncomfortable. Thomas, in this interpretation, began at last (one can almost detect the sigh of relief!) to write about what they disarmingly call 'real life'. But this claim, as more recent critics have observed, is another kind of simplification, one that ignores the dialectical interaction in Thomas's work between 'reel' and 'real' identified earlier in this chapter. In particular, it runs the risk of patronising Thomas by implying that he came to realise that what he had been doing up to that point had been an error, too 'obscure', however necessary from a developmental point of view. A better way of describing the undeniable change in his style in the 1940s, and the role of film in that change, might then be to say that, if Thomas's use of film in his 1930s poetry was *vertical* in nature – that is, it was of a kind which absorbed film technique in *depth*, at the level of poetic form – then in the 1940s he decided, as part of the populist (yet still Modernist-influenced) temper of the times, to use film *horizontally*, taking it as the model for a poetry that generated its complexities by dwelling on *surfaces* and the patterns that can be played across them.

However we decide to word it, what can be said is that Thomas was fascinated throughout his life by film, and the poetics of film, and that he strove in different ways to realise these in his work. Paradoxically, given the chance to write film scripts full-time during the war, he was limited by the demands of propaganda. After the war ended, however, and attracted by its lucrative prospects, he tried to make a full-time career of script-writing, and was given the chance to write more ambitious scripts than hitherto. Engaged by the producer Sidney Box for J. Arthur Rank's Gainsborough Films, which rode the brief boom in the British film industry between 1945 and 1948, Thomas wrote three full feature-length scripts for Rank, five scripts in all: a version of the Burke and Hare story, *The Doctor and the Devils*; an adaptation of the Irish classic *Twenty Years A-Growing*; the thriller-melodrama *The Three Weird Sisters* (1948); an adaptation of Joan Temple's stage play *No Room at the Inn* (1948); and an adaptation of Robert Louis Stevenson's story *The Beach of Falesà*. He also wrote some shorter scripts and treatments – *Betty London, The Shadowless Man, Me and My Bike* and *Rebecca's Daughters*.

None of these films were actually made in Thomas's lifetime; *The Doctor and the Devils* had to wait until 1986, and *Rebecca's Daughters* until 1992. However, *The Doctor and the Devils*, its dialogue interspersed with a description of setting and action, was published as a book in 1952, allegedly the first film-script ever to appear in this form before filming. It was well-received. Indeed, it was felt at the time that Thomas's treatment, like a contemporaneous one of *Tender is the Night* by Malcolm Lowry, was a new genre, blending drama, the novel and film in some radically new way. Bonamy Dobrée's review of it makes the point explicitly:

> His adventure in a new form, that of the published film-script before handling . . . is extraordinarily powerful, actual as only a poet can make it; and this new form makes us wonder whether this may not be a pointer towards the way novels may be written in future . . . It is written, of course, in film language; we 'dissolve to', the camera 'tracks back', we see someone 'in close up'; but we soon get used to all this, and adapt our imaginations to the whole movement, or the series of disjointed movements which make up the whole. The question arises: Do we need to see it on the film? Perhaps the answer is: We shall not need to see it only when the script is written so well as this one. That will be a rare occurrence, but a master in the art of the novel might well become a master in this new form.[5]

The quest for, and belief in, this 'new' genre is a fascinating historical curiosity; one can also see it in the contemporaneous adaptation of F. Scott Fitzgerald's *Tender is the Night* made by Malcolm Lowry, 'a 500-page filmscript with almost 100 pages of detailed explanation and comprising about six hours of movie time'.[6] Interestingly too, Dobrée's claims are echoed (but tempered in hindsight) by Julian Maclaren-Ross's account of the collaborative projects he and Thomas planned when they were working together at Strand Films:

> We . . . shared [an] ambition, which was to write a film script, not a Treatment . . . but a complete scenario ready for shooting which would give the ordinary reader an absolute visual impression of the film in words and could be published as a new form of literature. Carl Meyer, the co-author of *Caligari* and creator of many of the great early German silents, who invented the mobile camera . . . is said to have written such scripts, but neither Dylan nor I could get hold of [one] . . . the only ones we knew which almost succeeded in doing what we had in mind were those printed in *The Film Sense* by Sergei Eisenstein.
>
> The rules we laid down . . . were that the script had to be an original specially written in this form and not any kind of adaptation that actual film production must be possible. Our main obstacle consisted in the camera directions, which if given were apt to look too technical, and if omitted would lose the dramatic impact of, for instance, a sudden large close-up, which Dylan however hoped could be conveyed by one's actual choice of words. In fact we were attempting the well-nigh impossible, as anyone who has read the printed versions of *Marienbad* or *L'Immortelle* by Robbe-Grillet will realise, and perhaps Dylan himself in *The Doctor and the Devils* came as close to it as any writer ever will.

Dobrée makes too much of the novelty of what Thomas was doing; or, to be more charitable, he seems unaware of the extent to which Modernist authors (the Nighttown episode in *Ulysses* springs to mind, for example), had already done such things. Also, as Maclaren-Ross notes, the procedure would become a staple of postmodern fiction not long after Thomas wrote *The Doctor and the Devils*. Nevertheless, this written-through script, to give it another name, is powerful enough, a kind of knowing reworking of Dickens from a mid-twentieth century point of view. It focuses, that is, on matters which, while they arise from the work's location in early nineteenth century Edinburgh, rendered with Dickensian relish, were of particular importance in post-WWII Britain.[7] One is the question of means and ends: Doctor Rock, the high-flying Edinburgh anatomist and physician who is the work's central figure, mocks and flouts social convention, and justifies the use of dead bodies for dissection on the grounds of the advance of science. Although his critique of society is tonic, his need for a steady supply of recently-deceased bodies paves the way for his two most unscrupulous suppliers – the Burke and Hare equivalents, Fallon and Broom – to murder. Rock dramatises how a radical positivism, a belief that the ends justify the means, can lead to atrocities which a more 'backward' world-view would not so easily countenance. This was something very much in the mind of a world that had recently witnessed not just the savagery of the Nazis, but also the rise of Stalinism and the Soviet purges, and the destruction of German cities and use of atomic weapons on civilian populations by the liberal democracies. The other pressing issue of the time, the social crisis out of which the war had grown, is also present in Thomas's depiction of the wretchedness of the Edinburgh poor, which is suffused with anger as well as compassion, as Ackerman notes.[8] This was the anger that fuelled the creation of the Welfare State, which was in the process of being born as Thomas was writing his script.

Other of Thomas's films that were never made included a 1952 documentary for the Anglo-Iranian Oil Company (later Shell), intended to help stave off its nationalisation by the Iranian government. Cases such as this may tempt us to argue that the most interesting films Thomas ever wrote are those that he never got to make, or was not able to finish writing. What would we not give, for example, to have *The Shadowless Man*, 'a dark and fantastic romance of the German 1830s', as Thomas described it? Its story came from *Student of Prague*, one of the films he had mentioned in 'Salnady and Spajma' thirteen years before *The Shadowless Man* was written, in 1947. The most tantalising aspect of this unmade film is contained in the letter Thomas wrote to the film producer Benjamin Arbeid, who had read it: 'I did, of course, realise at the time how impracticable a subject it was in the light of Wardour Street's reaction to it. But your suggestion that I should try it out on Cocteau, I shall certainly do something about' (*CL*, 862). Like the opera libretto he was scheduled to write for Igor Stravinsky on the eve of his death, a Cocteau collaboration might at the very least have silenced the many critics who have claimed that Thomas is not worth taking seriously; unfortunately, there is no evidence that Thomas even sent it, and it remains one of film's (and literature's) great might-have-beens. Nevertheless, the real importance of film to Thomas, as I have argued, is in its influence on his other writing. Film, the Modernist art form *par excellence* was a crucial catalyst in his embrace of modernist experiment in 1934–6, and in his search for ways in which to recast it in more populist forms in the 1940s and 1950s.

Notes

[1] Constantine Fitzgibbon, *The Life of Dylan Thomas* (London: J. M. Dent & Sons, 1965), p. 62.

[2] See *CL*, 101, and Thomas's description of his heterogeneous everyday reading material: 'I seat myself in front of the fire and commence to read, to read anything that is near, poetry or prose, translations out of the Greek or the *Film Pictorial . . .*'.

[3] See the letter to Pamela Hansford Johnson of 'about 21 December 1933', in *CL*, 81: 'Nothing I can think of – including the personal delivery of Miss Garbo in a tin box – would please me so much as to spend Christmas with you.'

[4] John Ackerman, *A Dylan Thomas Companion: Life, Poetry and Prose* (Basingstoke; Macmillan, 1994), p. 106.

[5] Bonamy Dobrée, 'Two Experiments', *Spectator*, 190 (12 June 1953), 764.

[6] Ruth Perlmutter, 'Malcolm Lowry's Unpublished Filmscript of *Tender is the Night*', *American Quarterly*, vol. 28, no. 5 (Winter, 1976), 561.

[7] Another influence, given the Edinburgh location and nature of Dr Rock, is surely Robert Louis Stevenson's *Strange Case of Doctor Jekyll and Mr Hyde*.

[8] John Ackerman, *Dylan Thomas: The Filmscripts* (London: J. M. Dent), p. 103.

8

'IF WE ARE GONG TO CALL PEOTS BDA . . .': KINGSLEY AMIS AND DYLAN THOMAS

James Keery

'THE INFLUENCE OF MISTER DYLAN THOS.'

It was probably Philip Larkin who introduced Kingsley Amis to Dylan Thomas, since Amis was not at the Oxford English Club on a memorable night in 1941:

> Hell of a fine man: little, snubby, hopelessly pissed bloke who made hundreds of cracks and read parodies of everybody in appropriate voices . . . 'I'd like to have talked about a book of poems [by] a young poet called Rupert Brooke – it's surprising how he has been influenced by Stephen Spender . . .' There was a moment of delighted surprise, then a roar of laughter. Then he read a parody of Spender . . . which had people rolling on the floor. He kept this up all night.[1]

Larkin, the precocious and dedicated novelist who became, by default, one of the finest poets of the post-war period, and Amis, its finest novelist, possessed by the daemon of poetry, are both synonymous with the 1950s reaction against Thomas and the Apocalyptic style of the 1940s; yet, for Amis in particular, the disowned precursor remains an obsession. In 'After Goliath', the challenge to Thomas is enacted in an ironically triumphal context, but Amis's anxiety as to whether 'the right man lay in the dust' is more heartfelt than might appear.[2]

Larkin has acknowledged the influence of the 'New Apocalypse crowd' on *The North Ship* (1945);[3] whilst Amis's subsequent 'enthusiasm for [Thomas's] writing',[4] recorded and recanted in the same breath, permeates his first collection, *Bright November*, published in September 1947. As late as March 1946, he was writing to Larkin, quoting Hilly Bardwell's letters about their shared enthusiasms: 'thankyou so much for the Fats record [and] *The Map of Love*'.[5] Yet even before publication, in a letter to Larkin dated 9 January 1947, he had formulated the response to 'the influence of Mister Dylan Thos.', which, with help from his friends, he proceeded to impose on the literary world at large:

> I have traced the nastiness of my early words to the influence of Mister Dylan Thos. . . . I have only to see words like An old man's shank one-marrowed with my bone . . . to groan 8 laid. And if we are gong to call peots bda because of the fefect they have dha on Egnilsh peorty, then he is bad[.] (*Letters*, pp. 109–10)

The reaction against the 'influence' of Thomas and Apocalyptic poetry, which has become known as 'The Movement', was already, 'by 1950, becoming . . . conscious of its aims', as 'anti-Romanticism became an increasingly important part of its programme'.[6] It was Donald Davie, another important ideologist of the Movement, who declared that self-respecting poets 'were *in duty bound* to write as if . . . Dylan Thomas . . . had never existed';[7] but the extent to which such a reaction had been inaugurated and inspired by Amis may be demonstrated by tracing his polemical poem, 'Against Romanticism',[8] to its source in a contrast between Thomas and Robert Graves by a reviewer for a little magazine, in the autumn of 1946:

> To leave the rapt ecstasies of [Thomas's] personal vision for the more objective world delineated by Robert Graves is to find ourselves at once in a more temperate zone.[9]

On the spot, Amis trades 'Torrid images' and 'brain raging with prophecy' for 'a path leading out of sight, / And at its other end a temperate zone'.[10] Although even-handed in his response to the 'intensely personal exuberance' of 'what we have come to call the Apocalyptic poet', this critic anticipates the urbanity of the Movement attack: 'If fire is one of the things we ask from poetry, light is another; and . . . it

cannot be denied that he often leads us into the "palpable obscure"'.[11]
Thus, between completion and publication of *Bright November*, Amis
turns, once and for all, 'Against Romanticism', in a poem that 'enacts
the transition from Apocalypse to "Movement"'.[12] By contrast, John
Wain, who was to play a crucial role in the launch of the Movement
in 1953, as presenter of the BBC radio magazine *First Reading*,[13] was
still, in 1949, eager to acclaim the contributors to an Oxford anthology which 'sets a new standard, not only for Oxford, but for young
poets everywhere', as 'all Symbolists. // And all Romantics'.[14]

And for two generations, what Amis says goes. By 1957, a parodist of his own mordant villanelle, 'The Voice of Authority: A
Language Game' ('What goes is what I say O'Grady says'),[15] had got
the message:

> Now laugh. Shut up. Right, Lucky Jim says laugh
> . . .
> Now hiss. Lay off. Wait till I've said the words
> . . .
> What's bad's what I say Lucky Jim can't stand.[16]

Anxiety to repress what 'Lucky Jim can't stand' is made obligingly
explicit by a BBC producer, writing to Burns Singer about a poem on
Marcus Aurelius, in 1956:

> [O]ne particular point I want to take up is your reason for using old
> Marcus – and whether you couldn't have got what you say over in modern
> terms. This isn't my own line of argument, it's an objection that Kingsley
> Amis suggested to me and one you might like to answer in the broadcast.[17]

According to the *Sunday Times*, Amis was 'widely regarded as the
spokesman of the post-war generations'; and, for *The Daily Worker*,
'as much a part of the world of 1957 as television, rock 'n' roll and
the FA Cup'.[18] As Larkin wrote to a colleague about *The New Oxford
Book of Light Verse*, Amis's supplement to Larkin's own *Oxford Book
of Twentieth Century Verse*: 'We shall have stamped our taste on the
age between us in the end'.[19]

More particularly, as Zachary Leader observes, Amis was 'at the
heart of . . . the Movement, and complexly implicated in its various
schemes of self-promotion' (*Life*, p. 1). His keynote letter to Wain
('pity you're away; with you as general, the boys could move right into

control') is dated 6 November 1953 (*Letters*, p. 342), three days before the crucial stimulus of the death of Dylan Thomas. Amis's own collection of that year is subtitled *Eighteen Poems*, a direct challenge to Thomas's *18 Poems*, reinforcing the rebuke to neo-romantic splurges of emotion implicit in the title, *A Frame of Mind*.[20] Amis pursued Thomas, 'that crazy Welch fellow',[21] throughout his career, from use of the name 'Welch' to epitomise pretentiousness in *Lucky Jim*,[22] to the portrait of Brydan in *The Old Devils*.[23] His scathing review of Thomas's *Collected Letters* ends with a scarcely credible dismissal:

> Whatever it was that made so many people put up with all that for so long can hardly be expected to emerge now: this volume looks like being the last we shall hear of him.[24]

Yet the relationship, in *The Old Devils*, between the 'safely long dead'[25] Brydan and the Amis-surrogate Alun Weaver, culminates in artistic demolition by a candid friend (p. 340). My argument is that the life-long relationship between Amis and Thomas is equally grievous and profound.

The ironic achievement by Amis and Larkin of each other's greatest ambition has tended to cast Amis's mature poetry into the shade, let alone his Apocalyptic 'prentice work, to borrow the trademark Movement *mea culpa*:

> My hymn of doves, echoed upon this earth
> As fast as ears swinging beside the bell,
> Lives for a second echoing to birth,
> Strikes full on lips reft in a coloured sigh,
> Weaves in a skein of tears the distant heart;
> Makes us a mountain in a world of sky
> And vacant air; the hot blood lashes seed
> Unsilting channels in the absent shell.[26]

Rhyme apart, four lines from Thomas's sonnet, 'When all my five and country senses' might (without disrespect) be substituted for the last four of Amis's octave:

> My hymn of doves, echoed upon this earth
> As fast as ears swinging beside the bell,
> Lives for a second echoing to birth,
> Strikes full on lips reft in a coloured sigh[.]

> The whispering ears will watch love drummed away
> Down breeze and shell to a discordant beach,
> And, lashed to syllables, the lynx tongue cry
> That her fond wounds are mended bitterly.[27]

One line seems to transcend 'the luck of verbal playing':[28] 'Lives for a second echoing to birth'. The way 'echoing' actually does echo 'second' is almost worthy of Thomas:

> [Immortal Adam, after the first death,]
> Lives for a second echoing to birth.[29]

Yet this collection is routinely passed over in silence. Literally, in the 2009 symposium, *The Movement Reconsidered*: in the chapter on Amis's poetry, James Fenton devotes a page of sneers to Dylan Thomas and gives us an entire poem from '*The North Ship*' by 'the young Larkin', but not a single line by 'the young Kingsley Amis', not even a name-check for the book.[30] He is not alone in writing as though under instruction to ignore it, in the spirit of Amis's response to a suggestion that copies must be 'worth a bomb': 'Good. That'll keep its circulation nicely restricted.'[31]

Critics who do mention it speak with one voice, finding it immature and Audenesque. Clive James applauds the admission of six from *Bright November* into *Collected Poems*: 'Amis has done us a . . . service by not suppressing [them] . . . an object lesson in what a gifted young poet finds fascinating about an older master.'[32] Not a word on the poems influenced by Thomas, which Amis *has* suppressed! Similarly, in his superb biography, Leader hears only Auden in 'the wartime poems' (*Life*, p. 153), missing the significance, amongst the belongings of the Amis-character in the co-authored wartime novel, *Who Else Is Rank*, of a copy of *The Map of Love* by the 'smashing' Dylan Thomas.[33]

On message, Paul Fussell deplores 'unconscious parodies of someone else's voice, namely, Auden's'.[34] William H. Pritchard cites John Bayley on the second-hand competence of *The North Ship* and finesses *Bright November* as smartly as Fenton: 'A similar judgement might be passed on the presence of Auden in Amis's early poems.'[35] The sage generalisation disguises the fact that Pritchard, like James, has considered only the fraction of the evidence presented in *Collected Poems*, i.e. 'the first six' (p. 76).

'THE CHAMBOIS SHAMBLES'

The influence of Auden is thus agreed on all sides, whilst that of
Thomas is universally overlooked, unless, as by Neil Powell, it is
roundly denied: 'Kingsley was never tempted by "apocalyptic" excess,
nor did he share Philip's transitory admiration for Dylan Thomas.'[36]
The trouble is that, even for scholars as meticulous as Leader, the
1940s are still out of focus. The result is a failure to discriminate
between 'university stuff', in Fussell's summary, cited by Leader,
and 'army poems': 'Amis produced the kind of poems he came to
deplore: university stuff aimed not at the general reader but at clever
friends . . . wild for Auden, Eliot, and Donne.'[37] They were, but they
were also wild for sex, jazz and Dylan Thomas.

On the battlefield poetry in *Bright November*, critics have main-
tained radio silence. Again, Amis dismisses his own experience, as in
a 1953 letter to Larkin on his next novel: 'the Ormy is more or else
out of the question – I didn't do any fighting and I've forgotten what
I did do' (*Letters*, p. 321). Both Amis and Larkin tend to 'forget what
did' in the war, saying little about 'what happened to happen' to them,
Amis at the Falaise Gap, Larkin after the bombing of Coventry:
experiences comparable not only as visions of hell on earth, but in the
inglorious belatedness of the protagonists.[38] Both traverse the scene,
as conscious latecomers, in the safe but appalling aftermath. Thus,
according to one biographer, Amis 'saw no more of actual warfare
than he did of wirelesses': among the poets 'in the services' who 'got
nowhere near the war', Powell brackets him with Roy Fuller, who saw
more giraffes than Germans (p. 38).

A series of poems in *Bright November* tackles the nightmare
head-on. Several critics refer to the brief record of Amis's experience in *Memoirs* (pp. 86–8), but none mentions 'Elisabeth at
Chamboix':

> Hard to trace the form of Adam
> in a heap of sacking blown with gas;
> hard to credit with sensation
> source of midden odours that will pass . . .
>
> And of women you my dearest
> most astute to keep your limbs alive,
> clear of senseless putrefaction
> wisest in your living arts of love. (p. 18)

On 30 June 1944, Amis was a passenger in a jeep which drove off an American landing-craft into Normandy, three weeks after D-Day (*Life*, pp. 129–30). He was serving with a non-combatant signals unit, which never faced 'direct enemy fire', but, on its progress behind the armies across the battlefields, endured the constant sight of 'the terrible litter of German dead'.[39] His unit reached Falaise so soon after the slaughter that there had been 'no time even to bulldoze bodies to the roadside' (*Memoirs*, p. 86). Incredibly, the stench reached pilots in their planes.[40] 'Forty eight hours after the closing of the gap I was conducted through it on foot, to encounter scenes that could be described only by Dante. It was literally possible to walk for hundreds of yards at a time, stepping on nothing but dead and decaying flesh.' The author of this report is no journalist but Dwight D. Eisenhower.[41] 'Elisabeth at Chamboix' suggests a romantic tryst, but for all its idyllic connotations (*champs*, *bois*, *chambre*), the reference is to the village of Chambois ('s' not 'x'), south-east of Falaise, aka the 'Chambois Shambles'[42] – all too apt, in view of the hundreds of dead horses, 'upper lips drawn above their teeth as if in continuing pain', which Amis found 'almost more pitiful' than the soldiers (*Memoirs*, p. 86). '[Thoughts of] Elisabeth [from] Chamboix' gives the sense of the title, whilst spoiling its effect, which is, as another poem puts it, 'to reset / This pictured face in scenes of sacrifice'.[43] By placing her 'at' Chambois, Amis contrives a startling double-take, one of Hopkins's exploding tropes.

Amis reverts again and again to the 'stink of the lustless dead', overtly in 'Where Are You?' ('Nostrils contract at the bloated human wreck') (p. 17), surreally in 'Something Was Moaning in the Corner', cited entire:

> O muskrat, ramble through the living grass
> And coil the leaves on the abandoned bone;
> Bring to the midden your eliding grease
> And load the summer zephyrs with your bane.
>
> O viper, mad with coiling on a pin,
> Deadly Narcissus gazing on your scales,
> Vomit your naked young sentenced to pain
> And learn to love the bad sun where it scalds.
>
> O spider, crawl into my tiny heart
> And find your doom. The blood is vacant there.

> With needle legs prick my dull skin apart
> And build your web of sweet inhuman hair. (p. 14)

A unique fusion of the highly dissonant elements of irrepressible hilarity
and Apocalyptic sublimity; sex, poetry, jazz and mortality (specifically,
Elisabeth Simpson; Auden and Dylan Thomas; Sidney Bechet, Pee Wee
Russell and Louis Armstrong), and the 'midden odours' at Falaise,
a grim elucidation of the Dylanesque (and Shakespearean) fourth
line.[44] Each opening invocation names a record by one of Amis's (and
Larkin's) favourite musicians: *Muskrat Ramble* by Louis Armstrong
and His Hot Five, 1926;[45] *Viper Mad* by Sidney Bechet, 1938[46] ('On
me your voice falls as they say love should, / Like an enormous yes')[47]
and *Spider Crawl* by the Rhythmakers,[48] with Pee Wee Russell ('our
Swinburne and our Byron')[49] on tenor saxophone, 1932; while the title
is a line of another track from the legendary Rhythmakers sessions,
'Mean Old Bed Bug Blues' (*All What Jazz*, p. 108).

For Amis in his twenties, then, as for Colonel Manton in *The
Riverside Villas Murder*, 'Mean Old Bed Bug Blues' was, with sex, death
and poetry, 'about a quarter of my life'.[50] It is this song that crystallises
the influence, on Amis and Larkin alike, of the 'apocalyptic "twins"'[51]
in the title of Larkin's poem, 'Hard Lines, or Mean Old W. H. Thomas
Blues'.[52] A. T. Tolley dates it '1940?' (p. 74), but five lines, written 'yes-
terday', are cited in a letter of 20 March 1942;[53] while an April letter to
Amis about 'well-fused abortions made by Auden's language in Dylan
T.'s construction'[54] echoes the poem's admiring frustration:

> Lacking the wordy bloodstream at command,
> The green self-conscious spurt that drives the hand
> Of Dylan in his womb of whiskey rocked.
>   (*Early Poems and Juvenilia*, p. 73)

In another poem by Larkin from this period, 'The Returning', an
almost identical trope has the same position and driving rhythm as
the phrase 'Drives their red blood' in 'The force that through the
green fuse' (*Collected Poems*, p. 43): 'Another heart . . . Drives their
dry blood' (*Early Poems and Juvenilia*, p. 185).

In *Who Else Is Rank*, Amis reprises the theme of 'Mean Old
W. H. Thomas Blues' by christening the heroine 'Betty Russell', a
fusion of his lover, Elisabeth Simpson ('Betty' in letters to Larkin),
with the next most frequent name, that of Pee Wee Russell.[55] And

the intertextuality goes deeper. The title is not a question, but a noun-phrase, from *Julius Caesar*: 'I know not, gentlemen, what you intend, / Who else must be let blood, who else is rank'.[56] Mark Antony combines two meanings, *growing too luxuriantly* and *smelling too strongly*, with a cunning connotation of *seniority*: who else has grown so offensively great as to deserve to be cut down? Amis twists all three senses into an image of the 'bane' on the 'summer zephyrs' at Falaise, whilst also declaring a personal agenda, as yet unfocused, but already, to quote Karl Miller on Movement criticism, 'as judicial, as fault-findingly ambitious, and as youthfully and generationally vengeful, as any there has ever been'.[57] Mark Antony's vision of the Chambois Shambles – 'Cry havoc and let slip the dogs of war, / That this foul deed shall smell above the earth / With carrion men, groaning for burial' (III. 1. 273–5, pp. 76–7) – occurs in the same scene, which is in Shakespeare's best Apocalyptic vein:

> Thou art the ruins of the noblest man
> That ever livèd in the tide of times.
> Woe to the hand that shed this costly blood!
> Over thy wounds now do I prophesy –
> Which, like dumb mouths, do ope their ruby lips
> To beg the voice and utterance of my tongue[.] (III. 1. 256–61, p. 77)

'[T]ide of times' is a sly reversal of Thomas's 'tides of time' ('When once the twilight locks', *Collected Poems*, p. 53), whilst 'dumb mouths' is obviously nicked from 'The force that through the green fuse' (p. 43). Hence Thomas's intuitive understanding of *apophrades*,[58] the trope by which the precursor can appear to be ghost-writing in the style of his successor, as Brooke sounds as if 'he has been influenced by' Spender.[59] In this light, far from disposing of his opponent, Hotspur's retort to Glendower is just another Movement gibe at the Apocalyptic sublime: 'Glendower: I can call spirits from the vasty deep. / Hotspur: Why, so can I, and so can any man, / But will they come when you do call for them?'[60] Affirmative: in 'one of the mysteries of poetic style', 'the strong dead return, in poems as in our lives', but 'speaking in our voices'.[61]

'ANGELS ON HORSEBACK'

David Rees was right on the money when, in 1965, he focused on the parody of Thomas's verse in *That Uncertain Feeling*[62] as a key to

Amis's 'iconoclasm'.[63] '[L]ittle Bowen Thomas', 'buried . . . at bat-
light' in Gareth Probert's play (*That Uncertain Feeling*, p. 112), is first
cousin to 'Little Mr Tomkins', the *Spectator* alias gleefully adopted
by Amis in 1954, during the first public bunfight in the emergence
of the Movement, with *That Uncertain Feeling* on the stocks (*Life*,
pp. 294–7). This is the point at which the forties' sneer goes viral, to
be endlessly retweeted for sixty years.

Rees attributes to the 'integrity' of the Amis-character, John
Lewis, in the face of mock-Apocalyptic poetry, 'the same significance
for one's generation as, say, the tone of *Prufrock* or . . . *The Orators*
had for earlier generations', so that 'many of us today find it impossible to regard the Protean manifestations of Probert's attitude' with
anything other than dutiful contempt.[64] Lewis's epic 'reproach to all
Welshmen' about their 'phoney' culture, manned by 'literary dead-
beats, charlatans and flops' (pp. 108–10), transcends its inspiration,
The Martyr by Probert, humourless sibling of Rosie in *Under Milk
Wood*.[65] Lewis's belittlement of Probert, who 'sounded like an actor
pretending . . . to be Owain Glyndŵr in a play on the Welsh Children's
Hour' (p. 40), recalls Hotspur's disdain for Glendower's 'art': 'I think
there's no man speaks better Welsh'.[66] The parody of 'Jack Christ'
('Altarwise by owl-light')[67] as 'Dai Christ'[68] typifies the sleight of hand
by which Probert's prose is rigged to impute bogus 'Welchness',[69]
under sustained attack in the book, to Thomas himself. Dismissal of
'all those canonisations' takes care of the 'Holy-in-corner' saints of
'the Gorsedd', in whose garb Probert's hero, 'The Monk', is attired
(pp. 108–10), but also, more ambitiously, of the canon of modernism.
The marvellous nine-line highlight of *The Martyr* (or out-take from
'Altarwise by owl-light') is aimed at exactly the same targets:

> When in time's double morning, meaning death,
> Denial's four-eyed bird, that Petrine cock,
> Crew junction down the sleepers of the breath,
> Iron bled that dry tree at the place of rock,
> The son of dog snarled at the rat of love,
> Holy-in-corner of the tottered sky,
> Where angel tiered on angle swung above,
> Into each crack and crick and creek of eye,
> Angels on horseback wept with vinegar. (p. 108)

Amis's variations on themes by Thomas combine 'Time's nerve in
vinegar' from 'Altarwise by owl-light' (p. 85) with echoes of numerous

other poems and the unmistakable parody of a line from 'A Refusal to Mourn the Death, by Fire, of a Child in London' ('Nor blaspheme down the stations of the breath') into an Apocalyptic vision of Christ's passion (p. 172). Thomas's allusion to the use of Tube 'stations' as shelters, noted by Goodby, inspires the poignantly ridiculous puns on 'Crew(e) [J]unction' and railway 'sleepers'.[70] The fifth line is an equally unmistakable parody of a line from another Apocalyptic crucifixion, 'Golgotha', by J. F. Hendry: 'A set dog barking at the rat of heart'.[71] The 'son of dog' is also, obviously, Thomas as a young dog; and, by one of his own favourite Joycean tricks, son of God; whilst 'the rat of love', another of his internecine selves, is, at the same time, a self-portrait of the parodist as love-rat, forty years before the tabloid phrase was coined.[72]

Yet, with its echoes of George Barker ('O dog, my God!': 'from a better angle, / Like a double-headed angel'),[73] and direct quotations from Louis MacNeice and T. S. Eliot, the poem is not focused exclusively on Thomas, but zooms out to get three generations of modernism into shot. The allusion to 'Marina' ('Those who sharpen the tooth of the dog, meaning / Death')[74] transfers Eliot's curse on the secular satisfactions of violence, beauty, wealth and sex into a threat to his authority as 'the Pope of Russell Square';[75] while the quotation from *Autumn Sequel* imputes failure and betrayal to the poets of the 1930s, despite MacNeice's claim: 'Though denial / May please the Parrot and the Petrine cock, / Yet some still tell the truth in an hour of trial'.[76] The implication is that modernism, though apparently founded securely upon 'the Petrine rock'[77] of the papacy established by St Peter, the first pope, is, on the contrary, 'Tottering to Its Fall'.[78]

Amis's anti-modernism is paralleled by his exemplary swing to the right. He was still writing for the Fabian Society in 1957,[79] ten years before explaining 'Why Lucky Jim Turned Right',[80] but had already by the mid-1950s become a jewel in the crown of reascendant conservatism. *Spectrum: A Spectator Miscellany* (1956), co-edited by Ian Gilmour, proprietor since 1954, later a cabinet minister, features numerous other senior Conservative politicians, including Iain Macleod, Lord Hailsham, Randolph Churchill, Rab Butler, Norman St John-Stevas and Enoch Powell ('Pharos'), alongside George Gale, Evelyn Waugh and on across the spectrum, from blue to blue.[81] Yet non-alphabetical precedence is accorded to 'Thomas the Rhymer', Amis's attack on the 'apocalyptic' style of Dylan Thomas.[82]

In the verse-parody, the *coup de grâce* is administered in the final line, in which angelic horsemen shed bitter tears at the climax of the crucifixion, as narrated in John's gospel: 'When Jesus therefore had received the vinegar, he said, It is finished: and . . . gave up the ghost' (19: 30). For 'angels on horseback' is also the name of a delicacy, a hot *hors d'œuvre*, aristocratic pigs in blankets, with oysters instead of sausages. According to the *Washington Post*, 'the bivalves, bacon, vinegar and lemony *vin blanc* sauce hit all the right flavour notes'.[83] The collocation of oysters, vinegar and tears, in turn, recalls 'The Walrus and the Carpenter', in which Lewis Carroll's hypocritical Walrus devours the companions of their walk along the shore: '"A loaf of bread", the Walrus said, / "Is what we chiefly need: / Pepper and vinegar besides / Are very good indeed – / Now if you're ready, Oysters dear, / We can begin to feed" . . . "I weep for you", the Walrus said: / "I deeply sympathize". / With sobs and tears he sorted out / Those of the largest size'.[84] So modernism itself is, in its entirety, Apocalyptic nonsense, Bloomsbury hot air, an indulgence, of which nothing remains but shucks. And Amis leaves the crocodile tears to the Walrus: 'I'd like to think that the long period of modernism . . . is not only over but will be looked back on as a great fraud'.[85]

'WCH THE AMIS CHAR?'

The critical heritage, dire on the early poetry, redeems itself on *The Old Devils*. Leader reads it as an elegy for Larkin (*Life*, p. 746); Richard Bradford as an allegory of Amis's love for first wife;[86] Powell as a distribution of his terrors, angers, cruelty and remorse, 'the divided self transformed into fiction' (p. 228); Andrew James as revenge on Dylan Thomas, 'for leading him astray' (p. 183); and, most brilliantly, Bradford, again, as the revenge *of* Dylan Thomas, 'a kind of penitential rite' for 'four decades' of abuse (p. 375). Alun Weaver, professional Welshman on London television, 'embodiment of the Welsh consciousness',[87] or 'stage-Taffy' (p. 28), is, according to Amis himself, 'me': 'me coming back to Wales, or me as I used to be, or perhaps as I wanted to be'.[88] Spoiler alert: on return, Weaver picks up after forty years on friendships and affairs, notably with the wives of two of his cronies, until his sudden death leaves his wife free to return to her first love, a retired engineer. Their children fall in love, marry, and, as Larkin said of 'The Whitsun Weddings' (*Collected*

Poems, pp. 114–16), 'There's nothing to suggest that their lives won't be happy, surely? I defy you to find it!'[89]

Amis's name-games, from 'Betty Russell' to 'Jake Richardson' in *Jake's Thing*,[90] 'a deliberate reformulation of "Jim Dixon"',[91] culminate in *The Old Devils*. In the spirit of one of the author's notes, 'Keep the reader guessing – wch the Amis char?' (*Life*, p. 741), the novel is a reckoning with not one but several selves; and with Amis's drinking cronies, who were, almost to a man, trustees of the Dylan Thomas Estate like Amis himself. Weaver is outwardly modelled on Wynford Vaughan-Thomas, one of the cronies, author of 'Hiraeth in NW3', about homesickness for Wales, anthologised by Amis in *The New Oxford Book of Light Verse*[92] and of *Wynford Vaughan-Thomas's Wales* (1981),[93] prototype for a coffee-table book on *Brydan's Wales* by Weaver (p. 11). 'This book which I have been bold enough to call *My Wales*'[94] is full of Weaver-speak: 'do I see Wales through rose-coloured spectacles as a little Celtic paradise . . . ? The honest answer is "Yes"'.[95] Weaver's riff on what Wales means to him is in a similar vein: 'Many things grave and gay and multi-coloured but one above all: I'm coming home . . . Heart is where the home is' (p. 64). Just such 'Celtic claptrap about . . . My Wales!' is scorned by Owen Morgan-Vaughan in Dylan Thomas's screenplay for *The Three Weird Sisters*.[96] Weaver's books include '*Celtic Attitudes*'; and deceptively intelligent *hwyl* is exactly what is wrong with his shot at writing the real book he feels he has in him (pp. 295–6). Yet Amis's *hiraeth* is as genuine as Weaver's is dubious. In *Memoirs*, he recalls 'the early or middle 1950s' in Swansea as, '[i]n many ways', 'our best time': 'I miss it constantly and I miss those days . . . Often I wish I had never left' (p. 137). Now, 'Swansea has again become what it was . . . the piece of earth I know best, better than any part of London, and feel most at home in' (p. 139), a tribute reminiscent of John of Gaunt: 'This blessed plot, this [piece of] earth . . . this [Wales]'.[97] Except that the charged phrase is not of course from *Richard II*, but from that same scene of *Julius Caesar*: 'O pardon me, thou bleeding piece of earth' (III. 1. 254, p. 76). Conventional nostalgia is unconsciously 'coloured' with the anguish, remorse and violence of Antony's speech.

Another of the cronies was Swansea solicitor Stuart Thomas, a trustee (as was Vaughan-Thomas, whose decision to stand down in favour of Amis was under discussion as he drafted *The Old Devils*)[98] with a key role in the genesis of the book. 'The idea for it came to [Amis] during one of his regular summer visits to Swansea, as he "was putting his shoes on to go down to the Yacht Club" for a lunchtime drinking session with . . . Eve and Stuart Thomas',[99] before their acrimonious divorce and Stuart Thomas's expulsion from their 'little Garrick beyond Wales' (*Memoirs*, p. 138). At school with Dylan Thomas, as Weaver falsely claims to have been,[100] and a Burma veteran, Stuart Thomas has been described by an ex-student of Amis's as 'one of the most unpleasant men I've ever met', 'notoriously malevolent'.[101] His fictional redemption as Peter Thomas, the once and future partner of Rhiannon Weaver, is thus all the more poignant. Body double for Amis, also '[n]o-joke fat' (p. 170) by the mid-1980s, Peter is identifiable with Stuart Thomas by another, stranger coincidence: the marriage of his step-daughter, Rhiannon, in 1962, to Llewelyn, elder son of Dylan Thomas.[102] The marriage of the poet's son to the daughter of one of the old devils is, with the substitution of Weaver for Brydan, and the transfer of the name 'Rhiannon' from daughter to mother, an uncanny match for the marriage of Alun's son to Peter's daughter (pp. 35–57). One might even suggest a parallel between *The Old Devils* and a story from that 'smashing' collection, *A Map of Love*:

> Listen to the cock, cried Peter, and the sheets of the bed rolled up to his chin . . . Rhianon, with a sweet, naked throat, stepped into the room . . . She did not hear him, but stood over his bed and fixed him with an unbreakable sorrow. // Hold my hand, he said. And then: why are you putting the sheet over my face?[103]

Revivifying this romance, Amis even redeems the 'Petrine cock'!

'THE ORGAN-VOICE OF WALES'

Weaver owes his career to the bard known only as 'Brydan', an obvious variation on 'Dylan', with four of its five letters, altered to rhyme with the detested Dryden, tarred with the same brush as Thomas in 1947: 'I have got to the stage now with mr toss that I have only reached with Chaucer and Dryden . . . that of VIOLENTLY WISHING that the man WERE IN FRONT OF ME, so that I could be DEMONIACALLY RUDE to him about his GONORRHEIC RUBBISH'.[104]

This early self is incarnated in the novel as Charlie Norris, Alun's critic, victim and nemesis. He echoes the revulsion of the young

poet ('it's his influence that makes that stuff of yours . . . so awful')
(p. 306), giving explicit, almost equally hysterical expression to the
Oedipal anxiety of influence: 'if you want *Closing Time*[105] or *Coming
Home* or whatever it's called to be any good at all, you must scour
Brydan right out of it, so that not a single word reminds me of him
even vaguely. Whatever you think of him, you must write as if you
hated and despised him without reserve' (p. 306). Exactly as Amis
has, unrepentant even when, appointed a trustee, it was alleged that
he had 'spent the past 30 years . . . abusing Dylan Thomas'.[106] His
ironic refutation is a cynical admission of the charge: 'Actually . . . I
did find other things to do in those three decades' (*Letters*, p. 1133).
Charlie derides Brydan's style in the very voice of Amis: 'you can
stick the lot . . . the man in the mask and the man in the iron street.
All he'd done was juggle two phrases about' (p. 29). His disclaimer
– 'Not my field' (p. 28) – is belied by the apt variation on 'the man
in the wind and west moon'[107] and by the sweep of his attack on
Alun's draft: 'too much like Brydan . . . not just Brydan himself
but a whole way of writing' (p. 296). 'Amisian traits' (*Life*, p. 941)
include the boredom threshold of a delinquent; gourmet tastes; no-
joke alcoholism; and no-joke fear of the dark. Alun asks Charlie to
give his novel 'a free-from-bullshit certificate' (p. 294), then revenges
the wounding candour of the response by contriving, in his own
brutal words, to 'fuck him up by leaving him to come back here
on his own in the dark' (p. 320). Charlie's experience of howling,
inconsolable terror had been familiar to Amis, and to his nearest and
dearest, from his teens.[108] His verdict brings on a premonition of the
attack by which Alun is shockingly killed off (p. 340), precipitated
across a sofa in an ignominious parody of '[a] fearsome thrash with
Mrs No-holds-barred'.[109]

Alun rounds on a friend who harps on his 'poetical progenitor'
(p. 307), a snarl of fury from the lexicon of Harold Bloom.[110] In the
same technical vein, he reminds himself that 'the whole point' of
his writing is 'to set one's face against anything that could be called
modernism' (p. 285). In crisis, he makes an agonised effort to evaluate Brydan's poetry, becoming, in the process, indistinguishable from
his creator. Both had 'once spent most of an evening' with the poet;
and, when the chips are down, neither is sure of the answer to Alun's
question: 'talented charlatanry, or deeply flawed works of genius?'
(p. 303).[111] In one of his last letters to Larkin, Amis asked for his help
for the first time in decades:

I have as I may have said a Dylan-like character . . . safely long dead but some of the others bother about him. I wish you'd take your finger out and run me up half a dozen lines of sub-Thomas to come swimming back into someone's head. I think I could do it myself, though not as well, and there's no actual need for it anyway but it would be fun to have it there for a chap to wonder whether it was genius or piss. What about having a shot?[112]

In his last letter, Larkin apologises for being unable to comply, suggesting that Amis 'use that wonderful stuff from *That Uncertain Feeling*'.[113] Both Probert's verse and *The Old Devils* have the Celtic intricacy of the Book of Kells. As 'artistic heir' (p. 304) to the 'safely long dead' Brydan, Amis in the guise of Alun is comprehensively destroyed. If '[a] good poem about failure is a success',[114] however, so is a good novel about poetic defeat.

Amis's 'Mean Old Philip Thomas Blues' echo Thomas as often and as intimately as Larkin.[115] In his relief that 'the work of words went all right this morning' (p. 287), Alun alludes to the courageous poem in which Thomas outfaces the defeat suffered by Weaver: 'To surrender now is to pay the expensive ogre twice'.[116] Alun's reflections on 'how he was . . . making out as the organ-voice of Wales in Wales' (p. 282) go one further, echoing Larkin imitating Thomas: 'You may take me, young Amis, as the organ voice of old England. The genital-organ voice.'[117] Neither poet forgot a word that had ever passed between them; nor had Larkin lost his sense of affinity with Thomas, with whom he, too, once 'had a drink', after his performance at the English Club.[118] Comradely asides begin in the 1940s ('a "Pillar of the Swiss", as Dylan Thomas would spoonerise')[119] and are scattered throughout *Required Writing* ('the reading habits of Dylan Thomas matched mine – he never read anything hard'),[120] alongside a startling remark: 'I know it sounds absurd to say so, but I should say I had more in common with Dylan Thomas than with any other "famous writer"'.[121]

Amis's review of Thomas's letters, commending him to oblivion, appeared just as *The Old Devils* was 'entering its climacteric'.[122] This striking phrase from the same late letter seems to resonate with Larkin's approaching death (he died a fortnight later); and also with Amis's post-menopausal failure of desire. Peter and his wife 'had not touched each other for nearly ten years' (p. 163). Nevertheless, when Amis as 'sub-Brydan' poet is put to death, Amis as prodigal lover is reunited with his bride.[123] Peter and Rhiannon had not married. 'Like Hilly', who became Amis's first wife, Rhiannon 'got pregnant, but unlike Hilly she went through with the abortion'; unlike Alun, Hilly's undeceased husband was a member of the new household: '"Nay, stare not so", Amis wrote to Larkin . . . "Well, you'd be justified in staring a bit"'.[124] But there the dissimilarity ends. Constructed upon Amis's implausible return to cohabitation with Hilly, the scenario has the ring of fictional truth:

> Though you might not think so . . . and there was certainly a time when I forgot it myself, I've always loved you and I do to this day. I'm sorry it sounds ridiculous because I'm so fat and horrible, and not at all nice or even any fun, but I mean it. I only wish it was worth more. (p. 375)

A second redemption concerns the published but long-since-gone-quiet minor poet, Malcolm Cellan-Davies. In a restitution of dignity to Welsh culture, he is engaged, on the last page of the book, in a translation of '*Heledd Cariad*', 'a long poem by Cynddelw Mawr ap Madog Wladaidd (*c.*1320–?1388)',[125] 'more of an adaptation, actually, for among other adjustments he had altered the physical character-istics of the central figure to correspond with Rhiannon's' (p. 384). There is not a hint of a sneer. Troubled, 'in his conscientious way', by any slur on Brydan's poetry (p. 29), Malcolm would have been more in sympathy with an encomium in *The Daily Mirror*, by the author of the novel in which he appears:

> In almost everything Thomas wrote he created a particular kind of excite-ment no one else has matched, what seems a quite new sense that the realms of the imagination are infinite[.][126]

Higher praise would be hard to find, yet it dates from the same year as 'On the Scrounge'. If Charlie gives a voice within the novel to the jeering intelligence of the Movement, Malcolm speaks for dedication and generosity. 'If she had found love with Peter, he was glad' (p. 384). Reflecting on Rhiannon's marriage and on Alun's affair with his wife Gwen, he sorts out his collection of 'jazz records' (p. 384), 'exactly in line with Larkin's tastes', 'soundly anti-modernist', and thus tes-timony to 'the admirable character beneath his social awkwardness' (Powell, p. 224). The book ends with self-reflexive correspondences by which a Princess of the Powys dynasty becomes Rhiannon Weaver becomes Hilly Kilmarnock; a 'deeply flawed' (p. 303) charlatan becomes the 'embodiment' (p. 12) of artistic integrity; and the novel becomes a Welsh 'poem', 'the best tribute he could pay' (p. 384), not only to Hilly, but also to Larkin, one of whose warmest tributes to Thomas was occasioned by the news of his death:

> I can't believe D.T. is truly dead. It seems absurd. Three people who've altered the face of poetry, & the *youngest* has to die. I thought *The Times* did him proud.[127]

'Even Philip Larkin managed to extricate himself from the baleful influence of Kingsley Amis' (Lycett, p. 374). As we all must; as Amis himself succeeds in doing in *The Old Devils*. In the dream-like transformations at the heart of the book, artistic defeat and moral perdition are expiated by 'unjudging love'.[128]

As regards 'the world of [2020]', of which Dylan Thomas is 'as much a part' as Amis and Larkin, Instagram and *Match of the Day*, the 60-year-reign of the forties' sneer is drawing to a close. One would like to think 'that the long period of [anti-]modernism is not only over but will be looked back on' as a spectacular imposition. And the enmity between Movement principle and Apocalyptic sublimity is another. Millennial culture can accommodate both.

Notes

1 Philip Larkin, letter to J. B. Sutton (20 November 1941); *Selected Letters of Philip Larkin: 1940–1985*, ed. Anthony Thwaite (London: Faber and Faber, 1992), p. 28. It was Larkin, 'an extravagant admirer', who 'introduced Amis' to W. H. Auden; Paul Fussell, *The Anti-Egotist: Kingsley Amis, Man of Letters* (New York, NY: Oxford University Press, 1994), p. 168. Gwen Watkins records an earlier 'pyrotechnic display of wild, brilliant, anarchic comments on the contemporary literary scene', producing 'shrieks of laughter', 'cheering' and 'applause', at St John's College, Cambridge, on 13 February 1937; Gwen Watkins, *Dylan Thomas: Portrait of a Friend* (Llandysul: Gomer Press, 1983; Talybont: Y Lolfa, 2005), p. 53.

2 Kingsley Amis, *Collected Poems: 1944–1979* (London: Hutchinson, 1979; London: Penguin Books) pp. 77–8.

3 Lolette Kuby, *An Uncommon Poet for the Common Man: A Study of Philip Larkin's Poetry* (The Hague: Mouton, 1974), p. 160.

4 'I had lost all my earlier enthusiasm for his writing'; Kingsley Amis, *Memoirs* (London: Hutchinson, 1991; London: Penguin Books, 1992), p. 133.

5 *The Letters of Kingsley Amis*, ed. Zachary Leader (London: HarperCollins, 2000), p. 52.

6 Blake Morrison, *The Movement: English Poetry and Fiction of the 1950s* (Oxford: Oxford University Press, 1980), p. 25.

7 Donald Davie, cited Kenneth Allott, *The Penguin Book of Contemporary Verse* (Harmondsworth: Penguin, 2nd edn, 1962), p. 323.

8 Kingsley Amis, 'Against Romanticism', *A Case of Samples* (London: Gollancz, 1956); Amis, *Collected Poems: 1944–1979*, pp. 35–6.

9 [Neville Braybrooke?], 'Selected Notices', *The Wind and the Rain*, 3/3 (Autumn 1946), 158–70 (161) (anonymous, but, on stylistic and contextual grounds, almost certainly by the magazine's editor Braybrooke).

10 Kingsley Amis, 'Against Romanticism', *Collected Poems: 1944–1979*, pp. 35–6. Cf. Morrison, *The Movement* (p. 160): 'The poetic source is Robert Graves's "An English Wood", which like Amis's poem features a determinedly temperate landscape'; not, however, the word 'temperate'. Morrison proceeds to propose a 'critical study' by F. W. Bateson, prefaced by a poem entitled 'The Anti-Romantics', as a 'more direct source' (*English Poetry* (London: Longmans, 1950), p. ix). Amis's poem has not been assigned to a date prior to 1956, but in view of the date of the review in *The Wind and the Rain*, influence on Bateson by Amis appears more probable.

11 [Braybrooke?], 'Selected Notices', p. 161, citing John Milton, *Paradise Lost*, ed. Alastair Fowler (London: Longman, 1968 [1667]), Book II, line 406, p. 108. Note the performative confirmation of the post-war currency of the term 'Apocalyptic'.

12 Rob Jackaman, *The Course of English Surrealist Poetry Since the 1930s* (Lewiston, NY: Edwin Mellen, 1989), p. 102.

13 John Wain, *First Reading*, BBC Third Programme (26 April–24 September 1953).

14 John Wain, 'Oxford and After', review of *Oxford Poetry 1948* (Oxford: Blackwell, 1948), in *Outposts*, 13, edited by Howard Sergeant (Manchester, Spring 1949), pp. 22–3.

15 Amis, *Collected Poems: 1944–1979*, p. 65.

16 Geoffrey Strachan, 'Shooting New Lines', *Gemini*, 1 (Spring 1957), p. 65.

17 Gordon Wharton, letter to Burns Singer (3 July 1956), private archive. Wharton is one of the *New Lines* candidates rejected by Amis as 'pretty pisspoor', though 'far from spineless', in his role as de facto co-editor, in a letter to Robert Conquest, on 23 January 1955; Amis, *Letters*, p. 419.

18 J. W. Lambert, *Sunday Times* (6 January 1957); Arnold Kettle, *Daily Worker* (12 February 1957); both cited Zachary Leader, *The Life of Kingsley Amis* (London: Cape, 2006), p. 368.

19 Philip Larkin, letter to J. Norton Smith (14 April 1974), cited Leader, *Life*, p. 697.

20 Kingsley Amis, *A Frame of Mind: Eighteen Poems* (Reading: School of Art, Reading University, 1953). See listing and 'Bookseller Image', Blackwell's Rare Books (Oxford) *http://www.abebooks.co.uk* (accessed 17 April 2015). Dylan Thomas, *18 Poems* (London: The Sunday Referee and The Parton Bookshop, 1934).

21 Kingsley Amis, letter to Philip Larkin (29 April 1951), 'last week, that crazy Welch fellow came here to give a talk . . . frothing at the mouth with piss'; Amis, *Letters*, pp. 55–6.

22 Kingsley Amis, *Lucky Jim* (London: Gollancz, 1953 [January 1954]; London: Penguin Books, 1961), p. 7 and *passim*.

23 Kingsley Amis, *The Old Devils* (London: Hutchinson, 1986; London: Penguin Books, 1986), p. 11 and *passim*.

24 Kingsley Amis, 'On the Scrounge', *The Observer* (3 November 1985), in Kingsley Amis, *The Amis Collection: Selected Non-Fiction 1954–1990* (London: Hutchinson, 1990; London: Penguin Books, 1991), pp. 208–10 (p. 210).

25 Kingsley Amis, letter to Philip Larkin (17 November 1985); Amis, *Letters*, p. 1013.

26 Kingsley Amis, 'My hymn of doves', *Bright November* (London: Fortune Press, 1947), p. 12.

27 Dylan Thomas, *Collected Poems of Dylan Thomas: The New Centenary Edition*, ed. John Goodby (London: Weidenfeld & Nicolson, 2014), p. 99.

28 W. H. Auden, 'The Truest Poetry is the Most Feigning', *Collected Shorter Poems 1927–1957* (London: Faber, 1966), p. 317.

29 The concocted first line is intended to illustrate the affinity.

30 James Fenton, 'Kingsley Amis: Against Fakery', in *The Movement Reconsidered*, ed. Zachary Leader (Oxford: Oxford University Press, 2009), pp. 106–22 (p. 109).

31 Clive James, 'Profile 4: Kingsley Amis', *The New Review*, 1/4 (July 1974), 21–8; cited John McDermott, *Kingsley Amis: An English Moralist* (London: Macmillan, 1989), p. 15.

32 Clive James, 'The Examined Life of Kingsley Amis', *From the Land of Shadows* (London: Cape, 1982), pp. 141–7 (p. 141).

33 Andrew James, '*The Old Devils* or an Englishman's Attempt Write a Welsh Novel', in *Comparisons and Interactions Within/Across Cultures*, ed. Ludmilla Kostova, Iona Sarieva and Mihaela Irimia (Veliko Tarnovo, Bulgaria: St Cyril and St Methodius University Press, 2012), pp. 181–7 (p. 182): 'a "smeared" copy of Thomas's *The Map of Love* is on the bed of the Amisian character, Francis Archer, who calls the poet "smashing"'.

34 Fussell, *The Anti-Egotist*, p. 168.

35 William H. Pritchard, 'Entertaining Amis', in *Playing it by Ear: Literary Essays and Reviews* (Amherst, MA: Massachusetts University Press, 1994), pp. 75–83 (p. 76).

36 Neil Powell, *Amis & Son: Two Literary Generations* (London: Pan Macmillan, 2008), p. 49.

37 Fussell, *The Anti-Egotist*, p. 170. Leader, *Life*, p. 154. Compare Bradford's oddly condescending account: 'the time [Larkin] spent with Amis in Oxford was rather like a living parody of serious young writers honing their skills'; Richard Bradford, *Lucky Him: The Life of Kingsley Amis* (London: Peter Owen, 2001), p. 33.

38 Philip Larkin, 'Forget What Did', *Collected Poems*, ed. Anthony Thwaite (London: Faber and Faber and The Marvell Press, 1988), p. 184. Philip Larkin, 'Send No Money'; Larkin, *Collected Poems*, p. 146.

39 Kingsley Amis, interviewed by Ray Connolly, 'A Childhood: Kingsley Amis', *The Times* (24 September 1990); cited Leader, *Life*, p. 130.

40 J. Lucas and James Barker, *The Killing Ground: The Battle of the Falaise Gap, August 1944* (London: Batsford, 1978), p. 158.

41 Dwight D. Eisenhower, *Crusade in Europe* (New York, NY: Doubleday, 1948), p. 279.

42 Wolfgang Schneider, *Tigers in Normandy* (Mechanicsburg, PA: Stackpole Books, 2014), p. 357.

43 Kingsley Amis, '27 January 1946 (for G.W.)'; Amis, *Bright November*, p. 19.

44 The use of the word 'midden', in the same context of tainted air as the 'midden odours' of 'Elisabeth at Chamboix', suggests that this poem post-dates Falaise, despite Amis's 'Note' to the effect that the poems 'were written since October, 1943', bar six, of which this is one (*Bright November*, p. 2). Cf. William Shakespeare, *Measure for Measure*, I. 2. 121 (*c*.1603–4, ed. J. W. Lever, *The Arden Shakespeare* (London: Methuen, 1965), p. 15): 'Like rats that ravin down their proper bane'; Shakespeare, *Cymbeline*, IV. 2. 171–2 (*c*.1610, ed. J. M. Nosworthy, *The Arden Shakespeare* (London: Methuen, 1955), p. 127): 'they are as gentle / As zephyrs blowing below the violet'.

45 Brian Harker, *Louis Armstrong's Hot Five and Hot Seven Recordings* (New York, NY: Oxford University Press, 2011), p. 24.

46 John Chilton, *Sidney Bechet: The Wizard of Jazz* (London: Macmillan, 1987), p. 107.

47 Philip Larkin, 'For Sidney Bechet'; Larkin, *Collected Poems*, p. 83.

48 Philip Larkin, *All What Jazz: A Record Diary, 1961–68* (London: Faber and Faber, 1970), p. 108.

49 Philip Larkin, 'Introduction to *Jill*' (1975), *Required Writing: Miscellaneous Pieces 1955–1982* (London: Faber and Faber, 1983), pp. 17–26 (p. 22).

50 Kingsley Amis, *The Riverside Villas Murder* (London: Cape, 1973), pp. 156–7; noted by Powell, *Amis & Son*, p. 181.

51 Gabriel Pearson's claims for Thomas and Auden as 'apocalyptic "twins"' are cited in John Goodby, *The Poetry of Dylan Thomas: Under the Spelling Wall* (Liverpool: Liverpool University Press, 2013), p. 35.

52 Philip Larkin, *Early Poems and Juvenilia*, ed. A. T. Tolley (London: Faber and Faber, 2005), pp. 73–4.

53 Larkin, *Selected Letters*, pp. 32–3.

54 Philip Larkin, letter to Kingsley Amis (11 April 1942), cited Andrew Motion, *Philip Larkin: A Writer's Life* (London: Faber and Faber, 1993), p. 75.

55 Bradford, *Lucky Him*, p. 46.

56 Shakespeare, *Julius Caesar*, III. 1. 151–2 (*c*.1599, ed. T. S. Dorsch, *The Arden Shakespeare* (London: Methuen, 1955), p. 71.

57 *Karl Miller, Dark Horses: An Experience of Literary Journalism* (London: Picador, 1998), p. 32, cited Leader, *Life*, p. 309.

58 Harold Bloom, *The Anxiety of Influence* (New York, NY: Oxford University Press, 1973), pp. 139–55.

59 Dylan Thomas, at the Oxford English Club (November 1941), as reported by Philip Larkin (see n. 1).

60 Shakespeare, *King Henry IV Part 1*, III. 1. 50–2 (*c*.1596–7, ed. A. R. Humphreys, *The Arden Shakespeare* (London: Methuen, 1960), p. 90).

61 Bloom, *The Anxiety of Influence*, pp. 139, 141, 146.

62 Kingsley Amis, *That Uncertain Feeling* (London: Gollancz, 1955), p. 108.

63 David Rees, 'Re-Assessment: That Petrine Cock', *The Spectator* (28 August 1965), p. 20.

[64] Rees, 'Re-Assessment: That Petrine Cock', p. 20.

[65] Dylan Thomas, *Under Milk Wood: A Play for Voices* (London: Dent, 1954).

[66] Shakespeare, *King Henry IV Part 1*, III. 1. 45–7, p. 89.

[67] Thomas, *Collected Poems*, p. 85.

[68] Amis, *That Uncertain Feeling*, p. 109.

[69] Kingsley Amis, letter to Philip Larkin (26 November 1953), Amis, *Letters*, p. 345: [deploring] 'ignorant horsepiss about [Thomas's] Welchness'.

[70] John Goodby, 'Notes to the Poems'; Thomas, *Collected Poems*, p. 395.

[71] J. F. Hendry, *The Bombed Happiness* (London: Routledge, 1942), p. 37. Amis would have been aware that 'Golgotha' was a prime target of anti-Apocalyptic artillery.

[72] 'Amis, too, was an adulterer who loved his wife and family, but in his former role he was far more prodigious and calculating than Lewis'; Bradford, *Lucky Him*, p. 120. As regards his own 'reluctance to lie (if any)', to borrow a 'censorious' expression from 'On the Scrounge' (*The Amis Collection*, p. 208), Amis's letter to Larkin about a visit to R. A. Caton, shady proprietor of the Fortune Press, puts the boot on the other foot (12 September 1947): 'having once told him I was leaving Oxford last June to get him to hurry my book I was instantly caught up in a wind-tunnel of improvised deceit – about which he was censorious and watchful' (Amis, *Letters*, p. 140).

[73] George Barker, 'Sacred Elegies', 5, *Eros in Dogma* (London: Faber and Faber, 1944); Barker, *Collected Poems* (London: Faber and Faber, 1987), p. 149. Barker, 'To My Son', *Poetry* (Chicago), 78/6 (1951), p. 320; Barker, *Collected Poems*, p. 259.

[74] T. S. Eliot, *The Complete Poems and Plays of T. S. Eliot* (London: Faber and Faber, 1969), p. 109.

[75] Mary Trevelyan, *T. S. Eliot: The Pope of Russell Square* (London: Enitharmon Press, 2008).

[76] Louis MacNeice, *Autumn Sequel: A Rhetorical Poem in XXVI Cantos* (London: Faber and Faber, 1954); MacNeice, *Collected Poems*, ed. E. R. Dodds (London: Faber and Faber, 1966), p. 356.

[77] Alan Pryce-Jones, *The Bonus of Laughter* (London: Hamish Hamilton, 1987), p. 28.

[78] Joseph Fernandez, *Popery Tottering to Its Fall in 1866: Shewing what the Spirit of Popery Has Been, Now Is, and Will be Untill It Perishes from off the Face of the Earth* (London: Passmore and Alabaster, 1865).

[79] Kingsley Amis, *Socialism and the Intellectuals*, Fabian Society Tract 304 (London: Fabian Society, 1957).

[80] Kingsley Amis, 'Why Lucky Jim Turned Right', *Sunday Telegraph* (2 July 1967), in Kingsley Amis, *What Became of Jane Austen and Other Questions* (London: Cape, 1970), pp. 213–20.

[81] *Spectrum: A Spectator Miscellany*, ed. Ian Gilmour and Iain Hamilton (London: Longmans, Green, 1956).

[82] Kingsley Amis, 'Thomas the Rhymer', in *Spectrum*, ed. Gilmour and Hamilton, pp. 1–4 (p. 2).

[83] Deb Lindsey, 'Angels on Horseback', *The Washington Post* (1 August 2012) *http://www.washingtonpost.com* (accessed 17 April 2015).

84 Lewis Carroll, 'The Walrus and the Carpenter', *Through the Looking-Glass and What Alice Found There* (London: Merrell, 2006 [1872]), p. 39.

85 Michael Davie, 'Notebook: Lucky Jim discovers there's life after 60', *The Observer* (25 April 1982), p. 16. Amis describes Thomas as '[a] Bloomsburyite to his *dirty* fingernails' (26 November 1953), letter to Philip Larkin; Amis, *Letters*, p. 345.

86 Bradford, *Lucky Him*, p. 378.

87 Amis, *The Old Devils*, p. 12.

88 Andrew Dixon, 'Time Mellows an Old Devil', *News of the World* (14 September 1986); cited Leader, *Life*, p. 740.

89 Philip Larkin, 'An Interview with John Haffenden' (1981), *Further Requirements: Interviews, Broadcasts, Statements and Book Reviews 1952–85*, ed. Anthony Thwaite (London: Faber and Faber, 2001), pp. 47–62 (p. 57).

90 Kingsley Amis, *Jake's Thing* (London: Hutchinson, 1978).

91 Kingsley Amis, letter to John McDermott (25 April 1985); Amis, *Letters*, p. 997.

92 Wynford Vaughan-Thomas, 'Hiraeth in NW3', in *The New Oxford Book of English Light Verse*, ed. Kingsley Amis (Oxford: Oxford University Press, 1978), p. 273.

93 Wynford Vaughan-Thomas, *Wynford Vaughan-Thomas's Wales* (London: Michael Joseph, 1981).

94 Vaughan-Thomas, *Wynford Vaughan-Thomas's Wales*, cited on back of dust-jacket.

95 Vaughan-Thomas, *Wynford Vaughan-Thomas's Wales*, p. 17. In February 1986, between completion and publication of *The Old Devils*, 'Amis travelled to Swansea for Radio Wales to make a programme entitled "Amis on Wales"'; Leader, *Life*, p. 934.

96 Dylan Thomas, 'The Three Weird Sisters', *The Filmscripts*, ed. John Ackerman (London: Dent, 1995), p. 299.

97 William Shakespeare, *Richard II*, II. 1. 50 (*c*.1595, ed. Peter Ure, *The Arden Shakespeare* (London: Methuen, 1956), p. 53).

98 'Just before he wrote to Larkin (on 17 November 1985), Stuart Thomas, Amis's host in Swansea, had asked [Amis] to become one of the trustees of Dylan Thomas's literary estate' (Bradford, *Lucky Him*, p. 375), prompted, at a guess, by Amis's damaging dismissal, 'On the Scrounge' (3 November 1985). As well as exploiting Amis's professional expertise, Stuart Thomas may have preferred to have him inside pissing out.

99 Powell, *Amis & Son*, p. 223.

100 'At school with Brydan my eye' (Amis, *The Old Devils*, p. 49).

101 Clive Gammon, cited Leader, *Life*, p. 352.

102 Andrew Lycett, *Dylan Thomas: A New Life* (London: Weidenfeld & Nicolson, 2003), p. 382.

103 Dylan Thomas, 'The Visitor', *The Collected Stories*, ed. Walford Davies (London: Weidenfeld & Nicolson, 2014 [1983]), p. 31.

104 Kingsley Amis, letter to Philip Larkin (9 January 1947); Amis, *Letters*, p. 109.

105 Charlie's slight elides the true title of Alun's book with a memoir of Dylan Thomas, W. R. Rodgers, Julian Maclaren-Ross and other bibulous denizens of Soho by Dan Davin: *Closing Times* (Oxford: Oxford University Press, 1975).

106 Kingsley Amis, letter from 'a selectively pro-Welsh Englishman' to the editor of *The Sunday Times* (14 August 1994), in reply to a 'News Review' article by George Tremlett (7 August 1994); Amis, *Letters*, pp. 1132–3.

107 Dylan Thomas, 'And death shall have no dominion'; Thomas, *Collected Poems*, p. 23.

108 Leader, *Life*, p. 31: 'From childhood onwards Amis suffered from night terrors and screaming fits.' Leader compares a hair-raising 'description of Amis's howling' by his second wife, Elizabeth Jane Howard (Leader, *Life*, pp. 676, 742).

109 Kingsley Amis, 'Aberdarcy: the Chaucer Road'; Amis, *Collected Poems*, p. 115.

110 Arnold Bloom, 'Introduction', *Essayists and Prophets* (Philadelphia, PA: Chelsea House Publications, 2005), pp. xi–xii (p. xi).

111 Compare the curious equivocation in 'An Evening with Dylan Thomas', *The Spectator*, 1957, in Kingsley Amis, *What Became of Jane Austen? And Other Questions*, pp. 59–64 (p. 62): 'Although obviously without all charlatanry, he did here and there sound or behave like a charlatan'.

112 Kingsley Amis, letter to Philip Larkin (17 November 1985); Amis, *Letters*, pp. 1013–14.

113 Philip Larkin, letter to Kingsley Amis (21 November 1985); Larkin, *Selected Letters*, p. 758.

114 Philip Larkin, in Robert Phillips, 'An Interview with *Paris Review*' (1982), *Required Writing*, pp. 57–76 (p. 74).

115 Charlie's 'representations to himself while Garth quacked indefatigably on' include a variation on 'Dockery and Son' ('Life is first boredom, then fear'; Thomas, *Collected Poems*, p. 153): 'Life was first boredom, then more boredom' (p. 325). Leader identifies 'deeply felt echoes' of 'To the Sea', 'Church Going' and 'An Arundel Tomb'; Leader, *Life*, p. 745.

116 Dylan Thomas, 'On no work of words'; Thomas, *Collected Poems*, p. 104.

117 Philip Larkin, letter to Kingsley Amis (19 October 1943); Larkin, *Selected Letters*, p. 80.

118 Larkin, 'An Interview with *Paris Review*', p. 67.

119 Philip Larkin, letter to Kingsley Amis (19 October 1943); Larkin, *Selected Letters*, p. 79. The Helvetia in Old Compton Street, Soho, was 'popularly referred to as the Swiss pub'; Robert Fraser, *The Chameleon Poet: A Life of George Barker* (London: Cape, 2001), p. 215.

120 Philip Larkin, in Miriam Gross, 'An Interview with the *Observer*' (1979), *Required Writing*, pp. 47–56 (p. 53).

121 Larkin, 'An Interview with *Paris Review*', p. 67.

122 Kingsley Amis, letter to Philip Larkin (17 November 1985); Amis, *Letters*, p. 1013.

123 'Those poems are all sub-Brydan' (*The Old Devils*, p. 11). This dismissal by Gwen Cellan-Davies introduces the theme of poetic defeat on the first page of the novel.

124 Leader, *Life*, p. 743, citing a letter from Amis to Larkin (27 August 1981); Larkin, *Selected Letters*, p. 927.

125 'Cynddelw Mawr ap Madog Wladaidd' is a fictional composite of two real poets, Cynddelw Brydydd Mawr and Dafydd Bach ap Madog Wladaidd, both anthologised in *The Oxford Book of Welsh Verse in English*, ed. Gwyn

Jones (Oxford: Oxford University Press, 1977), p. vi. The elided (and mutated) 'Brydydd' dissociates this fictional true poet from 'Brydan', yet signals a submerged affinity. '*Heledd Cariad*' (Heledd Dear) is an imaginary part of the medieval *Heledd Cycle*, on which Thomas drew for 'The Woman Speaks'; Goodby, *The Poetry of Dylan Thomas: Under the Spelling Wall*, p. 77.

126 Kingsley Amis, *The Pleasure of Poetry: From His* Daily Mirror *Column* (London: Cassell, 1990), unpaginated. The final choice, for January 1985, is 'Light breaks where no sun shines'; Thomas, *Collected Poems*, pp. 46–7.

127 Philip Larkin, letter to Patsy Strang (11 November 1953); Larkin, *Selected Letters*, p. 218. Thwaite identifies the other two as Auden and Eliot.

128 Dylan Thomas, 'This side of the truth (for Llewelyn)'; Thomas, *Collected Poems*, p. 174.

9

'[E]RUPTIONS, FARTS, DAMPSQUIBS [AND] BARRELORGANS': ADMINISTRATING DYLAN THOMAS IN HIS CENTENARY YEAR

Kieron Smith

Visit Swansea and I defy you to avoid the ghosts of the city's most famous son. Jump off the train, and there he is on a mural on the platform wall, a disembodied head floating above the urban land-scape. Exit the station, and there he is again, covering the wall of a derelict pub; bigger this time, a looming, 15-foot high image, but unmistakably him.[1] Head south towards the city centre, down High Street and then Castle Street, and you'll soon stumble on the giant leaf-boat sculpture in Castle Gardens, inspired by 'Rain cuts the place we tread'.[2] Carry on south, down Wind Street, and you'll pass No Sign Wine Bar, one of numerous Swansea drinking holes claiming its connection; this one is allegedly immortalised as the 'Wine Vaults' in the short story 'The Followers'. Running alongside is Salubrious Passage: an ironic name, of course, and rendered in the same story 'Paradise Alley' (I wouldn't recommend walking down there). Carry on to the end of Wind Street and up ahead will be the old *Evening Post* building, the paper on which Thomas briefly worked as a junior reporter.[3] Just beyond that is the Marina, where you'll find the Dylan Thomas Theatre, the Dylan Thomas Centre, a statue of Captain Cat,[4] and, naturally, another of the man himself.[5]

Now you're just a five-minute walk from the bus station. On the way, you'll see Swansea's Civic Centre, outside which you might find council vehicles branded with Thomas's signature. At the station you can catch the number 5 Cwmdonkin Circular, a bus splashed with Thomas's image. This will take you up to 5 Cwmdonkin Drive, Thomas's birthplace. Close by is Cwmdonkin Park, haunt of the poet's youth, strewn with statues, plaques, and references to the poet. By now you'll probably need a drink. Wander back down the hill to the Uplands and chances are you'll end up in the Uplands Tavern, another Thomas haunt, with its obligatory Thomas 'snug', in which you can sit among framed photos, paintings, sketches, and collages of the poet. Lift your 'brass-bright' beer (that quote stencilled on the walls of too many pubs to mention) and, lo-and-behold, there he is, perfectly eliding the sacred and profane: a man with a legendarily troubled relationship with alcohol proudly brandished on your beer mat.

Thomas would surely have appreciated the irony of this superabundance. He seems not to have been precious about controlling his public image during his lifetime. In the 1930s and 1940s, you could walk into a bookshop and find him not only in the poetry section, but in fiction; out on the news stand he'd be found in newspapers and magazines; turn on the wireless and you'd have heard the boom of his voice; visit the cinema and you'd hear the unmistakable resonance of his writing in documentary films screened before the main feature. If you could afford a television in the years before the war, you might have caught him on screen. This capacity for uncontainable ubiquity can in one sense be understood as the extension of a poetics that is, in John Goodby's terms, 'premised on defiance of paraphrase, over-determination, boundary-breaking and "excess"'.[6] Just as Thomas's poetry 'confounds standard distinctions',[7] so too does his reputation: he continues to flummox straightforward categorisations of cultural distinction (elite/popular), nationality (Welsh/British), genre, and form. The quasi-authoritative quotability of his poetry in particular, combined with its lack of 'easily dated, specific sociocultural details',[8] means that lines can as easily be read in anthologies of twentieth century poetry as they can be heard in Hollywood blockbusters chronicling interstellar space exploration.[9]

While the ceaseless reification of Thomas across this endless array of contexts may, on the surface, appear as an inexplicably contradictory spectacle, there is, nevertheless, a set of priorities at work. As Guy Debord stated, 'the spectacle, though it turns reality on its head, is itself a product of real activity.'[10] Often, this 'real activity' is bluntly commercial. However, such processes of reification can also be promoted by the state; albeit by state administrations strongly skewed by commercial priorities. The year 2014 marked the centenary of Dylan Thomas's birth, and the year-long, state-subsidised yet commercially-focused festival that was organised to capitalise on this exemplified the pinnacle of the use of Dylan Thomas as a spectacular figure. It is not the aim of this chapter to evaluate the vast range of interpretations, reifications and performances of Dylan Thomas generated by artists and writers during 2014 and beyond; that would take another chapter – perhaps another book – entirely. It will, instead, focus on the strangely contradictory ways in which the idea of Dylan Thomas and, by extension, the idea of culture, was constructed and contested àt multiple administrative scales in Wales in the run up to, and during, 2014. To interpret the mechanisms at work, this chapter will utilise perspectives from cultural policy studies, a field broadly concerned with how, why, and to what ends 'culture' is 'administrated' at the level of state institutions in relation to wider, ever-changing socio-economic conditions. Informed also by cultural geography, it will examine the extra-textual 'traces' of Dylan Thomas, the 'marks, residues [and] remnants'[11] – often contradictory and overdetermined – that emerge in multiple contexts within what Henri Lefebvre called 'representational space' – that is, 'space as directly lived through its associated images and symbols . . . the space of "inhabitants" and "users"'.[12] It will argue that the strange ways in which Dylan Thomas has been reified in the realm of representational space in the years since his death can be traced to shifting, contradictory attitudes towards the administration of culture at the scales of the national and municipal in Wales.

Cultural policy, or the 'administration' of culture, is nothing new. As Theodor Adorno noted, '[w]hoever speaks of culture speaks of administration as well',[13] by which he implied that the very act of distinguishing 'culture' as a social phenomenon bespeaks a society whose organising principles are based not on the expression of human creativity as an end in itself – 'pure humanity' as Adorno called it[14] – but rather on 'the administrative view, the task of which, looking down from on high, is to assemble, distribute, evaluate and organize'.[15] In other words, the administration of culture has been in process as long as debates about the definition of culture have existed; indeed, for Adorno, these are two sides of the same coin. Nevertheless, it is possible to trace the emergence of the modern articulation of the administration of culture – specifically, state intervention in the production and promotion of the arts – to within the last one hundred years. Pre-war initiatives in Britain included the BBC (1927), the Standing Commission on Museums and Galleries (1931), and the British Film Institute (BFI, 1933),[16] but direct state sponsorship of the arts first emerged as an idea with the Council for the Encouragement of Music and the Arts (CEMA, 1940), a wartime initiative spearheaded by liberal economist J. M. Keynes. Keynes's vision of post-war British society was underpinned by the idea of a mixed economy of capitalist economic growth supported by state-sponsored public services and infrastructure, and this vision extended to his ideas about the cultural attitudes this society should adopt. Keynes, like many others at that time, felt that the populist commercial culture emerging out of a rapidly democratising industrial society posed a threat to the social fabric. He therefore advocated a programme of state sponsorship of the arts designed to uphold social values through 'universal opportunity for contact with traditional and contemporary arts in the noblest forms'.[17] CEMA would become the blueprint for the Arts Council of Great Britain (ACGB, 1946), the arms-length organisation tasked with distributing public funds to the arts until 1994, when it was separated into respective organisations for Wales, England, Scotland and Northern Ireland.

Dylan Thomas's connection with CEMA neatly illustrates the particular administrative priorities of cultural policy in that era, as well as his own peripherality in relation to post-war conceptions of cultural value. Established at a time when the definitions of 'high' and 'low' culture were being radically renegotiated, CEMA was designed not to cultivate new, emergent forms of creativity, but to utilise calcified notions of 'high' culture as the political instrument of a certain form of social organisation. It is therefore apt that Thomas, a well-established poet potboiling as a scriptwriter for the Strand Film Company in the 1940s, wrote the screenplay for the Strand production *CEMA* (1942), a documentary film showcasing the activities of the new organisation to the 'mass' public. Not deemed worthy of celebration on screen, Thomas's poverty forced him to labour behind the scenes of this new, soon to be popular cultural form. An artist subject to the whims of the labour market, he was de facto on the 'popular' side of the high-low divide that would dominate cultural discourse in Britain for at least the next three decades, a position confirmed by his work elsewhere as a popular radio broadcaster and general proto-celebrity *enfant terrible*. Indeed, during the 1960s, when debates continued to rage over the supposedly debased commercialisation of British culture, a time when the output of the ACGB was increased substantially in the service of bolstering the high arts,[18] Thomas was being appropriated by the very popular cultural icons that represented the threat.[19] The result, as Goodby notes, was that 'Thomas came to symbolize the threat of the middle-brow to many of the more mandarin and snobbish cultural arbiters, especially in England'.[20] Indeed in Wales, too, Thomas was deemed extraneous by an anglophone group of Welsh writers that were to utilise the new Literature Section of the newly-enhanced Welsh Arts Council[21] to promote Wales-focused writing as the basis for imagining the nation in a new light.[22]

However prescriptive the Keynesian view that 'culture' could, with the right policy mechanisms in place, assist the creation of a better society, this at least had at its core the conception that culture was something of inherent human value. Yet by the 1980s, a sustained era of deindustrialisation, mass unemployment and fiscal austerity in Britain resulted in a climate of 'entrepreneurialism' in which everything was commodifiable and nothing sacrosanct.[23] The result, as Jim McGuigan notes, was that 'the discourse of the market [predominated] in cultural policy as in everything else'.[24] The decline in the industrial and manufacturing base saw the rise of the discourse of the cultural and creative 'industries' to fill the gap, which in policy terms manifested in the recruitment of culture as a front for new forms of urban planning and regeneration based on 'high wage finance and business services, including design and other creative industries, and lower wage jobs in retail, tourism, and hospitality'.[25] In this context, the earlier sniffy distaste for Thomas gave way to a new-found enthusiasm for a figure whose commercial popularity was already very much proven.

The sum of these developments was that by the second decade of the twenty-first century, Thomas had been certified as a powerful brand of civic and economic development. As such, the centenary of his birth was anticipated with enthusiasm in the offices of social and cultural administration, particularly in Wales. Coincidentally, 2014 marked fifteen years since the arrival of devolution in Wales, and despite the 'astonishing speed' with which devolution had become an accepted part of the fabric of Welsh society,[26] the question of whether this political arrangement would bring material benefits to the people of Wales was very much in the air. Even as the first shockwaves of the 2008 economic crash receded, Wales still lagged woefully behind the rest of the UK by many measures of social wellbeing, with GVA stuck at around 72.3 per cent of the UK average at the end of 2013.[27] It is therefore unsurprising that at this time the idea of Dylan Thomas was enthusiastically welcomed by the Welsh Assembly Government (WAG).[28]

The central force driving this was a renewed faith in tourism and inward investment as a deliverer of wealth and wellbeing to Wales. Whilst at the time lacking any direct levers of revenue raising, WAG did have powers to devise its own tourism strategy and to 'support culture'.[29] With these limited powers in place, culture was inevitably enlisted in the service of the economy. In 2010, in the context of what it admitted were 'exceptional financial challenges',[30] WAG created a 'Major Events Unit' to create and attract 'mega-events' to Wales. Picking up on the recent widespread enthusiasm for 'mega-events' in Western economies as tools to attract tourism and foreign direct investment,[31] this new unit was set a remit to create 'a positive external reputation and brand image for Wales'[32] and 'deliver a series of economic, social, cultural and legacy benefits to Wales'.[33] These would be primarily major sporting events, but would also include musical and cultural festivals. In a sign of the extent to which economic concerns were now driving the cultural policy agenda, it was the Major Events Unit (MEU) that was tasked with 'steering' the celebration of Dylan Thomas's centenary. The MEU supplied £300,000, which was supplemented by £300,000 Arts Lottery Funding. ACW was tasked with administrating and distributing the funds among stakeholders and artists via a competitive application process. In total, ACW administered a sum in excess of £750,000. In addition to this, the Councils of Swansea, Ceredigion and Carmarthenshire contributed considerable funds of their own to the celebrations.[34]

As might be expected in this context, the ambitions for the centenary were framed by the steering group principally in economic terms. An early strategy document drew up seven key objectives that the centenary was to follow. Three of these objectives repeated essentially the same mantra relating to the centenary's potential to encourage tourism and inward investment.

[The] festival to mark the centenary of Dylan Thomas [*sic*] birth will be used

1.[. . .] to enhance Wales [*sic*] reputation as a world class events destination [. . .]

5.[. . .] to help raise Wales's international profile, as an inspirational, creative country to visit, invest in, and learn in, in key markets including London, and beyond, including USA [. . .]

6.[. . .] to drive visitor numbers and spend [. . .].[35]

The seventh objective outlined the ambition to stimulate 'the creative industries sector', and if we take the third objective's desire to use the centenary to stimulate 'reading and literacy projects' as evidence of a PISA-preoccupied Welsh Government convinced of the 'positive relationships between educational attainment and economic development',[36] then there was certainly a strongly economic dimension to this too. Only one of these objectives came close to treating Thomas's work as something of inherent, unquantifiable value rather than as an instrument of economic or social policy, though even this employed the thinly-veiled language of ceaseless growth: 'to help the people of Wales to recognise and celebrate Dylan Thomas and raise the profile of Dylan Thomas as a cultural icon within Wales'. (Quite how it was possible to 'raise the profile' of Wales's most famous and famously overdetermined cultural figure was not addressed.) The final objective specified the intention to use the centenary as an opportunity to 'engage with local areas associated with Dylan Thomas to help enhance community spirit.' This unenviably vague task was left to county councils to administer, and I will return to this point shortly.

These seven broad objectives were later fleshed out into fourteen key points in a later strategy document: *Dylan Thomas 100: A Symphony of Voices* (2012), which formed the outline for ACW's guide to artists and organisations seeking funding for centenary related activity.[37] The phrase 'symphony of voices' became the headline for much activity at this level, and while this document – compiled by writers and publishers – did more promisingly extend the vision beyond narrow economic and social instrumentalism to incorporate issues of language, interdisciplinary dialogue, artistic inspiration, and new media, what is notable is the extent to which the image and idea of 'Dylan Thomas' was stretched to fit the image of a unitary 'Wales'. This was, of course, a logical discursive consequence of a document commissioned at the level of devolved national government, especially a government at that time operating under a 'One Wales' coalition agreement between Welsh Labour and Plaid Cymru.[38] Indeed, the MEU strategy had been written with direct reference to the 'One Wales' agreement, and clearly stipulated its support only for events that would have an 'economic and socio-cultural impact at an all-Wales level'.[39] What is striking is the extent to which, at this level of cultural administration, any troubling sense of a figure with an at best complex, hybrid and unstable national identity is omitted in favour of an image of Thomas as straightforwardly, unproblematically 'Welsh'. The vision is by no means insular; the demands of Wales's positionality in a global economic marketplace are such that the 'international' dimension of the work was a key theme of the centenary's objectives. But the result is a conception of Thomas that is immaculately coterminous with – indeed, inseparable from – Wales and its landscape: his is a poetry with a 'home nation', 'rooted in the . . . landscape of Wales.'[40]

The phraseology of 'symphony of voices', a headline adopted in many Welsh Government and Arts Council of Wales steering documents, signals the desire to maintain a conceptual cohesion among the numerous activities that were to take place during the centenary year. This was further manifested in the branding logo commissioned by the Welsh Government. The final logo was a simple but effective image consisting of a monochrome illustration of Thomas (based on a Rollie McKenna photograph of Thomas dating from 1937), combined with a scan of the poet's signature. It was designed to be endlessly reproducible across a range of colour palettes and in every conceivable context (the tender document contains images of the logo on postage stamps, pin badges, pamphlets and T-shirts).[41] This was designed in response to a brief, written by Visit Wales, that emphasised the need to ensure 'consistent branding across a range of events and marketing, promotional and broadcast material'.[42] The branding was to support Visit Wales's 'vision', loudly proclaimed in the borderline aggressive language of competitive entrepreneurialism on the very front page of the brief: 'We want to change the status quo . . . We will not accept the received wisdom . . . Our marketing partners must share our commitment and vision.'[43] The branding functioned as a stamp of state endorsement of approved Thomas-related activity, including activity not awarded direct financial support by ACW.[44] It was to tie together the vast range of creative and commercial activity that took place during 2014 under a single banner that imaginatively connected 'Dylan Thomas' with an enterprising 'Wales' and its market-primed devolved government.

However, despite these efforts to construct a unified image and idea of Thomas for the centenary celebrations, the vision was elsewhere contested to meet the needs of different, perhaps even opposing, policy agendas, even among state administrations receiving funding from the same source. The result was that, at the level of city and county administration, a wholly different Dylan Thomas emerged, one that was required to speak not for the 'nation' but for the 'community', albeit a 'community' existing within an intensely competitive economic climate. The three councils of Ceredigion, Carmarthenshire and the City and County of Swansea (CCS) each received substantial funds from ACW to implement centenary activity. CCS received the largest sum, and, supplementing this with its own funds, engaged in the most intensive activities of the three.[45] The way it did so demonstrates some peculiar priorities, as well as clear tensions between cultural administration at the levels of the municipal and the national.

Swansea is no stranger to urban reifications of Dylan Thomas. Many of these can be traced to the new penchant for market-driven public policy that emerged wholesale in the 1980s, which resulted not only in a brazenly neoliberal agenda at the level of national government, but, at the same time, a shifting of fiscal responsibility out to cities and local authorities. Cities in particular were from this time 'expected to take on more responsibility for leveraging their own revenues'.[46] In effect, this meant competing with one another. In the area of cultural administration, this brought about the 'creative city concept' across the western world,[47] as cities sought to capitalise on culture as a means of branding and promoting themselves in the accelerated economic context of 'inter-urban competition for capitalist investment'.[48] Swansea is, by most measures, a 'small' or 'provincial' city,[49] and though barely smaller than Cardiff in terms of population, it lags far behind the capital economically.[50] This goes some way towards explaining the concerted resurrection of the image of Thomas in Swansea from the 1980s onwards, and the innumerable traces of him that we see in the city today, which happened not so much in the spirit of community development as an effort to survive an intensely competitive economic climate. In 1979, what was then Swansea City Council was in the process of redeveloping the docklands district of the city, and, as part of its new cultural initiative, gifted a derelict building in the area to Swansea Little Theatre. Naturally, the company named the new theatre after its most famous member on its opening in 1983.[51] Soon after, the statues of Thomas and Captain Cat sprang up in the new marina. In the early 1990s, Swansea jumped at the chance to host the 1995 UK Year of Literature and Writing, central to which was the creation of

'Tŷ Llên' ('Literature House'), a national literature centre for Wales. After a shambolic episode over the design of a new building,[52] the council settled on the refurbishment of its former Guildhall to house the centre. Although originally named 'Tŷ Llên', the city's designs on the building as another monument to its favourite son were made clear, as Nigel Jenkins noted, by the 'disproportionately huge' coat of arms embedded in the building's façade proclaiming it to be the Dylan Thomas Centre.[53] That this appropriation of Thomas as a frontispiece for urban economic regeneration persisted well into the new millennium is perhaps most crudely exemplified in the unabashedly economistic language of a study commissioned by the city in 2006: *Grab a Piece of the Action: A Tourism Strategy for the City and County of Swansea, 2006–2011*. Here Swansea is framed as a 'high quality environment', and Dylan Thomas a 'major brand' whose 'potential' must be 'maximised'.[54]

In keeping with this agenda, the City and County of Swansea embarked on a concerted campaign to maximise the regenerative potential of the Dylan Thomas centenary of 2014. It did so in a way that flaunted the directives of WAG to 'share' its 'commitment and vision'. Starting in early 2013, it convened a 'co-ordinating group' of local stakeholders, including civil servants, arts advocates, academics based at universities in the area, politicians, and representatives of local traders, who met regularly to discuss and shape progress. In this context, there was little effort to follow WAG's framing of Thomas as a 'national' figure. Rather, the emphasis was on constructing an image of Thomas that could benefit the local economy. This took the form of claiming Dylan Thomas as a figure with an almost spiritual connection to Swansea, and devising activities that would perform the idea of Thomas in these terms. There was discussion of Shakespeare's connection with Stratford-upon-Avon as the model of a cultural figure fused with a particular locality,[55] and some peculiar ideas were mooted to this end (including the invention of annual public rituals such as 'sounding church bells and ship horns at 11pm on 27 October',[56] or a 'torch-lit procession in Mumbles').[57] Thankfully, the actual celebrations avoided becoming a Welsh *Wicker Man*, though there was certainly a sacral quality to the way the centenary played out in Swansea. As Dean MacCannell has argued, cultural artefacts often move through a process of "sacralisation" in their construction as 'sacred objects' of the tourist 'ritual'.[58] Already an important figure in Swansea in 2014, Dylan Thomas was accelerated through the later phases of MacCannell's sacralisation process. For instance, Thomas's birthplace at 5 Cwmdonkin Drive, Uplands, had been refurbished and opened to the public some time ago, but 2014 saw the wholesale rebranding or 'enshrinement'[59] of the entire Uplands area, with new road signs erected proclaiming Thomas's connection with the suburb, and the poet's signature professionally graffitied on telephone network boxes. Such traces of Dylan Thomas have less the feel of a 'transgressive'[60] expression of local culture making its mark on a space than a somewhat phoney imposition. What MacCannell defines as the 'mechanical reproduction of the sacred object'[61] was secured by the CCS, who shunned the Welsh Government centenary logo in favour of its own commission. Notably, the brief for this commission made no mention of Thomas's Welshness, but instead made use of quotations that connected the writer with the particularity of his home city: 'Swansea is the best place' and 'This isn't like any other place'.[62] Indeed the branding imagery incorporated not only an image of Thomas and his signature, but the crucial words, unsubtly capitalised, 'SWANSEA ABERTAWE', in an effort to fuse the idea and image of Thomas with the city. CCS even staked its claim to Thomas in the realm of the digital, occupying the domain *www.dylanthomas.com*, which, amusingly, required the Dylan Thomas Estate's website *www.discoverdylanthomas.com* to announce itself as 'the official website'.[63] MacCannell suggests that the consummation of sacralisation occurs at the moment of 'social reproduction', when 'groups, cities, and regions begin to name themselves after famous attractions.'[64] The idea of renaming Swansea's railway station after Thomas was mooted by the coordinating group, though this was rejected by the rail authorities,[65] and, at the time of writing, the City and County of Swansea has not yet been renamed the City and County of Dylan Thomas.

MacCannell's description of this process of sacralisation is predicated on an analysis of the commodification of places and their culture in the service of the tourist industry, and this use of the Dylan Thomas brand in Swansea was certainly heavily informed by such priorities. However, as Kearns and Philo note, besides the 'economic logic of selling places' there is invariably also 'a more social logic at work' in the 'self-promotion of places'. They argue that place promotion simultaneously operates

> as a subtle form of socialization designed to convince local people, many of whom will be disadvantaged and potentially disaffected, that they are

important cogs in a successful community and that all sorts of 'good things' are really being done on their behalf.[66]

Swansea's substantial award from ACW was actually won on the grounds that it would take on part of the responsibility for 'enhanc[ing] community spirit', and its efforts to do this in tandem with its economic agenda are evident in the branding image it commissioned.[67] It is an attractive image, incorporating an illustration in which Thomas stares proudly into the middle distance, his head held high (though at closer inspection he does appear somewhat bleary-eyed). It is colourised in light pastels, soft pinks, blues and greens, merging into coloured polygons that pleasingly distort the right side of the illustration.[68] The overall effect is an eye-catching image that proclaims a certain synthetic quality, as if announcing itself as a self-consciously benign 'reimagining' of a not uncontroversial figure. Indeed, research conducted in the early 2000s found that the perception of Dylan Thomas in Swansea was almost entirely negative, with one Council Officer noting that 'We're up against . . . a general kind of dislike of Dylan within Swansea, that he was a drunk, or he was obnoxious, that he borrowed money and never gave it back, he was generally uncouth.'[69] Similarly, the Council's then Chair of Leisure suggested that the people of Swansea considered Thomas a 'drunken yob'.[70] The 2014 image reconstructs Thomas as a benevolent figurehead for the city, a brand that aims to position him as not only a 'unique selling point' and a 'robust mental image for the target audiences', in the words of an employee of CCS's Tourism and Marketing department, but simultaneously as an almost spiritual, paternal presence around the city, guiding Swansea towards its future.[71] The imagery was duly reproduced *ad nauseam* across the city's urban geography: it could (and, as of 2019, still can) be seen on buses, beer mats, banners hung from bridges, and even somewhat absurdly on the sides of the entire fleet of the council's civic amenity vehicles. Notably, the imagery is never seen alongside the Welsh Government's DT100 logo.

Many critiques of the ways in which state and municipal cultural planning plays out in the twenty-first century focus on the limitations of policies that prioritise 'inter-city competition, place-making and leveraging in middle-class populations and inward investment' at the expense of the 'wider goals of holistic and socially inclusive cultural planning'[72] – that is, the potential for culture to enrich and transform everyday lives. For instance, as Graeme Evans notes, in the administration of culture at the level of urban cultural planning, there is often a 'mismatch' between 'areas receiving and benefiting from urban revitalization through culture and related forms of cultural consumption, and those most in need socially and economically'.[73] If, as we have seen, CCS was tasked with the job of implementing the centenary of Thomas's birth in a way that 'engages with local areas . . . to help enhance community spirit', then there is evidence to suggest a 'mismatch' between those who benefited and those who did not. The community representatives present at the co-ordination group meetings included both the MP and the AM for Swansea West – historically the wealthier side of the city – and city councillors and business representatives from the middle-class suburbs of Uplands and Mumbles. No such representatives attended from Swansea East. Moreover, while there was talk in early meetings of the 'jobs' that might be created through the increased 'economic traffic' through the city,[74] the meetings contained no other discussion of how the inhabitants of the city might benefit from the celebrations, or of how the festival might enhance 'community spirit'. As Jim McGuigan has noted, in the realm of public policy the term 'culture' is often evoked alongside the word 'community' without addressing precisely how the two concepts interact or intersect. 'Instead of naming the source of trouble unequivocally,' says McGuigan, such discourse 'opt[s] for a positively idealistic advocacy of cultural development. It becomes, thus a rather vague solution to problems that are not made quite clear.'[75]

All this is not to suggest that the Dylan Thomas Centenary was an unmitigated disaster from which no good came. In Swansea, the celebrations were a catalyst in the council's successful bid for a Heritage Lottery Fund grant of close to £1m to upgrade the Dylan Thomas Centre and fund learning and outreach programmes that worked with, among others, asylum seekers and refugees, programmes that have continued long after the centenary year.[76] 'Developing Dylan 100' was an outreach programme coordinated by Literature Wales, and took established writers to schools in Wales to deliver creative writing workshops.[77] At a time when GCSE English Literature is no longer a core subject in Welsh schools, it would be churlish to suggest that this was anything other than a positive achievement. Moreover, ACW funded an enormous range of activities that reimagined Thomas and his work in new ways; one major highlight was *Dylan Live*, an enthralling, collaborative spoken-word and musical performance that explored Thomas's legacy in Wales and the USA. Indeed, the creative dialogues enabled by the centenary and the innumerable events that took place in 2014 are, rightly, impossible to quantify.

Neither is this to deny the place of the state administration of culture. As Adorno wrote in an indispensable essay on these matters, 'culture suffers damage when it is planned and administrated; when it is left to itself, however, everything cultural threatens not only to lose its possibility of effect, but its very existence as well'.[78] In an era of aggressive neoliberalism, in which cultural and media institutions are being absorbed into vast global conglomerates, the areas of social life in which meaningful cultural activity can take place are under threat. These same forces are, in identifiable ways, reshaping the conceptions and definitions of culture and creativity adopted by state institutions that exist to serve the public interest. The superabundance of state-funded activity that took place around DT100 exemplified a conception of culture grossly skewed by commercial and economistic priorities. Indeed, it could be said that Thomas was paradoxically absent from much of the discussion. Frequently, the phrase 'Dylan Thomas' stood in to signify an identifiable brand for commercially-focused state activity. Hannah Ellis, granddaughter of Thomas and member of the Welsh Government DT100 steering committee, tellingly remarked that at committee meetings, attendees desperately avoided referring to Thomas as a 'brand', 'apologising profusely if they accidentally did.'[79] This reveals just how largely commercial considerations loomed in these discussions: despite the performance of abashed contrition, this commercialism was precisely the agenda pursued by the Welsh Government, and still is. 'Dylan Day' has now become an annual event, and every year Wales witnesses a new 'major event'-inspired festival, from the promotion of other globally-recognised Welsh cultural figures (even those with only circumstantial cultural connections with Wales, such as Roald Dahl)[80] to pan-Wales 'themes' (see the 2017 'Year of Legends' and the 2018 'Year of the Sea'). Coercing cultural activity into taking shape around annual macro-themes such as these should be understood as a manifestation of 'the desire of capital to foreground forms of creativity that promise the new'.[81] It is happening at the expense of real opportunities to look for alternative, progressive conceptions of culture and creativity.

Perhaps one place to start in this search might be the actual writings of the figure at the centre of the discussion. As John Goodby reminded readers in an article published halfway through the centenary year, Thomas may have been an 'entertainer and a performer' but he was 'at root a daring modernist poet'.[82] He also had some ideas about culture and its relationship to society. Some of these are explored in a 1938 letter to Henry Treece, who had at that time been showing Thomas drafts of what would become his book-length study *Dylan Thomas: 'Dog among the fairies'* (1949). In this letter, Thomas interestingly takes umbrage with Treece's suggestion that his was a poetry with 'no social awareness,' that was 'out-of-contact with . . . society' (*CL*, 310). While he concedes that his poetry is 'not concerned with politics', he does so only insofar as 'politics' is understood narrowly as 'supposedly the science of achieving and "administrating" human happiness' (*CL*, 310). Thomas instead affirms that he is in fact 'extremely sociable', by which he does not, in this instance at least, mean that he enjoys spending time in pubs, but rather that he thinks that

> a squirrel stumbling at least of equal importance as Hitler's invasions, murder in Spain, the Garbo-Stokowski romance, royalty, Horlick's, lynchlaw, pit disasters, Joe Lewis, wicked capitalists, saintly communists, democracy, the Ashes, the Church of England, birthcontrol, Yeats's voice, the machines of the world I tick and revolve in, pub-baby-weather-governement-football-youth-and-age-speed-lipstick, all small tyrannies, means tests, the fascist anger, the daily, momentary lightenings, eruptions, farts, dampsquibs, barrelorgans, tinwhistles, howitzers, tiny death-rattles, volcanic whimpers of the world I eat, drink, love, work, hate and delight in. (*CL*, 310)

There is, as M. Wynn Thomas observes elsewhere in this collection, a breathless comic energy conspicuously on display here, in part as a riposte to those contemporary poets of the 'Auden generation' for whom political poetry must adopt a tone of solemn seriousness. But these lines can also be read as an impassioned defence of Dylan Thomas's own poetics: one that mischievously evades direct political statements, but whose broader, serious implication is that a narrow, 'regimental' conception of politics engenders a narrow, 'regimental' culture, and vice versa. He appears to advocate a conception of the 'political' that is not reducible to that which can be administered, but rather a more 'sociable' one that does not hold fast to arbitrary conceptual boundaries, and instead encompasses a more diffusive sense of the relations between culture, self and society. In keeping with an approach to language that is obsessed by excess, boundary-breaking and overdetermination, this is not a relativist conception of the political but one that destabilises arbitrary distinctions, and instead emphasises the decentred relationality – and connectedness – of self and society.

If culture must be 'administrated', we would perhaps benefit from an approach that is more diffuse, decentred, excessive. Notably, Adorno pointed towards a definition of culture closer to Thomas's view, and this was one that resulted in an approach to cultural policy that avoided rigid, regimented determinism. He spoke of 'the spontaneous consciousness not yet totally in the grips of reification', which is 'still in a position to alter the function of the institution within which this consciousness expresses itself'.[83] Dylan Thomas is, in the current climate, close to being 'totally in the grips of reification'. If we are to retain a conception of the human spontaneity that his work embodied, we would do well to allow the object of cultural policy – culture itself – to have some bearing on the process of that which administrates it. Adorno advocated the creation of 'centres of freedom';[84] perhaps this could take the form of policy that dispenses with the obsession with monolithic major events that enlist cultural figureheads as brands for cultural activity designed to fit the needs of the market. Rather, cultural activity could be promoted in the broader sense of 'creativity' as, in Edensor et al.'s terms, as 'social and *sociable*, culturally specific and communally produced . . . located in innumerable social contexts' (my emphasis).[85] Intriguingly echoing Thomas's own words, such an approach might help destabilise the currently symbiotic relationship between cultural administration and narrowly economic considerations, and allow us to imagine other ways of engaging with this world we all 'eat, drink, love, work, hate and delight in'.

Notes

[1] Designed by Pete Fowler.
[2] Designed by Amber Hiscott.
[3] At the time, this was the *South Wales Daily Post.*
[4] Created by Robert Thomas.
[5] Created by John Doubleday. Urban legend has it that this statue, after it was put up, became known as 'A Portrait of the Artist as Someone Else'.
[6] John Goodby, *The Poetry of Dylan Thomas: Under the Spelling Wall* (Liverpool: Liverpool University Press, 2013), p. xv.

7 Goodby, *Under the Spelling Wall*, p. 36.
8 Goodby, *Under the Spelling Wall*, p. 450.
9 *Interstellar* (Christopher Nolan, 2014).
10 Guy Debord, *The Society of the Spectacle*, trans. by Donald Nicholson-Smith (New York: Zone Books, 1995 [1967]), p. 14.
11 Jon Anderson, *Understanding Cultural Geography* (London: Routledge, 2010), p. 5.
12 Henri Lefebvre, *The Production of Space*, trans. Donald Nicholson-Smith (Oxford: Blackwell, 1991 [1974]), p. 39.
13 Theodor Adorno, 'Culture and Administration', in *The Culture Industry* (London: Routledge, 2001 [1978]), p. 107.
14 Adorno, 'Culture and Administration', p. 108.
15 Adorno, 'Culture and Administration', p. 107.
16 Graeme Evans, *Cultural Planning: An Urban Renaissance?* (London: Routledge, 2001), p. 87.
17 J. M. Keynes, quoted in David Bell and Kate Oakley, *Cultural Policy* (London: Routledge, 2014), p. 18.
18 The ACGB budget increased threefold between 1964 and 1970. See Jim McGuigan, *Rethinking Cultural Policy* (Maidenhead: Open University, 2004), p. 39.
19 See, for example, the cover of the Beatles' *Sgt Pepper's Lonely Hearts Club Band* (1967).
20 Goodby, *Under the Spelling Wall*, p. 4.
21 The Welsh Arts Council, in existence from 1967 to 1994, was effectively a sub-committee of the umbrella Arts Council of Great Britain. It was awarded further funds and responsibilities in 1967, including a Literature Section, directed by Meic Stephens. Arts Council of Wales, the autonomous organisation that replaced the Welsh Arts Council, was created in 1994. Throughout its history, its name in Welsh has remained *Cyngor Celfyddydau Cymru*.
22 Tony Conran, '*Poetry Wales* and the Second Flowering', in M. Wynn Thomas (ed.), *Welsh Writing in English* (Cardiff: University of Wales Press, 2003), p. 234.
23 David Harvey, 'From Managerialism to Entrepreneurialism: The Transformation in Urban Governance in Late Capitalism', *Geografiska Annaler*, 71/1 (1989), 3–17.
24 McGuigan, *Rethinking Cultural Policy*, p. 42.
25 Carl Grodach, 'Urban cultural policy and creative city making', *Cities*, 68 (2017), 82.
26 Martin Johnes, *Wales Since 1939* (Liverpool: Liverpool University Press, 2012), p. 438.
27 See *https://www.ons.gov.uk/economy/grossvalueaddedgva/bulletins/regional grossvalueaddedincomeapproach/2014-07-07* (accessed 6 February 2018).
28 Prior to the Wales Act 2014, the Welsh Government was known as the Welsh Assembly Government. I will here refer to it by the name used during the years with which this chapter is concerned.
29 The power to devise an autonomous tourism strategy separate from the British Tourist Authority had originally been transferred to the Wales Tourist Board under the Tourism (Overseas Promotion (Wales)) Act 1992. These

were later transferred to the Welsh Assembly Government under the Wales Tourism Board (Transfer of Functions to the National Assembly for Wales and Abolition) Order 2005. Visit Wales was the department created to implement these new powers. Moreover the Government of Wales Act 2006 Section 61 outlines the powers pertaining to 'the support of culture'.

30 *Event Wales: A Major Events Strategy for Wales 2010–2020* (Welsh Government, 2010), p. 25.

31 Chris Rojek, *Event Power: How Global Events Manage and Manipulate* (London: Sage, 2013).

32 *Event Wales*, p. 3.

33 *Event Wales*, p. 3.

34 Correspondence with Arts Council of Wales as a result of Freedom of Information Request *https://www.whatdotheyknow.com/request/237995/response/587372/attach/4/K%20Smith%20reply.pdf?cookie_passthrough=1* (accessed 6 February 2018).

35 'Summary of Overall Objectives' (2012); made available by Freedom of Information Request, *https://www.whatdotheyknow.com/request/237988/response/586051/attach/3/ATISN%208952%20Kieron%20Smith%20Dylan%20Thomas%20100%20Reply.pdf?cookie_passthrough=1* (accessed 6 February 2018).

36 Gareth Rees and Chris Taylor, 'Is There a 'Crisis' in Welsh Education?', *Transactions of the Honourable Society of the Cymmrodorion*, 20 (2014), 99.

37 *Dylan Thomas 100: A Symphony of Voices Funding Information Pack* (Arts Council of Wales, 2012); made available by Freedom of Information Request, *https://www.whatdotheyknow.com/request/dylan_thomas_centenary_policy_2#incoming-587372* (accessed 6 February 2018).

38 *One Wales: A progressive agenda for the government of Wales* (Welsh Assembly Government, 2007).

39 *Event Wales*, p. 5.

40 *Dylan Thomas 100: A Symphony of Voices* (Parthian and Tinderbox Consultants, 2012), p. 2; made available by Freedom of Information Request, *https://www.whatdotheyknow.com/request/dylan_thomas_100#incoming-586051* (accessed 6 Feburary 2018).

41 *Welsh Government/Visit Wales Tender* (Celf Creative, 2012); made available by Freedom of Information Request, *https://www.whatdotheyknow.com/request/correspondence_with_celf_creativ#outgoing-739438* (accessed 23 February 2018).

42 *Dylan Thomas 100 – Festival Logo Brief* (Visit Wales, 2012), p. 3; made available by Freedom of Information Request, *https://www.whatdotheyknow.com/request/correspondence_with_celf_creativ#outgoing-739438* (accessed 23 February 2018).

43 *Dylan Thomas 100 – Festival Logo Brief.*

44 *A Symphony of Voices Funding Information Pack*, p. 7.

45 CCS received £100,000 from ACW. *Arts Council of Wales 2013/14 Reports and Annual Statements*, available at *http://www.arts.wales/c_annual-reports/reports-and-financial-statements-2013-14* (accessed 23 February 2018).

46 Tim Edensor, Deborah Leslie, Steve Millington and Norma M. Rantisi (eds), *Spaces of Vernacular Creativity: Rethinking the Cultural Economy* (London: Routledge, 2009), p. 3.

47 Grodach, 'Urban cultural policy and creative city making', 83.
48 Harvey, 'From Managerialism to Entrepreneurialism', 10.
49 Peter Hall, quoted in David Bell and Mark Jayne, *Small Cities: Urban Experience Beyond the Metropolis* (London: Routledge, 2006), p. 4.
50 In 2013, Swansea's population was 240,332 to Cardiff's 351,710 (roughly 68.3% of Cardiff's), yet its GVA stood at 48.3% of that of Cardiff. See *https:// www.ons.gov.uk/economy/grossvalueaddedgva/datasets/regionalgvaibylocal authorityintheuk* (accessed 23 February 2018).
51 See *https://www.dylanthomastheatre.org.uk/about-us* (accessed 6 February 2018).
52 Nigel Jenkins, *Real Swansea* (Bridgend: Seren, 2008), p. 73.
53 Jenkins, *Real Swansea*, p. 74.
54 *Grab a Piece of the Action: A Tourism Strategy for the City and County of Swansea, 2006–2011* (Stevens Associates and the City and County of Swansea, 2006)
55 'Dylan Thomas Swansea Abertawe 2014 – Co-ordinating Group Minutes 12.09.14'; made available by Freedom of Information Request, *https://www.whatdotheyknow.com/request/dylan_thomas_centenary_ policy#outgoing-423842* (accessed 23 February 2018).
56 'Dylan Thomas Swansea Abertawe 2014 – Co-ordinating Group Minutes 25.10.13'; made available by Freedom of Information Request, *https://www.whatdotheyknow.com/request/dylan_thomas_centenary_ policy#outgoing-423842* (accessed 23 February 2018).
57 'Dylan Thomas Swansea Abertawe 2014 – Co-ordinating Group Minutes 6.12.13'; made available by Freedom of Information Request, *https://www.whatdotheyknow.com/request/dylan_thomas_centenary_ policy#outgoing-423842* (accessed 23 February 2018).
58 Dean MacCannell, *The Tourist: A New Theory of the Leisure Class* (Berkeley: University of California Press, 2013 [1976]), p. 44.
59 MacCannell, *The Tourist*, p. 45.
60 Tim Cresswell, *In Place/Out of Place: Geography, Ideology and Transgression* (Minnesota: University of Minnesota Press, 1996).
61 Cresswell, *In Place/Out of Place*, p. 45.
62 'Design brief' (City and County of Swansea, 2013); made available by Freedom of Information Request, *https://www.whatdotheyknow.com/request/ correspondence_with_design_compa#outgoing-730220* (accessed 23 February 2018).
63 See *www.discoverdylanthomas.com* (accessed 23 February 2018).
64 MacCannell, *The Tourist*, p. 45.
65 'Dylan Thomas Swansea Abertawe 2014 – Co-ordinating Group Minutes 10.10.14'; made available by Freedom of Information Request, *https://www.whatdotheyknow.com/request/dylan_thomas_centenary_ policy#outgoing-423842* (accessed 23 February 2018).
66 Gerry Kearns and Chris Philo, *Selling Places: The City as Cultural Capital, Past and Present* (Oxford: Pergamon, 1993), p. 3.
67 The imagery can be seen at *www.dylanthomas.com*.
68 The style is remarkably similar to that employed by São Paulo mural artist Eduardo Kobra. See *www.eduardokobra.com* (accessed 23 February 2018).

[69] Helen Watkins and David Herbert, 'Cultural Policy and Place Promotion: Swansea and Dylan Thomas', *Geoforum*, 34/2 (2003), 256.

[70] Watkins and Herbert, 'Cultural Policy and Place Promotion', 257.

[71] 'Dylan Thomas Swansea Abertawe 2014 – Co-ordinating Group Minutes 25.10.13'; made available by Freedom of Information Request, *https://www.whatdotheyknow.com/request/dylan_thomas_centenary_policy#outgoing-423842* (accessed 23 February 2018).

[72] Graeme Evans and Jo Foord, 'Small Cities for a Small Country: Sustaining the Cultural Renaissance?', in David Bell and Mark Jayne, *Small Cities: Urban Experience Beyond the Metropolis* (London: Routledge, 2006), p. 154.

[73] Graeme Evans, *Cultural Planning: An Urban Renaissance?*, p. 257.

[74] 'Dylan Thomas Swansea Abertawe 2014 – Co-ordinating Group Minutes 01.03.13'; made available by Freedom of Information Request, *https://www.whatdotheyknow.com/request/dylan_thomas_centenary_policy#outgoing-423842* (accessed 23 February 2018).

[75] McGuigan, *Rethinking Cultural Policy*, p. 100.

[76] Correspondence with City and County of Swansea as a result of Freedom of Information Request. Available at *https://www.whatdotheyknow.com/request/dylan_thomas_centenary_policy#outgoing-423842* (accessed 23 February 2018).

[77] See *http://www.developingdylan100.com/* (accessed 23 February 2018).

[78] Adorno, 'Culture and Administration', p. 108.

[79] See *https://www.discoverdylanthomas.com/dylan-thomas-brand-cultural-icon-exploited-sell-wales* (accessed 23 February 2018).

[80] See *http://gov.wales/about/cabinet/decisions/previous-administration/2015/apr-jun/culture/eh0358/?lang=en* (accessed 23 February 2018).

[81] Edensor et al, *Spaces of Vernacular Creativity: Rethinking the Cultural Economy*, p. 8.

[82] John Goodby, 'And I am dumb(ed down) to tell'?': Dealing with the Dylan Thomas centenary', *Poetry Wales* 50/2 (2014).

[83] Adorno, 'Culture and Administration', p. 131.

[84] Thomas, 'Letter to Henry Treece, 6 or 7 July 1938', p. 310.

[85] Edensor et al., *Spaces of Vernacular Creativity: Rethinking the Cultural Economy*, p. 8.

Bibliography

Ackerman, John, *Welsh Dylan: Dylan Thomas's Life, Writing and his Wales*
    (Bridgend: Seren, 1979)
Ackerman, John, *Dylan Thomas: His Life and Work* (Basingstoke:
    Macmillan, 1990 [1964])
Ackerman, John, *A Dylan Thomas Companion: Life, Poetry and Prose*
    (Basingstoke; Macmillan, 1994)
Adorno, Theodor, 'Culture and Administration', in *The Culture Industry*
    (London: Routledge, 2001 [1978])
Agamben, Giorgio, *The End of the Poem: Studies in Poetics*, trans. Daniel
    Heller-Roazen (Stanford, CA: Stanford University Press, 1999)
Allott, Kenneth, *The Penguin Book of Contemporary Verse* (Harmondsworth:
    Penguin, 2nd edn, 1962)
Amis, Kingsley, *Bright November* (London: Fortune Press, 1947)
Amis, Kingsley, *Lucky Jim* (London: Gollancz, 1953)
Amis, Kingsley, *A Frame of Mind: Eighteen Poems* (Reading: School of Art,
    Reading University, 1953)
Amis, Kingsley, *That Uncertain Feeling* (London: Gollancz, 1955)
Amis, Kingsley, *A Case of Samples* (London: Gollancz, 1956)
Amis, Kingsley, *Socialism and the Intellectuals*, Fabian Society Tract 304
    (London: Fabian Society, 1957)
Amis, Kingsley, *What Became of Jane Austen and Other Questions* (London:
    Cape, 1970)
Amis, Kingsley, *The Riverside Villas Murder* (London: Cape, 1973)
Amis, Kingsley (ed.), *The New Oxford Book of English Light Verse* (Oxford:
    Oxford University Press, 1978)
Amis, Kingsley, *Jake's Thing* (London: Hutchinson, 1978)

Amis, Kingsley, *Collected Poems: 1944–1979* (London: Hutchinson, 1979)

Amis, Kingsley, *The Old Devils* (London: Hutchinson, 1986)

Amis, Kingsley, *The Pleasure of Poetry: From His* Daily Mirror *Column* (London: Cassell, 1990)

Amis, Kingsley, *The Amis Collection: Selected Non-Fiction 1954–1990* (London: Hutchinson, 1990)

Amis, Kingsley, *Memoirs* (London: Hutchinson, 1991)

Amis, Kingsley, *The Letters of Kingsley Amis*, ed. Zachary Leader (London: HarperCollins, 2000)

Anderson, Jon, *Understanding Cultural Geography* (London: Routledge, 2010)

Anonymous, 'Selected Notices', *The Wind and the Rain*, 3/3 (Autumn 1946)

Auden, W. H., 'The Truest Poetry is the Most Feigning', *Collected Shorter Poems 1927–1957* (London: Faber, 1966)

Auden, W. H., *The Dyer's Hand and Other Essays* (London: Faber, 1975)

Barfoot, Rhian, *Liberating Dylan Thomas: Rescuing a Poet from Psycho-sexual Servitude* (Cardiff: University of Wales Press, 2014)

Barker, George, *Collected Poems* (London: Faber and Faber, 1987)

Barthes, Roland, *Image Music Text*, trans. Stephen Heath (London: Fontana, 1977 [1967])

Bateson, F. W., *English Poetry* (London: Longmans, 1950)

Bell, David, and Mark Jayne, *Small Cities: Urban Experience Beyond the Metropolis* (London: Routledge, 2006)

Bell, David, and Kate Oakley, *Cultural Policy* (London: Routledge, 2014)

Bloom, Harold, *The Anxiety of Influence* (New York, NY: Oxford University Press, 1973)

Bloom, Harold, *Essayists and Prophets* (Philadelphia, PA: Chelsea House Publications, 2005)

Bowlby, Rachel, *Everyday Stories* (Oxford: Oxford University Press, 2016)

Bradford, Richard, *Lucky Him: The Life of Kingsley Amis* (London: Peter Owen, 2001)

Brinnin, John Malcolm, *Dylan Thomas in America* (New York: Avon, 1955)

Brown, Tony, 'Glyn Jones and the Uncanny', *Almanac: Yearbook of Welsh Writing in English*, 12 (2007–8), 89–114

Bryony Randall, 'Modernist Literature and the Everyday', *Literature Compass*, 7/8 (2010), 824–35

Carroll, Lewis, *Through the Looking-Glass and What Alice Found There* (London: Merrell, 2006 [1872])

Childs, Peter, *Modernism* (London: Routledge, 2000)

Chilton, John, *Sidney Bechet: The Wizard of Jazz* (London: Macmillan, 1987)

Cleverdon, Douglas, *The Growth of Milk Wood* (New York: New Directions, 1969)

Conran, Tony, '*Poetry Wales* and the Second Flowering', in *Welsh Writing in English*, ed. M. Wynn Thomas (Cardiff: University of Wales Press, 2003), pp. 222–54

Cox, E. B. (ed.), *Dylan Thomas: A Collection of Critical Essays* (London: Prentice-Hall, 1966)

Cresswell, Tim, *In Place/Out of Place: Geography, Ideology and Transgression* (Minnesota: University of Minnesota Press, 1996)

Davies, James, *Dylan Thomas's Swansea, Gower and Laugharne* (Cardiff: University of Wales Press, 2000)

Davies, James A., 'Dylan Thomas and his Welsh Contemporaries', in *Welsh Writing in English*, ed. M. Wynn Thomas (Cardiff: University of Wales Press, 2003), pp. 120–64

Davies, Walford, *Dylan Thomas* (Milton Keynes: Open University Press, 1986)

Davies, Walford, *Dylan Thomas: Writers of Wales* (Cardiff; University of Wales Press, 2014 [1972])

Davin, Dan, *Closing Times* (Oxford: Oxford University Press, 1975)

Debord, Guy, *The Society of the Spectacle*, trans. Donald Nicholson-Smith (New York: Zone Books, 1995 [1967])

Derrida, Jacques, *Acts of Literature*, ed. Derek Attridge (New York and London: Routledge, 1992)

Dobrée, Bonamy, 'Two Experiments', *Spectator*, 190 (12 June 1953), 763–4.

Drakakis, John, *British Radio Drama* (Cambridge: Cambridge University Press, 1981)

Dylan Thomas 100: A Symphony of Voices (Parthian and Tinderbox Consultants, 2012)

Eagleton, Terry, *How to Read a Poem* (Oxford and Malden, MA: Blackwell, 2007)

Edensor, Tim, Deborah Leslie, Steve Millington and Norma M. Rantisi (eds), *Spaces of Vernacular Creativity: Rethinking the Cultural Economy* (London: Routledge, 2009)

Eisenhower, Dwight D., *Crusade in Europe* (New York, NY: Doubleday, 1948)

Eliot, T. S., *The Complete Poems and Plays of T. S. Eliot* (London: Faber and Faber, 1969)

Ellis, Hannah (ed.), *Dylan Thomas: A Centenary Celebration* (London: Bloomsbury, 2014)

Emig, Rainer, *Modernism in Poetry: Motivations, Structures and Limits* (London: Longman, 1995)

Evans, Graeme, *Cultural Planning: An Urban Renaissance?* (London: Routledge, 2001)

Evans, Graeme and Jo Foord, 'Small Cities for a Small Country: Sustaining the Cultural Renaissance?', in David Bell and Mark Jayne, *Small Cities: Urban Experience Beyond the Metropolis* (London: Routledge, 2006), pp. 151–68

Event Wales: A Major Events Strategy for Wales 2010–2020 (Welsh Government, 2010)

Fernandez, Joseph, *Popery Tottering to Its Fall in 1866: Shewing what the Spirit of Popery Has Been, Now Is, and Will be Untill It Perishes from off the Face of the Earth* (London: Passmore and Alabaster, London, 1865)

Ferris, Paul, *Dylan Thomas* (London: Hodder and Stoughton, new edn 1999)

Fitzgibbon, Constantine, *The Life of Dylan Thomas* (London: J. M. Dent & Sons, 1965)

Freud, Sigmund, *The Penguin Freud Library*, vols 1–15, trans. J. Strachey (London: Penguin, 1990–3)

Freud, Sigmund, *The Uncanny*, trans. David McLintock (Harmondsworth: Penguin, 2003)

Fussell, Paul, *The Anti-Egotist: Kingsley Amis, Man of Letters* (New York, NY: Oxford University Press, 1994)

Gilmour, Ian and Iain Hamilton (eds), *Spectrum: A Spectator Miscellany* (London: Longmans, Green, 1956)

Goodby, John, *The Poetry of Dylan Thomas: Under the Spelling Wall* (Liverpool: Liverpool University Press, 2013)

Goodby, John, '"And I am dumb(ed down) to tell"?: Dealing with the Dylan Thomas centenary', *Poetry Wales* 50/2 (2014)

Goodby, John, *Discovering Dylan Thomas: A Companion to the 'Collected Poems' and Notebook Poems* (Cardiff: University of Wales Press, 2017)

Goodby, John and Lyndon Davies (eds), 'Introduction', in *The Edge of Necessary: An Anthology of Welsh Innovative Poetry 1966–2018* (Llangattock: Aquifer, 2018)

Goodby, John, and Adrian Osbourne (eds), *The Fifth Notebook of Dylan Thomas: Annotated Manuscript Edition* (London: Bloomsbury, 2020)

Goodby, John and Chris Wigginton, '"Shut, too, in a tower of words": Dylan Thomas's modernism', in Alex Davis and Lee M. Jenkins (eds), *Locations of Literary Modernism: Region and Nation in British and American Modernist Poetry* (Cambridge: Cambridge University Press, 2000), pp. 89–112.

Goodby, John and Chris Wigginton (eds), *Dylan Thomas: New Casebook* (Basingstoke: Palgrave, 2001)

Goodby, John and Chris Wigginton, 'Welsh Modernist Poetry: Dylan Thomas, David Jones and Lynette Roberts', in *Regional Modernisms*, ed. James Moran and Neal Alexander (Edinburgh: Edinburgh University Press, 2013), pp. 160–83

Grodach, Carl, 'Urban cultural policy and creative city making', *Cities*, 68 (2017)

Grosz, Elizabeth, 'Julia Kristeva', in Elizabeth Wright (ed.), *Feminism and Psychoanalysis: A Critical Dictionary* (Oxford: Blackwell, 1992), p. 199

Harker, Brian, *Louis Armstrong's Hot Five and Hot Seven Recordings* (New York, NY: Oxford University Press, 2011)

Harvey, David, 'From Managerialism to Entrepreneurialism: The Transformation in Urban Governance in Late Capitalism', *Geografiska Annaler*, 71/1 (1989)

Hendry, J. F., *The Bombed Happiness* (London: Routledge, 1942)

Homer, Sean, *Jacques Lacan* (London: Routledge, 2005)

Jackaman, Rob, *The Course of English Surrealist Poetry Since the 1930s* (Lewiston, NY: Edwin Mellen, 1989)

James, Andrew, '*The Old Devils* or an Englishman's Attempt Write a Welsh Novel', in Ludmilla Kostova, Iona Sarieva and Mihaela Irimia (eds), *Comparisons and Interactions Within/ Across Cultures* (Veliko Tarnovo, Bulgaria: St Cyril and St Methodius University Press, 2012), pp. 181–7

James, Clive, *From the Land of Shadows* (London: Cape, 1982)

Jarvis, Matthew, 'Devolutionary Complexities: Reading Three New Poets', in Matthew Jarvis (ed.), *Devolutionary Readings: English-Language Poetry and Contemporary Wales* (Oxford: Peter Lang, 2017), pp. 113–14.

Jenkins, Nigel, *Real Swansea* (Bridgend: Seren, 2008)

Johnes, Martin, *Wales Since 1939* (Liverpool: Liverpool University Press, 2012)

Jones, Glyn, *The Dragon has Two Tongues*, ed. Tony Brown (Cardiff: University of Wales Press 2001 [1968])

Kearns, Gerry, and Chris Philo, *Selling Places: The City as Cultural Capital, Past and Present* (Oxford: Pergamon, 1993)

Kerschner, R. B., *Dylan Thomas: The Poet and His Critics* (Chicago: American Library Association, 1976)

Kristeva, Julia, *Tales of Love*, trans. Leon S. Roudiez (New York: Columbia University Press, 1987)

Kuby, Lolette, *An Uncommon Poet for the Common Man: A Study of Philip Larkin's Poetry* (The Hague: Mouton, 1974)

Larkin, Philip, *All What Jazz: A Record Diary, 1961–68* (London: Faber and Faber, 1970)

Larkin, Philip, 'Introduction to *Jill*', *Required Writing: Miscellaneous Pieces 1955–1982* (London: Faber and Faber, 1983)

Larkin, Philip, 'Forget What Did', *Collected Poems*, ed. Anthony Thwaite (London: Faber and Faber and The Marvell Press, 1988)

Larkin, Philip, *Selected Letters of Philip Larkin: 1940–1985*, ed. Anthony Thwaite (London: Faber and Faber, 1992)

Larkin, Philip, *Further Requirements: Interviews, Broadcasts, Statements and Book Reviews 1952–85*, ed. Anthony Thwaite (London: Faber and Faber, 2001)

Larkin, Philip, *Early Poems and Juvenilia*, ed. A. T. Tolley (London: Faber and Faber, 2005)

Lefebvre, Henri, *The Production of Space*, trans. Donald Nicholson-Smith (Oxford: Blackwell, 1991 [1974])

Lewis, Peter, 'The Radio Road to Llareggub', ed. John Drakakis, *British Radio Drama* (Cambridge: Cambridge University Press, 1981), pp. 72–110.

Lucas, J., and James Barker, *The Killing Ground: The Battle of the Falaise Gap, August 1944* (London: Batsford, 1978)

Lycett, Andrew, *Dylan Thomas: A New Life* (London: Weidenfeld & Nicolson, 2003)

MacCannell, Juliet Flower, 'Sigmund Freud', in Julian Wolfreys (ed.), *Modern European Criticism and Theory: A Critical Guide* (Edinburgh: Edinburgh University Press, 2006), pp. 57–67.

MacCannell, Dean, *The Tourist: A New Theory of the Leisure Class* (Berkeley: University of California Press, 2013 [1976])

MacNeice, Louis, *Collected Poems*, ed. E. R. Dodds (London: Faber and Faber, 1966)

Marcus, Laura, and Peter Nicholls (ed.), *The Cambridge History of Twentieth-Century English Literature*, vol. 1 (Cambridge: Cambridge University Press, 2005)

Maud, Ralph, *Where Have the Old Words Got Me? Explications of Dylan Thomas's Collected Poems* (Cardiff: University of Wales Press, 2003)

McDermott, John, *Kingsley Amis: An English Moralist* (London: Macmillan, 1989)

McGuigan, Jim, *Rethinking Cultural Policy* (Maidenhead: Open University, 2004)

Miller, Karl, *Dark Horses: An Experience of Literary Journalism* (London: Picador, 1998)

Milton, John, *The Works of John Milton* (Hertfordshire: Wordsworth, 1994)

Morrison, Blake, *The Movement: English Poetry and Fiction of the 1950s* (Oxford: Oxford University Press, 1980)

Motion, Andrew, *Philip Larkin: A Writer's Life* (London: Faber and Faber, 1993)

Muldoon, Paul, *The End of the Poem: Oxford Lectures in Poetry* (London: Faber and Faber, 2006)

Netzley, Ryan, 'Milton's Sonnets', in Thomas N. Corns (ed.), *A New Companion to Milton* (Oxford and Malden, MA: Wiley Blackwell, 2016), pp. 270–81

One Wales: A progressive agenda for the government of Wales (Welsh Assembly Government, 2007)

Peach, Linden, *The Prose Writing of Dylan Thomas* (London: Macmillan, 1988)

Perlmutter, Ruth, 'Malcolm Lowry's Unpublished Filmscript of *Tender is the Night*', *American Quarterly*, 28/5 (Winter, 1976)

Perloff, Marjorie, *Poetry On & Off the Page: Essays for Emergent Occasions* (Evanston: Northwestern University Press, 1998)

Powell, Neil, *Amis & Son: Two Literary Generations* (London: Pan Macmillan, 2008)

Pritchard, William H., 'Entertaining Amis', in *Playing it by Ear: Literary Essays and Reviews* (Amherst, MA: Massachusetts University Press, 1994)

Pryce-Jones, Alan, *The Bonus of Laughter* (London: Hamish Hamilton, 1987)

Randall, Bryony, *Modernism, Daily Time and Everyday Life* (Cambridge: Cambridge University Press, 2007)

Rees, Gareth and Chris Taylor, 'Is There a 'Crisis' in Welsh Education?', *Transactions of the Honourable Society of the Cymmrodorion*, 20 (2014)

Roberts, Lynette, *Collected Poems*, ed. Patrick McGuinness (Manchester: Carcanet, 2005)

Rojek, Chris, *Event Power: How Global Events Manage and Manipulate* (London: Sage, 2013)

Royle, Nicholas, *Jacques Derrida* (London and New York: Routledge, 2003)

Royle, Nicholas, *The Uncanny* (Manchester: Manchester University Press, 2003)

Schneider, Wolfgang, *Tigers in Normandy* (Mechanicsburg, PA: Stackpole Books, 2014)

Shakespeare, William, *Julius Caesar*, eet al. T. S. Dorsch, *The Arden Shakespeare* (London: Methuen, 1955)

Shakespeare, William, *Cymbeline*, ed. J. M. Nosworthy, *The Arden Shakespeare* (London: Methuen, 1955)

Shakespeare, William, *Richard II*, ed. Peter Ure, *The Arden Shakespeare* (London: Methuen, 1956)

Shakespeare, William, *King Henry IV Part 1*, ed. A. R. Humphreys, *The Arden Shakespeare* (London: Methuen, 1960)

Shakespeare, William, *Measure for Measure*, ed. J. W. Lever, *The Arden Shakespeare* (London: Methuen, 1965)

Soja, Edward, *Thirdspace: Journeys to Los Angeles and Other Real-and-Imagined Places* (Oxford: Blackwell, 1996)

Tedlock, E. W. (ed.), *Dylan Thomas: The Legend and the Poet* (London: William Heinemann, 1960)

Thomas, David N. (ed.), *Dylan Remembered, Vol. 1: 1914–1934* (Bridgend: Seren/NLW, 2003)

Thomas, Dylan, *Adventures in the Skin Trade* (London: Dent, 1955)

Thomas, Dylan, *Portrait of the Artist as a Young Dog* (London: Dent, Guild Books, 1956)

Thomas, Dylan, *Early Prose Writings*, ed. Walford Davies (London: Dent, 1971)

Thomas, Dylan, *Quite Early One Morning: Poems and Stories*, ed. Aneirin Talfan Davies (London: Dent, Aldine Paperbacks, 1974)

Thomas, Dylan, *The Collected Letters*, ed. Paul Ferris (London: Paladin, 1987)

Thomas, Dylan, *The Notebook Poems 1930–1934*, ed. Ralph Maud (London: Dent, 1990)

Thomas, Dylan, *The Broadcasts*, ed. Ralph Maud (London: Dent, 1991)

Thomas, Dylan, *The Filmscripts*, ed. John Ackerman (London: Dent, 1995)

Thomas, Dylan, *The Notebook Poems 1930–1934*, ed. Ralph Maud (London: Dent/Everyman, 1999)

Thomas, Dylan, *Under Milk Wood*, ed. Walford Davies (London: Penguin, 2000)

Thomas, Dylan, *Collected Letters*, ed. Paul Ferris (London: Dent, 2000)

Thomas, Dylan, *Collected Poems 1934–53*, ed. Walford Davies and Ralph Maud (London: Phoenix, 2000)

Thomas, Dylan, *A Child's Christmas in Wales* (London: Orion, 2014)

Thomas, Dylan, *The Collected Poems of Dylan Thomas: The New Centenary Edition*, ed. John Goodby (London: Weidenfeld & Nicolson, 2014)

Thomas, Dylan, *Collected Stories*, ed. Walford Davies (London: Weidenfeld & Nicolson, 2014)

Thomas, M. Wynn, *Corresponding Cultures* (Cardiff: University of Wales Press, 1999)

Trevelyan, Mary, *T. S. Eliot: The Pope of Russell Square* (London: Enitharmon Press, 2008)

Vaughan-Thomas, Wynford, *Wynford Vaughan-Thomas's Wales* (London: Michael Joseph, 1981)

Wain, John, *Outposts* (ed. Howard Sergeant), 13 (Manchester, Spring 1949)

Watkins, Gwen *Dylan Thomas: Portrait of a Friend* (Llandysul: Gomer Press, 1983)

Watkins, Helen, and David Herbert, 'Cultural Policy and Place Promotion: Swansea and Dylan Thomas', *Geoforum*, 34/2 (2003), 249–66

Williams, Daniel G., 'Welsh Modernism', in Brooker et al., *The Oxford Handbook of Modernisms* (Oxford: Oxford University Press, 2010)

Williams, Daniel G., '"Speaking with the Elgin Marbles in his Mouth?": Modernism and Translation in Welsh Writing in English', *Translation Studies*, 9/2 (2016), 183–97

Williams, Daniel G., 'In Paris or Sofia? Avant-Garde Poetry and Cultural Nationalism after Devolution', in Matthew Jarvis (ed.), *Devolutionary Readings: English-Language Poetry and Contemporary Wales* (Oxford: Peter Lang, 2017), pp. 115–56

Williams, Keith, 'Post-war Radio Broadcast', in Laura Marcus and Peter Nicholls (eds), *The Cambridge History of Twentieth-Century English Literature*, vol. 1 (Cambridge: Cambridge University Press, 2005)

Wolfreys, Julian (ed.), *Modern European Criticism and Theory: A Critical Guide* (Edinburgh: Edinburgh University Press, 2006)

Wood, Michael, *Yeats and Violence* (Oxford: Oxford University Press, 2010)

Wright, Elizabeth (ed.), *Feminism and Psychoanalysis: A Critical Dictionary* (Oxford: Blackwell, 1992)

Wright, Elizabeth, *Psychoanalytic Criticism: A Reappraisal* (Cambridge: Polity Press, 2006)

INDEX